THE NEW CLARENDON SHAKESPEARE

Under the general editorship of

R. E. C. HOUGHTON, M.A.
Fellow and Tutor of St. Peter's Hall
Lecturer in English Literature, Oriel College, Oxford

	Edited by
As You Like It	ISABEL J. BISSON
Coriolanus	B. H. KEMBALL-COOK
Hamlet	GEORGE RYLANDS
Henry IV, Part I	F. A. B. NEWMAN
Henry IV, Part II	WILLIAM R. RUTLAND
Henry V	R. F. W. FLETCHER
Julius Caesar	R. E. C. HOUGHTON
Macbeth	BERNARD GROOM
Merchant of Venice	R. F. W. FLETCHER
Midsummer Night's Dream	F. C. HORWOOD
Much Ado about Nothing	PHILIP WAYNE
Richard II	J. M. LOTHIAN
Romeo and Juliet	R. E. C. HOUGHTON
The Tempest	J. R. SUTHERLAND
Twelfth Night	J. C. DENT
The Winter's Tale	S. L. BETHELL (*Shortly*)

(11/55)

THE NEW CLARENDON SHAKESPEARE

THE WINTER'S TALE

Edited by

S. L. BETHELL

Senior Lecturer in English
University College, Cardiff

OXFORD
AT THE CLARENDON PRESS
1956

Oxford University Press, Amen House, London E.C.4

GLASGOW NEW YORK TORONTO MELBOURNE WELLINGTON
BOMBAY CALCUTTA MADRAS KARACHI CAPE TOWN IBADAN

Geoffrey Cumberlege, Publisher to the University

PRINTED IN GREAT BRITAIN
AT THE UNIVERSITY PRESS, OXFORD
BY CHARLES BATEY, PRINTER TO THE UNIVERSITY

PREFACE

THE *New Clarendon* Shakespeare aims primarily at presenting the text in such a way that it can be easily read and understood. The language of Shakespeare presents considerable difficulties to the beginner, difficulties which are constantly overlooked by readers familiar with the plays. But the answers of examination candidates, even at the university stage, often reveal unexpected ignorance of common Elizabethan usage and vocabulary. In this edition, therefore, the main emphasis has been placed on the interpretation of words and phrases, rather than on such linguistic matter as received much space in the old Clarendon Press editions of Clark and Wright. The notes have been divided, short glosses being placed below the text, while the more difficult passages are reserved for the commentary at the end. The latter, in the introductions to each scene and in the notes on individual lines, also gives full attention to points of literary and dramatic interest which have rightly come to the fore in modern teaching of English literature. Discussion of the true text and a few other more difficult notes are printed in smaller type within square brackets. The commentary and the introduction are supplemented by a substantial selection from the best criticism of the play, both old and new: a feature in which this edition of Shakespeare follows the plan set by the Clarendon English series. Here some matter will be found suitable for more advanced students, and the inclusion of varying opinions will provide material for reflection and comparison. It is the belief of the General Editor that students can best be taught to criticize by the provision of material which they can use as a starting-point as well as a model.

ACKNOWLEDGEMENTS

THE editor wishes to acknowledge his debt above all to the New Variorum edition of *The Winter's Tale* by H. H. Furness; also to the *Oxford English Dictionary* and to the following further editions of *The Winter's Tale:* the new Cambridge (Sir Arthur Quiller-Couch and J. Dover Wilson), the Arden (F. W. Moorman), the Yale (F. E. Pierce), Heath's (H. B. Charlton), the Granta (J. H. Lobban). A special word of thanks is due to the general editor for his great patience, for much valuable criticism and advice, and for many helpful suggestions.

The editor is also grateful to the following for permission to reprint passages from copyright works:

Messrs. Chatto & Windus, Ltd., and Harcourt, Brace & Company, Inc., U.S.A. (Lytton Strachey: *Books and Characters*); Messrs. Chatto & Windus, Ltd. (E. M. W. Tillyard: *Shakespeare's Last Plays*); Messrs. A. P. Watt & Son on behalf of the Owner of the Copyright (John Bailey: *Shakespeare*); The Clarendon Press (J. W. Mackail: *The Approach to Shakespeare*, Richard G. Moulton: *Shakespeare as a Dramatic Artist*, and Richard Noble: *Shakespeare's Use of Song*); Messrs. Routledge & Kegan Paul, Ltd. (Edward Dowden: *Shakespeare: A Critical Study of his Mind and Art*); Messrs. George Allen & Unwin, Ltd.(D. G. James: *Scepticism and Poetry*); The Cambridge University Press (J. Dover Wilson: *The Essential Shakespeare, The Winter's Tale*, ed. by J. Dover Wilson, Sir Arthur Quiller-Couch: *Shakespeare's Workmanship*, and Caroline F. Spurgeon: *Shakespeare's Imagery*); Messrs. Ginn & Company, Ltd. (H. N. Hudson: *Shakespeare: his Life, Art and Characters*); Messrs. Macmillan & Co. Ltd. (Sir Walter Raleigh: *Shakespeare*); Messrs. Constable & Company, Ltd. (Stopford A. Brooke: *On Ten Plays of Shakespeare*); Messrs. John Murray, Ltd. (Sir Sidney Lee: *A Life of William Shakespeare*); Messrs. Sidgwick & Jackson, Ltd. (E. K. Chambers: *Shakespeare: A Survey*).

The picture of the Fortune Theatre on page 6 is reproduced from *The Globe Restored*, by Walter C. Hodges, by kind permission of Messrs. Ernest Benn, Ltd.

The text of *The Winter's Tale* here printed is complete.

CONTENTS

LIST OF ILLUSTRATIONS

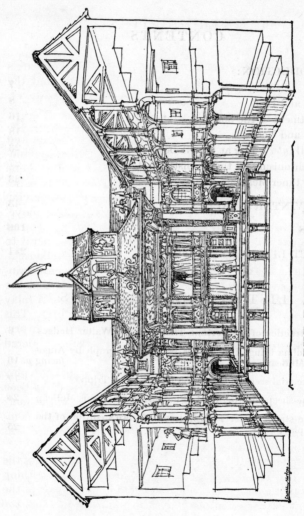

THE FORTUNE THEATRE

A reconstruction by Mr. C. Walter Hodges. The theatre was built in 1600, one year later than the Globe, at which most of Shakespeare's plays were performed, and burnt down in 1621

INTRODUCTION

DATE

In order to understand the development of Shakespeare's thought and art we need to know all we can about the dating of the plays. Documentary evidence is, however, scanty and doubtful.

(i) There exists a manuscript *Booke of Plaies* by Dr. Simon Forman, an odd character who was both doctor and fortune-teller. It was discovered by Collier, an early nineteenth-century scholar who perversely eked out his genuine and important finds with an occasional forgery. It is believed, however, to be genuine. Dr. Forman reports having seen 'the Winters Talle at the glob 1611 the 15 of maye' and seems to have been chiefly struck by the character of Autolycus, from whom he derived the practical moral to 'beware of trustinge feined beggars or fawninge fellouse'.

(ii) The Revels Office looked after the king's entertainments, and its account book for 1611–12 records that the King's Players, Shakespeare's company, acted 'A play called ye winters nighte Tayle' on 5 November 1611. This account book also was discovered only in the last century, but, though long regarded as a forgery, it is now considered authentic.

If we allow the evidence above, it appears that the play was in existence in 1611. And it is unlikely to have been produced much earlier without some notice of the fact: Shakespeare was chief playwright to the king's own company, and a play by him, in the latter part of his life, was probably something of an event.

So much for *production*. We have no external proof of the date when *The Winter's Tale* was *written*. There is nothing to indicate a date before which it could not exist except the novel it is based on, and that was published in 1588, too early to be any real help. It has been suggested that Shakespeare put the dance of the twelve satyrs into Act IV, Scene iv because it had already won applause as part of Jonson's masque *Oberon*, presented at Court on 1 January 1611. The servant introducing the dancers says that 'one three of them . . . hath danced before the king' and this might refer at least as much to King James as to King Polixenes—being one of the many instances of a reference to both play world and real world ambiguously wrapped up in a single phrase. So, it is argued, Shakespeare must have written the play after 1 January 1611. But he might easily have inserted the dance after writing the play: it is the sort of revision that we should expect from a practical man of the theatre. Moreover, there is no proof that such a dance was anything of a novelty in a time when satyrs, nymphs, and the whole paraphernalia of 'pastoral' were in constant literary use. Surely the best argument for the date of composition is that it would be very shortly before the date of first production: a successful dramatist does not have to wait long for production, and a quick writer like Shakespeare would not brood long over his work when he had once embarked on it. Stylistic evidence points, as we shall see, to the last period of Shakespeare's writing. The most likely date of composition would appear to be late 1610 or early 1611, and, although we cannot be certain of any of the dates involved, it is very probable that *The Winter's Tale* was written between *Cymbeline* and *The Tempest*.

TITLE AND PLOT

The term 'winter's tale' was used by Elizabethans and Jacobeans to mean something rather like an 'old wives' tale': a story that we know to be untrue yet still enjoy hearing as a way to pass a long winter's evening. Mamillius begins a winter's tale in *The Winter's Tale*: 'A sad tale's best for winter,' he says; 'I have one of sprites and goblins' (II. i. 25). The very title of our play warns us not to take its events too seriously.

In spite of this, critics have complained that the story is incredible. They have also objected to the plot, the plan of the story, as being untidy: it sprawls, with a great gap of sixteen years in the middle; and half-way through the play we take up a new set of characters and return again to the old only when we have almost lost interest in them. We shall later see that Shakespeare had his reasons for this apparent carelessness. Here, meanwhile, is the plot briefly analysed.

I. i. Camillo, chief counsellor of Leontes, king of Sicilia, exchanges courtesies with Archidamus, a Bohemian nobleman in the train of King Polixenes, visiting Leontes. They discuss the popularity of the young Sicilian prince Mamillius.

I. ii. Polixenes, although urged by his boyhood friend Leontes to prolong his holiday, says he must go home. Leontes asks his queen Hermione to try to persuade him to stay and, when she succeeds, becomes suddenly jealous. He tells Camillo that Hermione has been unfaithful to him with Polixenes and orders him to poison the royal visitor. Camillo cannot believe anything against the virtuous Hermione but, pretending to fall in with Leontes' wishes, reveals the plot to Polixenes and plans to escape with him to Bohemia.

II. i. Leontes, furious at the escape of Polixenes and Camillo, denounces Hermione before the court as an adultress, asserting Polixenes to be the father of the child she is going to have, and commands her to be imprisoned. Hermione rebuts the charge with quiet dignity and, as she is escorted to prison, Antigonus and other lords protest strongly against Leontes' action. He tells them that he has sent to the oracle at Delphos to seek Apollo's counsel in the matter.

II. ii. Antigonus' wife, Paulina, visits the prison and offers through Hermione's attendant, Emilia, to carry the newly born princess to Leontes, who may perhaps be softened by the sight of his innocent child.

II. iii. Paulina presents the baby to Leontes, who refuses to own it. She, with her husband and other courtiers, remonstrates with him until, driven almost mad by their opposition, his nerves frayed by worry and loss of sleep, he bids Antigonus take the child away to a desert place and leave it exposed to the elements.

III. i. The returning messengers describe the temple of Apollo which they have visited.

III. ii. Leontes puts Hermione on trial for high treason. She appeals to the oracle of Apollo. The messengers have just arrived and the oracle is read, acquitting Hermione, Polixenes, and Camillo of all blame, accusing Leontes of jealousy and tyranny, and declaring that 'the king shall live without an heir if that which is lost (i.e. the infant princess) be not found.' Leontes blasphemously refuses to believe the oracle and directs that the trial proceed. Immediately a servant enters and announces the death of Mamillius. Leontes at once acknowledges that he has sinned and is being punished. Hermione faints and is assisted from the scene. Paulina quickly returns and says that the queen, too, is dead. Leontes, deeply afflicted, determines to lead a life of penitence and devotion to his wife's memory.

III. iii. Antigonus with the infant princess lands on the coast of Bohemia. He is pursued and killed by a bear; the child is discovered by a shepherd and his clownish son; and the ship that has brought them perishes in a storm with all hands.

IV. i. Time himself enters to bridge the gap of sixteen years, during which Leontes has faithfully led his life of penitence, and the princess Perdita has grown up as daughter to the old Shepherd.

IV. ii. Camillo wishes to return to Sicilia, where the penitent Leontes is now reconciled to Polixenes, but the latter dissuades him. Both are concerned about Polixenes' son, the crown prince Florizel, whom they think to have fallen in love with a shepherd's daughter.

IV. iii. Autolycus, a rascally ex-courtier, plays a confidence trick on the Clown and picks his pocket.

IV. iv. At the sheep-shearing feast Florizel, disguised as a shepherd, and Perdita, dressed as queen of the feast, are about to be betrothed, but Polixenes, present with Camillo in disguise, interrupts the ceremony and threatens punishment for all concerned, if the match be not instantly broken off. Camillo, still anxious to return to Sicilia, assists the escape of Florizel and Perdita to that country, intending to inform Polixenes and accompany him in pursuit of them. Autolycus, who as pedlar and cutpurse has thriven well at the feast, is compelled to exchange clothes with Florizel. After the refugees have departed for the coast, Shepherd and Clown enter on their way to the king with a bundle of the things found with the infant Perdita and which will prove that she is not the Shepherd's daughter. Autolycus, hoping to serve Florizel and profit by the occasion, presents himself to them as a courtier and, under pretence of leading them to Polixenes, spirits them away to the prince's ship.

V. i. In Sicilia his courtiers try to persuade Leontes to remarry, but, vehemently supported by Paulina, he resists their entreaties. Florizel arrives with Perdita, whom he introduces as a Libyan princess. Leontes receives them joyfully, but a messenger soon enters with news that Polixenes has arrived in pursuit of his son, who has eloped with a shepherd's daughter. The young pair have not yet had an opportunity to marry, and Florizel begs Leontes to

intercede for them with his father, that he may be allowed
the wife of his choice. The now saintly king of Sicilia
consents.

v. ii. Through the affected chatter of certain Sicilian
courtiers we learn how Leontes has discovered his daughter
by means of the Shepherd's bundle and of the meeting of
the two kings.

v. iii. Leontes, with Florizel and Perdita and his whole
court, visits the house of Paulina to see a newly made
statue of Hermione. The statue apparently comes to life
and proves to be Hermione herself, who has lived apart
from her husband until the discovery of Perdita, thus
obeying the oracle's behest that 'the king shall live without an heir if that which is lost be not found'. Leontes and
Hermione are reunited; Florizel and Perdita are to marry;
and so are Paulina and Camillo. All wrongs have been
forgiven and righted, and there is to be general rejoicing.

'AN OLD TALE'

In the title of the play Shakespeare calls attention to its
incredibility: it is a 'winter's tale'. And within the play
he gives a commentary which does not seem very complimentary to his own story. When the courtiers discuss the
revelation of Perdita's identity and the remarkable chain of
events that led up to it—which is, of course, the story the
audience have seen enacted—the second gentleman observes: 'this news which is called true is so *like an old tale*,
that the verity of it is in strong suspicion' (v. ii. 28). Later
in the same scene we have:

> *Second Gent.* What, pray you, became of Antigonus that
> carried hence the child?
> *Third Gent. Like an old tale* still, which will have matter
> to rehearse, though credit be asleep and not an ear open.
> He was torn to pieces with a bear.
>
> (v. ii. 58)

And in the last scene Paulina speaks of Hermione:

> That she is living,
> Were it but told you, should be hooted at
> *Like an old tale*; but it appears she lives,
> Though yet she speak not.

(v. iii. 115)

'Like an old tale'! It *is* an old tale that Shakespeare is telling, and through his characters he seems to admit that it is incredible, boring ('not an ear open') and more liable to be 'hooted at' than applauded. Why does he criticize the story in this way, and why did he bother to dramatize it, if he had so poor an opinion of it?

The surprising thing is that in the last phase of his career, after the succession of great tragedies, Shakespeare wrote a whole series of plays based on romantic and incredible 'old tales'. First, it seems, he tinkered with someone else's play about *Pericles, Prince of Tyre*, making it ready for the King's Men to perform. There he found the story of a lost baby princess who turns up years afterwards, and of her mother who revives after a long coma, as if returning from the dead. These themes, of finding a lost one and of return from the dead, figure largely in the three plays that followed: *Cymbeline*, *The Winter's Tale*, and *The Tempest*. Thus, while recognizing its weaknesses, Shakespeare went on dramatizing this same type of story. Why?

(i) Was he, at forty-seven, cynical, disillusioned, despairing of reality, determined to amuse himself with fairy tales and beautiful verse? Hardly, for there is a strong tang of reality in his fairy tales: Leontes' jealousy is quite as real and as horrible as Othello's. And the verse, as we shall see, does not lead us into an unreal world but with its images and references anchors us firmly in Shakespeare's own times.

(ii) Was he acting as a shrewd business-man, with an eye on the box-office? Romances, it is said, were growing

popular on the stage with the work of those rising col-
laborators, Beaumont and Fletcher. Was Shakespeare
'cashing in' on a new fashion ? We do not in fact know how
many Beaumont and Fletcher romances had appeared
before *Cymbeline*. Probably not many; perhaps only one.
And Shakespeare was already fairly well-to-do, even con-
templating retirement, so that he is unlikely to have set
aside his own tastes for the sake of money. In any event
Shakespearian romance is not sentimental like that of
Beaumont and Fletcher, and the resemblances are very
superficial.

(iii) It may be that, for Shakespeare, these old tales,
however silly and inconsequential on the surface, expressed
in story form what he believed about life—about God and
Man and Nature—and that in adapting them for the stage
he subordinated plot and character to the main function of
conveying an 'inner meaning'. This, it would seem, is the
only hypothesis which accounts satisfactorily for the references to 'an old tale' and its incredibility, to which we have
referred, and for similar references throughout the text of
The Winter's Tale.

(*a*) *Such references 'distance' the story and keep the audience
detached and critical.* When a character in a novel exclaims
'Why, it's just like a novel!', even though the remark may
be strictly realistic, the effect on the reader is to remind
him that it is, after all, *only* a novel. In recent years film
comedians have exploited for purposes of humour the
precarious interrelation between real world and film world,
cutting momentarily across the accepted 'dramatic illusion'. 'This is the best gag in the whole picture,' said
Groucho Marx, looking up while gagging the engine-driver
in *The Marx Brothers Go West*. Comedians on the wireless
use a similar technique when they joke about their script.
The effect is to remind us that it is 'only a picture' or
'only a radio show'. Three and a half centuries ago Shake-

speare did the same sort of thing. In *The Winter's Tale* it is unusually frequent: we have the three references to 'an old tale', Mamillius' tale which is 'best for winter', and a number of theatrical metaphors of the 'All the world's a stage' type, which will be pointed out individually in the notes. Such references, reminding the audience that the play is only a play, prevent them from becoming too absorbed in the action. Surely Shakespeare wanted them to remain detached and critical in order to see beyond the mere events of the story to the meaning that lies behind them.

(*b*) *The same references* not only get the audience into the proper frame of mind for perceiving an inner meaning, but also *convey something of that inner meaning themselves and so suggest what should be our approach to the play as a whole*. Shakespeare frequently presents a multiplicity of worlds one inside another, like a stage magician's boxes. For instance, in *A Midsummer Night's Dream* and *Hamlet* he has a play within the main play, and this main play is itself, of course, performed in a theatre in the 'real' world. But 'all the world's a stage': what we call the real world is itself a mere theatrical performance, a shadow show, when compared with the still-more-real world of eternity. In *The Winter's Tale* the references we are considering create, perhaps more strongly than in any other play, this sense of the mysterious multiplicity of life, which impresses us most strongly in Mamillius' tale. We hear him begin it: 'There was a man . . . Dwelt by a churchyard' (II. i. 28)—a man, we cannot help thinking, rather like the penitent Leontes later, who daily visited his wife's tomb. From these specific references it appears that life, according to Shakespeare, is mysterious and complex. It may well be that he could better express his interpretation of life by means of a 'winter's tale', a fairy tale, than by a more sober and factually convincing narrative. Fairy tales and legends have their origin in primitive myths and so contain in symbolic form early beliefs about the nature of the universe. That is why we often feel, when reading them, that they mean more than they say in so many words. *The Winter's Tale*, as we shall see in the next section, is based on such a story, and we shall go on to a further consideration of whether Shakespeare used this likely material as a means of stating his 'philosophy' and, if so, what that philosophy might be.

TREATMENT OF THE SOURCE

The source of Shakespeare's plot is a prose romance by Robert Greene, published in 1588 as *Pandosto: The Triumph of Time* and republished in 1607 with the title changed to *Dorastus and Fawnia*. In Act III, Scene ii, Shakespeare quotes the words of the oracle from his source: 'and the king shall live without an heir'. This proves that he used the first edition, for in the editions of 1607 and later 'live' is changed to 'die'.

Certain elements in the story, the Arcadianism (idealized life among the shepherds), the mixture of love story and adventure, especially by sea, and, above all, the oracle theme, might be traced back through the Renaissance into the field of Greek prose romance, Christian and pre-Christian; and the oracle theme itself goes back farther, to the epic and drama of classical Greece, centuries before Christ.

There is no need to summarize Greene's story, since Shakespeare has followed it fairly closely. We may, however, learn something of the dramatist's intentions by noting the main points wherein the plot of *The Winter's Tale* differs from its source. (i) Greene allows Pandosto (Shakespeare's Leontes) to grow gradually jealous as he sees his queen lavishing attentions on the royal visitor. Shakespeare makes the jealousy occur suddenly and un-accountably, emphasizing the mystery of evil and of human

1. Act II, Sc. iii. Paulina brings Leontes his baby
(John Gielgud and Flora Robson at the Phoenix Theatre, 1951)

2. Act III, Sc. ii. The trial scene. 'This news is mortal to the queen.'

(Old Vic, 1955)

personality. (ii) In *Pandosto* the baby princess is set adrift alone in an open boat. Shakespeare introduces Antigonus and the bear, thus rendering his story more incredible, confusing us by making comedy out of a tragic incident (see below, p. 27), and supplying a religious reference (see III. iii. 116 and note). (iii) Shakespeare is responsible for the homely side of the sheep-shearing feast (see below, p. 32) and is sole inventor of Autolycus. (iv) Greene makes Pandosto fall in love with his own daughter without knowing who she really is. Shakespeare removes this unpleasantness, of which only a trace remains in the dialogue (see v. i. 223 and note). (v) In *Pandosto* the queen dies and Pandosto himself finally commits suicide, being overcome by remorse. Shakespeare revives Hermione, reuniting her to Leontes in the 'statue' scene, which is derived from the legend of Pygmalion, well known in those days. (Also, in the play, Bohemia and Sicilia have changed places: Pandosto was king of *Bohemia*. And the characters' names are changed: Shakespeare borrows several from Sidney's famous pastoral romance, the *Arcadia*, which would be well known to the more cultivated members of his audience. These changes are not of any consequence, nor are the reasons for them clear.)

Shakespeare makes his story pleasanter and happier than the original. In one respect his version is more like real life: his country folk are modelled on the Warwickshire peasants he knew so well, not on the conventional figures of Greene's pastoral scenes. But he increases the element of the marvellous in the plot, stressing the mystery of life, both of the evil which invades it and of the providential ordering of events by which good is brought out of evil. Pandosto had remorse, not true penitence, and so took his own life—an act which, in Shakespeare's day, was thought to lead to almost certain damnation. Leontes by true penitence gains even more than the happiness his sin had

lost him. *Pandosto* was also called *The Triumph of Time*,
but *The Winter's Tale* with its strong religious hope might
well be called the Triumph of Eternity.

TEXT AND VERSE

The Winter's Tale appeared in print for the first time in
1623 in the first folio edition of Shakespeare's works, edited
by his friends and fellow actors, Hemynge and Condell. It
is now generally agreed that this was, by the standards of
the times, a carefully prepared volume and that, allowing
for the inevitable vagaries of copyists and printers, it
represents pretty closely what Shakespeare wrote. Since
the play had not appeared earlier in quarto, as had so
many of the others, we have only one clearly authoritative
text. In the present edition the first folio has been followed
except where it seems impossible to make sense of it. In
such places we have adopted the emendations that appear
most likely, on textual and historical grounds, to be what
Shakespeare wrote or intended to write. We have not, however, followed the punctuation of the first folio, which is
more likely to be the printer's than Shakespeare's and would
undoubtedly confuse the average reader, since its conventions are very different from our own. The punctuation
given here is that of the Oxford one-volume edition,
except where the present editor regards it as misleading:
in such cases he has reverted, where possible, to the first
folio.

Stylistically this is a difficult play. In his early works
Shakespeare wrote an involved and artificial style, which
he simplified as his dramatic powers grew. In *Hamlet* and
the so-called 'dark comedies', however, he introduced a
new type of difficulty. It is no longer the style of a brilliant
young man who enjoys making a simple subject awkward
for the sake of the intellectual exercise; it is the style of a
mature mind at grips with profound problems. In *Othello*

and *Lear* exploration and experiment are replaced by insight and assurance, and the style clears again; but from *Macbeth* onwards we move into a third kind of difficulty, which is due, not to a young man's 'smartness' nor to intellectual puzzlement, but to the effort to present as fully as possible the writer's understanding of life as variety in unity. In this attempt to see life as a multiple pattern of interrelated worlds of experience—we have spoken above of the relation of play world to real world and of the latter to the even more real world of eternity—Shakespeare was not unique but shared the attitude and intention of many of his contemporaries. We are accustomed to think of him as an 'Elizabethan', and scholars have added to the confusion by using this term to cover the whole period up to the closing of the theatres in 1642. But we should remember that Shakespeare was a not much older contemporary of John Donne; his greatest plays were written under James I; and by 1611, when *The Winter's Tale* appeared, the 'metaphysical' type of poetry had been written in this country for upwards of fifteen years. The style of *The Winter's Tale* can best be understood as one version of the poetry of 'metaphysical wit', which dominated England and the greater part of Europe in the first half of the seventeenth century.

(i) Rhythms for the most part are not smooth and regular as in the early plays, nor do they so directly suggest the rhythms of ordinary speech as do those of Shakespeare's middle period. We are aware of the blank verse pattern and we can hear at the same time the tones of speech, but the total effect is new, a blank verse which is tense, springy, contorted. Among the means employed to achieve this are a daring use of harsh sound to express harsh feelings, the frequent omission of words properly required by the syntax—this is called 'ellipsis'—and a sometimes violent distortion of word order; e.g.:

Polixenes . . .
      My affairs
  Do even drag me homeward ; which to hinder
  Were in your love a whip to me ; my stay
  To you a charge and trouble : to save both,
  Farewell, our brother.
Leontes.   Tongue-tied our queen ? speak you.
               (I. ii. 23)

(ii) The vocabulary, although admitting words hallowed by poetic custom, covers the whole range of ordinary subjects and affairs. In imagery and reference we have crab-apples (I. ii. 102), hat-blocks (I. ii. 225), a spider (II. i. 39), a negro's tooth (IV. iv. 362), none of which is traditionally poetic but all of which are put to poetic use.

(iii) The several characteristics of 'metaphysical wit' can also be found in *The Winter's Tale*. In this sense—in which we shall constantly be using the term—'wit' is not necessarily humorous but signifies a capacity for perceiving the relations subsisting among various objects. In expression it is always metaphorical : perceiving a relation between A and B, it goes on to state A in terms of B or vice versa. 'Metaphysical wit' is expressed in a special kind of metaphor, called a 'conceit'. Here the two terms (A and B) are very different or, as we say, 'remote', from one another and are brought together in such a way as to surprise and delight the reader, while pointing to a real—and frequently analogical—relationship between them. Polixenes' final 'thank you' is meant, like a nought at the end of a row of figures, to multiply all that have gone before (I. ii. 6) : here is a new and surprising parallel between courtesy and arithmetic. All wit has about it an element of fiction, feigning, or false reasoning, and yet this falsity is used to state a truth. Florizel says, that, when he sees Perdita dancing, he wishes she might become a wave of the sea and always move in the same rhythm (IV. iv. 140).

But no lover would really be happy to have his beloved transformed into a wave. The logic is false, for it is based on the assumption that, if a thing is good, the more we have of it the better. This may be true in general, but it is not true of all particulars: e.g. it does not apply to doses of medicine. Nor does it apply to Perdita's dance rhythm, for she has other valuable qualities which will not be perceived if she does nothing but dance, whether she be changed into salt water or not. Yet by an absurd statement we are made vividly to apprehend a truth: the beauty of Perdita as she dances—and there may be a poetic hint at a relation between Perdita and the sea, Perdita, who is dressed like Flora, the life-bringing goddess of spring, and the sea, the source of all life and parent of the love-goddess Aphrodite, who was foam-born, as Perdita might seem to have been.

What we have so far said about style applies to the play in general. But here and there the normal style is modified for specific purposes. For example, in Perdita's flower speech there is something of the crisp, early beauty of *A Midsummer Night's Dream*, though this combines with other elements to make the result more thoughtful and more richly mature; in the speeches of the old Shepherd rural simplicity is suggested by a combination of slow, awkward rhythms with plain but forceful diction; and in the statue scene there is a different type of simplicity attained by quiet regular rhythms and the use of words easy to understand in their dictionary sense but of profound religious significance. These and other modifications of style will be dealt with in the notes.

With its 'tough' rhythms, and imagery drawn from the workaday world of Shakespeare's own time, the style of *The Winter's Tale* is wholly different from the remote, pastoral, and 'poetical' beauty affected by Fletcher in his *Faithful Shepherdess*, which was produced probably in 1609 or 1610 and might be regarded as in some ways anticipating

the rural scenes of *The Winter's Tale*. Here is a passage
from Fletcher's pastoral play:

> Oh, you are fairer far
> Than the chaste blushing morn, or that fair star
> That guides the wandering seaman through the deep;
> Straighter than the straightest pine upon the steep
> Head of an aged mountain, and more white
> Than the new milk we strip before day-light
> From the full-freighted bags of our fair flocks;
> Your hair more beauteous than those hanging locks
> Of young Apollo!

Fletcher uses imagery drawn from the landscape, occupations and religion of a mythical Arcadia, so that the effect
of his play is to withdraw the audience into a world of make-
believe. Shakespeare, with a tale of wild impossibilities,
equally remote from reality, expresses himself in terms of
the rural and industrial occupations of Jacobean England,
with its crab-apples and hat-blocks. This is not a type of
verse designed to help us escape from the problems of life:
indeed, as we have seen, it conveys something of life's
complexity by the wit with which it joins together remote
and very different mental worlds. Moreover, this same
kind of verse is spoken by most of the characters most of
the time. Whereas in some plays characters are differen-
tiated one from another by the sort of verse put into their
mouths (contrast, for example, the verse of Othello with
that of Iago), in *The Winter's Tale* only the old Shepherd is
given a characteristic style. The jealous Leontes, the faithful Florizel, the gracious Hermione, even the forthright
Perdita, all speak with twisted rhythms, 'realistic' vocabulary, and metaphysical wit. The style represents Shakespeare's mind, not the character's; indeed, it draws our
attention *away from* the speaker to what is spoken about;
and, surprisingly in such a simple story, we find the dialogue
frequently dwelling on themes of philosophical importance:

the relation between imagination and reality, in connexion with Leontes' jealousy, or between art and nature, in Perdita's argument with Polixenes. Shakespeare, then, recognizes the story to be silly, and is not primarily concerned with character, but frequently introduces philosophical themes and employs throughout a style that expresses a complex reading of experience. This apparent discrepancy between plot and character on the one hand and thought and style on the other would disappear if the characters 'stood for' something and the story possessed an 'inner meaning'.

'THE WINTER'S TALE' AT THE GLOBE

The Globe theatre, where Dr. Forman saw our play, was very different from the theatre of today. Its essential feature, as in all Elizabethan theatres (see illustration on p. 6), was a large platform stage thrust out among the audience. Entrance to this stage was by doors at the back. About other features there is some doubt. There *may have been* at the back of the main platform an 'inner stage' which could be concealed by a curtain and so contain a small 'set' that did not need to be shown to the audience until required. If there were no inner stage, such a set would presumably be erected in a stage tent, a curtained-off area of the main platform where equally it could remain concealed until the appropriate time. Above the platform at the back the gallery might house spectators or an orchestra or it might at times have been used as a further acting area, an 'upper stage'. Certainly, some scenes involved appearances on one or more upper levels, e.g. where battlements are stormed, or the balcony in *Romeo and Juliet*. There is, however, no occasion for an upper stage in *The Winter's Tale*. In the 'statue' scene Hermione would be posed in the inner stage, if there was one; otherwise in a 'tent' on the main platform, where all the rest of the play would certainly take place.

At the Globe the audience surrounded the stage closely on three sides, in the yard and in the galleries; on the fourth side some might be seated in the gallery at the back; and even *on* the stage, at the edge, the gallants of the day occupied movable stools and showed off their splendid clothes in rivalry with the actors. The play was thus seen from all angles, in the round, like a modern circus performance. There was no curtain to the platform, so that stage mechanics, such as the carrying on and off of properties, were visible to the audience. It was not a 'bare' stage, as scholars used to assert; it may well have been highly decorated; but it remained a *decorated stage*, not a stage *disguised* as something else. There was no scenery, though properties and costume provided an ample and colourful spectacle. (Think of the sheep-shearing feast with its rustic finery; Perdita as a sort of May Queen; Florizel in a rich pseudo-rustic garb which can transform Autolycus into a courtier later; the saltiers who 'have made themselves all men of hair'; the dancing; the pedlar and his pack. Here are colour and movement in plenty.) Although a penthouse covered most of the stage and kept the actors' costumes out of the rain, and the galleries were roofed over, the yard was open to the sky and plays were acted by daylight. We can now see the chief difference between an Elizabethan and a modern theatre. In the usual modern theatre the audience sit back in the dark and watch the actors over a gulf, the orchestra pit, as they perform within a well-lit picture-frame and against scenery which simulates reality. This situation makes for the maximum of 'dramatic illusion'. We do not quite run for the police when the villain enters with a gun—there is something deep inside us which still says 'This isn't true'; but we come very near to the sort of excitement we should have if we were peering through a

3. Act IV, Sc. iv. The sheep-shearing feast
(Phoenix Theatre, 1951)

4. Act V, Sc. iii. The statue scene
Frontispiece from Rowe's edition of the play, 1709

window at a real villain armed with a genuine automatic. The Elizabethan stage, on the other hand, always looks like a stage, and the audience gets its illusion of reality, not by the passive contemplation of an illuminated moving-picture, but by active participation, by attending to the story and its significance as it is conveyed in the poetry spoken by the actors. The modern, 'naturalistic' theatre affects the nervous system as happenings in real life affect it; the Elizabethan theatre appeals to the emotions by way of the intelligence, since the poetry must be understood for the drama to be appreciated. In the modern theatre, if the dramatic illusion is shattered, the whole effect is gone. The Elizabethan theatre, however, showing the play to the audience nakedly *as* a play and relying on their co-operative intelligence to create out of it a play world—not by lighting in a picture-frame but by poetry in the imagination—can afford to cut across the dramatic illusion, to let it go and take it up again. And the audience, active and alert, is simultaneously aware of play world and real world, so that the playwright can work upon this double awareness, sometimes leading them imaginatively into the world of his story, sometimes abruptly reminding them of the real world (as most obviously in the choric speech of Time in *The Winter's Tale*), often playing the one against the other, requiring the audience to be at *the same time* aware of both (as in the references to 'an old tale' or to the world as a stage). Shakespeare frequently uses this double awareness that his type of theatre made possible, and we have seen that he seems especially to insist on it in *The Winter's Tale*, as though he did not wish the audience to be too absorbed in the story, perhaps because he wanted them to be looking out for his deeper meaning.

The normal tendency of the Elizabethan theatre toward a conventional rather than a naturalistic type of drama is further reinforced in *The Winter's Tale* by the use of obvious, amateurish, or perhaps at times old-fashioned, dramatic technique. The late Harley Granville-Barker, noting a similar tendency in *Cymbeline*, described it as 'a sophisticated, not a native artlessness, the art that rather displays art than conceals it'. The Elizabethan drama began by being highly conventional and became more natural as writers and actors gained experience. Thus, in its early years there was much 'direct address', i.e. the actor stepped forward and told the audience who he was supposed to be, what sort of fellow he was, and what he intended to do. Later 'soliloquies' were less obvious than this, although Shakespeare never wholly gave up direct address, using it very effectively for Iago, for example, and for the Clown in *Lear*. But *The Winter's Tale* is full of crude and obvious technique: the long direct addresses of Autolycus (IV. iii. 1; IV. iv. 593, 667, 823); the assumption that disguise cannot be seen through, a convention a good deal strained with Autolycus donning and doffing his false beard and with Polixenes and Camillo at the feast unrecognized even by Florizel; the awkward excuses by which characters move back-stage to allow others to converse as if unheard or to address the audience, in Act IV, Scene iv, when the escape is being planned. We may add the meandering way in which the story is told, the gap of sixteen years, the dropping of one set of characters for another—the apparent clumsiness commented on by various critics. Unless Shakespeare was losing his grip—and we have seen good reason to believe that he was not—these technical crudities must have been deliberate and the effect one of burlesque, as if a modern play were to be written and produced with strong reminiscences of *East Lynne*, or *Sweeney Todd, the Demon Barber of Fleet Street*, with a stage-villain twirling his moustaches and stage-whispering across the footlights. No doubt the creaky technique produces an imitation *naïveté* appropriate to the unreal, stagey plot of *The*

Winter's Tale. But it also helps to remind us that the play is only a play, to disengage our minds from the story and to keep us alert to its possible significance.

That this use of crude technique is deliberate and that Shakespeare was never surer of his powers is further emphasized by the technical adroitness with which he rings the changes between comedy and tragedy. What ought to be tragic he makes comic: the scene in which Paulina presents the infant Perdita to Leontes starts seriously enough but gradually becomes almost music-hall farce, as Paulina goads Leontes, and the irritable king jeers at Antigonus for being unable to control his wife; then the tone changes again with Leontes pronouncing his terrible doom upon the helpless baby. Later, the death of Antigonus and the loss of the ship become comic in the mouth of the Clown ('nor the bear half dined on the gentleman' (III. iii. 102)). On the other hand, the old Shepherd, faced with the fury of Polixenes, suddenly grows in dignity: though generally a comic figure, he rises almost to tragic heights as he fears he may never fill a grave beside his ancestors. Tragic is comic and vice versa: all depends on the point of view. Shakespeare is again playing with the multiversity of things, using tricks of the theatre (e.g. presenting Antigonus' death only in the dialogue of the Clown) to point to the ambiguity of human experience. Perhaps what seems most tragic, like being eaten by a bear, is not tragic at all, if we could see with the vision of God!

ANACHRONISM AND THE REALISTIC PASTORAL

An anachronism is a mistake about time: if, in a novel or a play, we were to make Queen Elizabeth ring up Sir Walter Raleigh on the telephone, that would be an anachronism. Several of these apparent blunders have been noted in *The Winter's Tale*. Presumably the events of the

story are meant to take place in a pre-Christian era, yet
Hermione speaks of her father as Emperor of Russia. In
classical times Russia was uncivilized and there was no
emperor. This may be a natural mistake for Shakespeare
to have made, but what about Julio Romano? He was an
Italian, a disciple of Raphael, and died in 1546, but the
Third Gentleman ascribes to him the supposed statue of
Hermione. Can Shakespeare possibly have thought that
an artist who lived within his own century and had an
obviously Italian name really lived over sixteen hundred
years earlier? Surely, if he knew of Julio Romano at all, he
could not make a mistake like that. More obvious, and
more significant, is the mingling of Christian references
with other phrases suggesting classical paganism. We hear
frequently of 'the gods', Hermione appeals to Apollo, and
Phoebus and Dis (Pluto) are named in Perdita's flower
speech. Yet there are references to original sin (see I. ii. 74
and note) and to Judas the betrayer of Our Lord (I. ii. 419);
and Perdita, commenting on her pagan flower speech, likens
herself to a player in 'Whitsun pastorals' (IV. iv. 134).

   The truth is that in Shakespeare's time there was no
'historical method' laid down for the playwright: anachronisms did not exist, because there was no rule that
characters in a past period must refer only to people and
objects that they could really have known about. Shakespeare did not think that Julio Romano was an ancient
Greek or that a pagan king could know about the betrayal
of Our Lord before it happened. But he probably did not
mingle past and present so *deliberately* as would a modern
writer attempting a similar technique. When Mr. Eliot
made the four knights in *Murder in the Cathedral* justify
their action in speeches full of modern clichés, he was
reacting against a clearly defined historical naturalism. In
1611 there was no historical naturalism to react against.
We cannot know to what degree Shakespeare was aware of

what he was doing, but we can see what he did. The dramatic convention about history was not unlike that which holds in pantomime today, where a medieval Dick Whittington may make a joke about something in our modern world, perhaps bus queues, without at all distressing the historical sensibility of the audience. Shakespeare exploited this situation, bringing past and present, pagan and Christian worlds, together. It is yet another means by which story world and real world are kept alongside one another in the mind of the audience. The characters in the story are seen as contemporary and relevant to *us*: they 'talk our language'. (This is literally true, for the Gentlemen in Act v, Scene ii, for example, are a parody of the courtiers of Elizabeth and James, talking the silly courtier jargon which Shakespeare had already ridiculed in a series of characters from Don Armado in *Love's Labour's Lost* to Osric in *Hamlet*.) If the characters talk our language, perhaps the story, when probed, will be of significance for us, too. At the same time our modern problems, put back into an old tale, are distanced, given a framework, so that we can see them in better perspective: modern jargon sounds silly in an ancient legend, and modern jealousy looks silly in a classical king. Furthermore, the mingling of times produces a timelessness, just as the eccentric geography produces a placelessness, which sets the story right outside the normal world. It is not about this or that person who really lived; they are figures in a legend, a myth. And myths have a religious interpretation.

A clue to Shakespeare's possible meaning lies in the mixture of pagan and Christian already mentioned. Far from being peculiar to Shakespeare, this mixture was a common feature of European literature in the period after the Renaissance; it is to be found, for example, in Milton's *Lycidas*. Medieval thought dealt chiefly with the *supernatural*, with divine grace; and medieval art, though indulging at times in a pagan exuberance, for the most part has a guilty attitude towards the delights of this world and fixes its contemplation on the divine as something *opposed to* the earthly. The Renaissance, in its enthusiasm for classical and pagan antiquity, was concerned particularly with the *natural* order, displaying a new interest in physical beauty, human achievement, the varying picture of our earthly life. Christianity had always acknowledged that God's creation was good but knew that it contained an element of corruption also, since the time when Satan and his rebel angels fell through selfish pride, and man subsequently, yielding to temptation, began to live a life of self-assertion instead of the self-discovery and self-development he would have found by living in obedience to God. After the first enthusiasm of the Renaissance had spent itself, a wiser generation wished to do justice both to the 'humanism' it had fostered and to the 'otherworldliness' of the preceding age. The Middle Ages had undervalued the glories of the creation; the Renaissance had neglected the miracle of our redemption. The later sixteenth and earlier seventeenth centuries tried to produce a Christian humanism, a balanced picture in which natural and supernatural should be seen as parts of one divine order. For the creation, though corrupted by the Fall, was redeemed by Our Lord upon the Cross and is now in process of restoration through the operation of divine grace in the Church. Also, since both natural and supernatural orders were produced by the same God, they must be governed by fundamentally the same laws and so have the relationship of *analogy* one to the other. It was therefore believed that the natural, visible creation might be taken as expressing symbolically the supernatural, invisible, and eternal world (e.g. a human king is analogous to God, who is the King of Heaven—although the analogy is very different from any subsisting between two earthly creatures).

The 'pastoral' tradition in literature began in ancient Greece, with writers who presented the shepherd life of the region of Arcadia, not as it was known to be but as it was imagined to have been in a mythical golden age, when gods and goddesses walked the earth and nymphs and satyrs haunted the streams and woods. But poets often used these simple Arcadians and their talk about their loves or their flocks to present, in a covert way, satire upon contemporary political and social affairs. The pastoral form was revived at the Renaissance, and in the next generation the golden-age Arcadia came to stand for the natural order, without the corruption of sin as also without the special insights of Christian revelation (e.g. the satyrs in *The Faerie Queene*, Book I). Sometimes the shepherds would debate political matters in allegorical form, as did their classical prototypes—the superiority of pastoral simplicity to courtly ambition was a favourite theme—and sometimes religious questions, adding, by means of allegory, the supernatural to the natural order which they already represented (e.g. Spenser's *Shepheardes Calender*, Iulye). Or Arcadia might stand for the natural order restored by grace and glorified: it is easy to use the pastoral as a symbol of Heaven when Our Lord is himself the Good Shepherd (see *Shepheardes Calender*, Iune:

> O happy *Hobbinoll*, I blesse thy state,
> That Paradise hast found, whych *Adam* lost;

also, much later, Marvell's *Dialogue between Thyrsis and Dorinda*). So, when we find pastoral conventions in Shakespeare, as in Act IV, Scene iv of *The Winter's Tale*, we may expect some suggestion of uncorrupted nature, together with some use of the natural order to express the supernatural. Also there might be a political or social significance. In the next section we shall see how all these elements form part of a consistent interpretation of the whole play.

Meanwhile we must note that Shakespeare uses the pastoral convention with a difference. Even as early as *As You Like It* he brought out the unreality of this literary tradition by introducing a couple of genuine if exaggeratedly clownish rustics, William and Audrey, in contrast with Silvius and Phebe, the usual Arcadian types. In *The Winter's Tale*, although the setting is Arcadian, his country folk—Perdita excepted—are of his own time and from his native county of Warwickshire. The pastoral tradition is thus modified in two ways: (*a*) It is not pure Golden Age or Eden that is presented: there is a suggestion of sinless innocence, of Eve before the Fall, in Perdita; but Autolycus and the comic triangle formed by the Clown, Mopsa, and Dorcas remind us that the serpent had intruded into man's earthly paradise—in the hint of Eden sin is not forgotten. (*b*) The same contrast of innocence and fall is underlined, and carried over into the sociological field, by contrasting the older and younger generations of rustics. The Shepherd looks back to better days, when his old wife lived, but the younger generation run after the newest gawds from the city and are well versed in the latest ballads. Shakespeare had experienced the invasion of his beloved countryside by middle-class businessmen, the early stages of that urbanization of England which some people are beginning to deplore. It seemed to him that a wholesome feudal tradition, which held the various social classes distinct yet united in mutual service, was being replaced by money-grubbing, trickery, inhumanity, and disorderly confusion. The last point is demonstrated when the Clown becomes 'a gentleman born' (v. ii. 136). Shakespeare's social commentary is thus presented directly, not by way of allegorical dialogue. And this gradual corruption of rural life, sin in its sociological aspect, is dovetailed into the wider religious theme of the play, which we must now endeavour to explain.

THE 'INNER MEANING'

In recent years a number of scholars have been studying Shakespeare's plays historically, trying to see them in relation to the rest of the literature and the thought of his times. And some of these scholars have come to believe that a Shakespeare play is intended to convey an 'inner meaning', that it is not just a moving story arousing general reflections upon our human destiny, but that it is designed to express a particular doctrine or combination of doctrines, religious, social, and political. In the last plays, it would seem, this inner meaning has become all-important and the more immediately dramatic qualities of dialogue, character, and situation are subordinated to it much more decidedly than in even the later tragedies. Shakespeare criticism, however, is not and cannot be an exact science, and there are scholars today who reject the theory of 'inner meanings' as false or not proven; of them most would probably be content with the nineteenth-century criticism which found hints of 'reconciliation' in the last plays but avoided detailed interpretation. In this edition the views of earlier critics, as well as of some contemporaries, are quoted (on pp. 231 ff.), and the reader may form his own opinion. In what follows the present editor proposes to explain why he favours the theory of inner meanings and to give his own interpretation of *The Winter's Tale*.

Undoubtedly the search for inner meanings was a customary activity in Shakespeare's day. Sermon-going was popular and the Scriptures were much studied. For all except the anabaptist extremists the normal method of scriptural exegesis was by way of allegorical and other 'hidden' significances. The Israelites crossing the river Jordan under the leadership of Joshua were a type of the faithful led by Christ ('Joshua' and 'Jesus' are different forms of the same name) through the water of baptism

4123.15   C

into the promised land of the Church. Jordan also signifies the stream of death across which Our Lord leads his people into the Kingdom of Heaven. (The two interpretations are related, Baptism itself being a sort of death, the death of the 'old man', death to sin.) In the theatre 'morality' plays (like *Everyman*) were still performed at times: their characters were personified virtues and vices and other abstractions, and the dialogue and action of such plays had to be interpreted in order to be understood at all—the story was clearly not enough. Poetry such as Spenser's *Faerie Queene* was still full of allegory, and even classical poetry was given an allegorical interpretation.

In such circumstances it would not be surprising if Shakespeare, too, sought to express an inner meaning. Not that he ever employed strict allegory, for that is a method which, as it were, divides the mind of writer and reader. Since everything that happens or is said has to mean something else as well as its obvious meaning, the writer may not develop his story naturally but has to adjust it to an allegorical significance not inherent in the story itself. And the reader is kept hopping between two mental operations: if he becomes too absorbed in events and characters or in the beauty of expression in so far as it relates to the story, he tends to forget the allegory; if he attends to the allegory closely, the other qualities of the work evade him. It is fortunate that Shakespeare never assumed the shackles of formal allegory; but the *essence* of allegory—its conveying two or more layers of meaning at one time—is to be found in the late romances, though the means employed are *symbolic* rather than *allegorical*. The precise difference must be explained. Allegory presents a point-to-point relationship between story and significance: Joshua = Our Lord; Jordan = Baptism; Canaan = the Church. A symbol, however, is an object taken from the natural world (or the imagination) and representing a group of

interrelated significances, not all of which need be present
to the mind at one time. Going back to our illustration, we
may take the river Jordan not only as part of an allegory
but as being in itself symbolic. For it is not merely an
object with two particular significances, baptism and death:
it has a wider range of meaning, which gathers about those
two notions. As the river was geographically the border
between one land and another, it implies the crucial change
in passing from paganism to Christianity or from this
world to the next. Its waters suggest drowning and
oblivion, hence forgetfulness of the cares of this life or of
the sins of the past. The ever-moving waters resemble the
constant flow of time, which must be passed to reach the
stability of eternity—in heaven or the Church. Jordan is a
symbol, drawing together a number of ideas about life and
death, indeed fusing life and death into one: from the
'drowning' of Baptism the candidate rises to a new life
which is centred on the eternal, not the transient, and from
the drowning of death the Christian soul rises to the fulfilment of what is prefigured in the Church. This Jordan
symbol is used in popular hymnody as well as in the subtle
devotional poetry of George Herbert: *Jordan* is the title of
two poems in Herbert's *Temple*. All allegory has something
of the symbolic about it, and usually the more symbolic it
is, the higher its value as poetry. In *The Winter's Tale*
Shakespeare eschews continuous allegory and employs
symbol, with, however, touches of allegory here and there.
Moreover, he brings new life to his expression of religious
truth by avoiding the traditional symbols of Bible and
Church and creating a new symbolic medium out of pagan
romance. Thus, for example, the sea takes the place of
Jordan in Shakespeare's symbolic pattern: it is crossed in
passing from sinful Sicilia to the paradise of Bohemia,
which corresponds to the transition from Leontes jealous
to Leontes penitent, from fall to restoration and recovery

(see notes, p. 196). Among characters Perdita has the most complex symbolic function. She is 'the lost one', as her name signifies—the good life that Leontes forfeited through sin and regained through penitence: as such she represents natural goodness, the spirit of fertility, the beauty of land and sea, the spring season, true love. Whether Shakespeare thought it out in this way or not, he must have felt it so, for that is what he put into his poetry about Perdita and into the poetry that she speaks. Having established the means by which Shakespeare expresses his inner meaning, we are now in a position to state in outline the interpretation of Leontes' story.

The jealousy of Leontes is sin. It comes to him mysteriously, as if from outside. Sin often does thus arise unheralded in the soul and, although within, it comes originally from outside the sinner. It is not a part of the creation at all but is, strictly, as the theologians say, 'nothing': it is *not* being, creation; it *is* not-being, destruction. Satan and sin are the negative power which, opposing the *order* of the universe, tries to break it down to its primal chaos once more. Leontes' sin is deadly, for it consists in a complete reversal of values: he takes good for evil, the gracious love ('charity') and friendship of Hermione for Polixenes he mistakes for evil lust. Mistaking in this one great matter, he mistakes in everything. He thinks he is clever to have seen through the deceit of the supposed lovers and that others are fools not to have done so. But it is he who is deceived, and the others are in the right. He is isolated in a dream-world of his own making, where everything is seen askew as in a distorting-mirror. This is not just the way of Leontes' sin but of all sin: Shakespeare presents in this tale of far-off times the truth about what sin does in every man and what it has done in the universe at large, obscuring the truth and admitting disorder.

Sin is unreal, 'nothing'; it rests entirely on a mistaken

judgement, taking good for evil and evil for good. But it is infinitely dangerous: 'My life stands in the level of your dreams', says Hermione (III. ii. 80). Leontes plans her death, condemns the innocent Perdita to destruction and would have poisoned Polixenes, if he could, and made a murderer out of Camillo. As it is, Mamillius dies, Hermione goes into voluntary seclusion, the court mourns, and the country is left without an heir—all because of the sin of one man. The position of the king as head of the State means that his sin is especially widespread in effect, but we are surely to understand that all sin has wide and unlooked-for consequences.

The oracle, introduced by Cleomenes and Dion in terms arousing religious awe, reminds us of the divine Providence overruling all things. When Leontes defies its pronouncement (sin sets us against God), he is at once punished in the death of Mamillius and the supposed death of Hermione; and Paulina, who as well as being a lively character in the story seems almost to symbolize Leontes' conscience, bids him yield to despair. In contrast, however, with Greene's Pandosto, who had only remorse, Leontes has already repented in the practical, Christian way; for immediately upon the death of Mamillius he had declared his intention of seeking reconciliation with his queen, Polixenes, and Camillo. Now, believing Hermione dead, he shows such distress that Paulina, after her condemnatory speech, is moved to encourage him, and he determines to devote himself to his wife's memory. That he did in fact reconcile himself with Polixenes and Camillo we learn later. This moment of 'conversion' is also the turning-point of the play. Perdita is symbolically the life of grace that Leontes has lost: she represents, in fact, the natural goodness which was corrupted in Adam and restored in Christ— which in the individual Christian is renewed by baptism and thereafter repeatedly lost through sin and found again

through sacramental grace. Mamillius, who so much re-
sembled him is, in a sense, the old Leontes who has died, as
in every Christian the 'old man' must die (so says St. Paul)
that the new, or renewed, man may live. All this is a mere
hint or suggestion: it is not allegory or Mamillius would
have been a bad boy, not a good one. But now Leontes is
repentant and Hermione, in order that the oracle may be
fulfilled and the king live without an heir until the lost one
be found, embarks on a self-imposed discipline of seclusion
from her husband and from the world. Sixteen years of
ascetic self-denial on the part of Leontes and Hermione are
necessary before happiness can be restored. Because sin
has corrupted the rich beauty of our earthly life, we must
exercise self-denial in order to enter upon its riches and
perceive its beauty. Otherwise we misprize them as Leontes
did at first and turn their good into evil.

Perdita, the pastoral May Queen, represents, as we have
said, natural goodness, the untried innocence of Eden,
which comprises also the notions of spring, fertility, natural
beauty, true love. She is what Leontes was before he
learned 'the doctrine of ill-doing' (i. ii. 70), and she and
Florizel typify the love that Hermione and Leontes should
have enjoyed but for the catastrophic entry of sin into
their world. So, likewise, they represent what we should
all be but for that same catastrophic entry of sin into the
universe and the soul of man. They have, moreover, a
sociological significance, taking up the traditional pastoral
opposition of court and country. Leontes with his jealousy,
Polixenes with his pride, both indicate a degree of corruption and over-sophistication as characterizing the court.
It is capable of salvation only through the engrafting upon
it of the rural virtues, the simple honesty of the old
Shepherd. (This is the grafting process advocated by
Polixenes (see iv. iv. 88 and note).) The country itself,
however, is far from perfect: Autolycus' victims are stupid

boors. The grafting process is mutually necessary and the
proper fusion of court and country is symbolized in the
marriage of Florizel and Perdita, and indeed in Perdita
herself, who is both princess and shepherdess, 'the queen
of curds and cream' (IV. iv. 161).

So, when Perdita, that 'peerless piece of earth' (v. i. 94),
returns to Sicilia, she is welcome 'as is the spring to the
earth' (v. i. 152): the images used show that she represents
the return of the rural virtues to a civilization that needed
them. (Shakespeare must have felt that, even then, England was in danger of losing her integrity by allowing a
developing civilization to overthrow the traditional pieties
of the countryside.) Also she, or she and Florizel, symbolize the renewed, restored life which Leontes and Hermione are to share, since by divine grace the one had
wrought out his penitence aided by the self-effacing devotion of the other. Renewed life and a healthy soul come
to people and to kingdoms only by self-denial; and self-
denial takes two forms, the penitence of the sinner and the
self-devotion of the saint. (Normally both will be found in
the same person, for each one is both saint and sinner.)
Hermione, then, comes back as from the dead, and the
hushed and gracious verse of the statue scene speaks of the
resurrection of the Christian to eternal life here and hereafter. One of the silly gentlemen, describing the opening of
Perdita's bundle, says that the king and Camillo 'looked
as they had heard of a world ransomed or one destroyed'
(v. ii. 15), which indicates that Shakespeare had in mind the
ransoming of the world by Our Lord and that destruction
at the Last Day from which the New Jerusalem will arise.
And in the last scene the word of resurrection is spoken by
Paulina:

> Bequeath to death your numbness, for from him
> Dear life redeems you.
>
> (v. iii. 102)

Such would appear to be the 'inner meaning' of *The Winter's Tale*: Shakespeare's mature interpretation of life is that of the Christian faith. But it must be well understood that the paragraphs written above are no substitute for the play itself. They are merely a clue to enable you to read or hear the play with greater understanding. It is only as you attend to the play as a whole, submitting to the power of its poetry, that you will be able to enter into that experience of life's meaning, which Shakespeare himself had and which he is prepared to pass on to you under the symbol of a 'winter's tale'.

DRAMATIS PERSONÆ

LEONTES, King of Sicilia.
MAMILLIUS, young Prince of Sicilia.
CAMILLO,
ANTIGONUS,
CLEOMENES, } Lords of Sicilia.
DION,
POLIXENES, King of Bohemia.
FLORIZEL, his Son.
ARCHIDAMUS, a Lord of Bohemia.
A Mariner.
A Gaoler.
An old Shepherd, reputed Father of Perdita.
Clown, his Son.
Servant to the old Shepherd.
AUTOLYCUS, a Rogue.

HERMIONE, Queen to Leontes.
PERDITA, Daughter to Leontes and Hermione.
PAULINA, Wife to Antigonus.
EMILIA, a Lady, } attending the Queen.
Other Ladies,
MOPSA, } Shepherdesses.
DORCAS,

Sicilian Lords and Ladies, Attendants, Guards, Satyrs, Shepherds
Shepherdesses, &c.

Time as Chorus.

SCENE.—*Sometimes in Sicilia, sometimes in Bohemia.*

THE WINTER'S TALE

ACT I

Scene I

Enter CAMILLO *and* ARCHIDAMUS.

Archidamus. If you shall chance, Camillo, to visit Bohemia, on the like occasion whereon my services are now on foot, you shall see, as I have said, great difference betwixt our Bohemia and your Sicilia.   **4**

Camillo. I think, this coming summer, the King of Sicilia means to pay Bohemia the visitation which he justly owes him.

Archidamus. Wherein our entertainment shall shame us: we will be justified in our loves: for, indeed,—

Camillo. Beseech you,—   **10**

Archidamus. Verily, I speak it in the freedom of my knowledge: we cannot with such magnificence—in so rare —I know not what to say. We will give you sleepy drinks, that your senses, unintelligent of our insufficience, may, though they cannot praise us, as little accuse us.   **15**

Camillo. You pay a great deal too dear for what's given freely.

Archidamus. Believe me, I speak as my understanding instructs me, and as mine honesty puts it to utterance.

---

2 **on the . . . occasion :** i.e. in the train of his king.   **6**
Bohemia : the King of Bohemia.   8–9 **Wherein . . . loves :** We shall not be able to give you such a good time as you have given us : you must take the will for the deed.   13–15 **We will . . . accuse us :** We shall drug you so that, not perceiving our inadequacy, you will not criticize even though you cannot praise us [*N*].   16–17 **You pay . . . freely :** There is no need for polite speeches (already implied in 'beseech you' above).

Camillo. Sicilia cannot show himself over-kind to 20
Bohemia. They were train'd together in their child-
hoods; and there rooted betwixt them then such an
affection which cannot choose but branch now. Since
their more mature dignities and royal necessities made
separation of their society, their encounters, though 25
not personal hath been royally attorneyed with inter-
change of gifts, letters, loving embassies; that they have
seem'd to be together, though absent, shook hands, as
over a vast, and embrac'd, as it were, from the ends of
opposed winds. The heavens continue their loves!   30

Archidamus. I think there is not in the world either
malice or matter to alter it. You have an unspeakable comfort of your young Prince Mamillius: it is a gentleman of
the greatest promise that ever came into my note.   34

Camillo. I very well agree with you in the hopes of him.
It is a gallant child; one that indeed physics the subject,
makes old hearts fresh; they that went on 'rutches ere he
was born desire yet their life to see him a man.

Archidamus. Would they else be content to die?   39

Camillo. Yes; if there were no other excuse why they
should desire to live.

Archidamus. If the king had no son, they would desire to
live on crutches till he had one.

[*Exeunt.*

24 **royal necessities :** the needs of their (respective) kingdoms.
26 **royally attorneyed :** nobly performed by proxy (attorney =
substitute).   29 **vast :** wide, waste sea [*N*].   32 **malice or
matter :** ill will or facts for it to work on [*N*].   33 **it :** perhaps
because referring to a child.   34 **note :** notice.   36 **physics the
subject :** is as good as a tonic to the people.

Scene II

Enter LEONTES, POLIXENES, HERMIONE, MAMILLIUS,
CAMILLO.

Polixenes. Nine changes of the wat'ry star hath been
The shepherd's note since we have left our throne
Without a burden: time as long again
Would be fill'd up, my brother, with our thanks,
And yet we should for perpetuity   5
Go hence in debt: and therefore, like a cipher,
Yet standing in rich place, I multiply
With one 'We thank you' many thousands moe
That go before it.
   Leontes.   Stay your thanks awhile,
And pay them when you part.
   Polixenes.   Sir, that's to-morrow.   10
I am question'd by my fears, of what may chance
Or breed upon our absence, that may blow
No sneaping winds at home, to make us say,
'This is put forth too truly!' Besides, I have stay'd
To tire your royalty.
   Leontes.   We are tougher, brother,   15
Than you can put us to 't.
   Polixenes.   No longer stay.
   Leontes. One seve'night longer.
   Polixenes.   Very sooth, to-morrow.
   Leontes. We'll part the time between 's then; and in that
I'll no gainsaying.
   Polixenes.   Press me not, beseech you, so.

1–2 **Nine . . . note :** The shepherd has noted nine moons; i.e. It
is nine months (**wat'ry star :** the moon, which controls the tides).
5 **for perpetuity :** for ever.   6 **cipher :** nought [*N*].   8 **moe:** more
(plural).   12–13 **that . . . No :** lest [*N*].   13 **sneaping :** nipping.
15–16 **We are . . . to 't :** We are too 'tough' for you to drive us to
that extreme.   17 **seve'night :** week.   18 **part the time :** split
the difference.   19 **I'll no gainsaying :** I'll take no refusal.

There is no tongue that moves, none, none i' th' world 20
So soon as yours, could win me: so it should now,
Were there necessity in your request, although
'Twere needful I denied it. My affairs
Do even drag me homeward; which to hinder
Were in your love a whip to me; my stay   25
To you a charge and trouble: to save both,
Farewell, our brother.

    Leontes.   Tongue-tied our queen? speak you.

    Hermione. I had thought, sir, to have held my peace
        until
You had drawn oaths from him not to stay: you, sir,
Charge him too coldly: tell him, you are sure   30
All in Bohemia's well: this satisfaction
The by-gone day proclaim'd: say this to him,
He's beat from his best ward.

    Leontes.   Well said, Hermione.

    Hermione. To tell he longs to see his son were strong:
But let him say so then, and let him go;   35
But let him swear so, and he shall not stay,
We'll thwack him hence with distaffs.

[*To* POLIXENES.] Yet of your royal presence I'll adventure
The borrow of a week. When at Bohemia
You take my lord, I'll give him my commission   40
To let him there a month behind the gest
Prefix'd for's parting: yet, good deed, Leontes,
I love thee not a jar o' th' clock behind
What lady she her lord. You'll stay?

31–32 **this satisfaction . . . proclaim'd**: we heard this good
news yesterday.   33 **ward**: defence.   35, 36 **But**:
only.   39 **borrow**: loan.   41 **let him there**: stay there
(either from let = allow or let = hinder, delay.   **gest**:
allotted time.   42 **good deed**: indeed.   43 **jar o' th' clock**:
a tick (used metaphorically for the smallest quantity: cf. a jot, an
iota).   43–44 **behind . . . lord**: less than any lady loves her
lord [*N*].

Polixenes. No, madam.

Hermione. Nay, but you will?

Polixenes. I may not, verily. 45

Hermione. Verily!
You put me off with limber vows; but I,
Though you would seek t' unsphere the stars with oaths,
Should yet say, 'Sir, no going'. Verily,
You shall not go: a lady's 'verily' 's 50
As potent as a lord's. Will you go yet?
Force me to keep you as a prisoner,
Not like a guest; so you shall pay your fees
When you depart, and save your thanks. How say you?
My prisoner, or my guest? by your dread 'verily', 55
One of them you shall be.

Polixenes. Your guest, then, madam:
To be your prisoner should import offending;
Which is for me less easy to commit
Than you to punish.

Hermione. Not your gaoler then,
But your kind hostess. Come, I'll question you 60
Of my lord's tricks and yours when you were boys:
You were pretty lordings then?

Polixenes. We were, fair queen,
Two lads that thought there was no more behind
But such a day to-morrow as to-day,
And to be boy eternal.

Hermione. Was not my lord 65
The verier wag o' th' two?

Polixenes. We were as twinn'd lambs that did frisk i'
th' sun,

---

47 **limber** : weak [*N*]. 48 **unsphere** : put out of their regular
course. 51 **yet** : still. 57 **import offending** : imply that I
had committed a crime against you. 62 **lordings** : young lords.
63 **behind** : to follow. 65 i.e. that we should go on being boys
for ever.

And bleat the one at th' other: what we chang'd
Was innocence for innocence; we knew not
The doctrine of ill-doing, nor dream'd   70
That any did. Had we pursu'd that life,
And our weak spirits ne'er been higher rear'd
With stronger blood, we should have answer'd heaven
Boldly, 'not guilty'; the imposition clear'd
Hereditary ours.
   Hermione.   By this we gather   75
You have tripp'd since.
   Polixenes.   O! my most sacred lady,
Temptations have since then been born to's; for
In those unfledg'd days was my wife a girl;
Your precious self had then not cross'd the eyes
Of my young playfellow.
   Hermione.   Grace to boot!   80
Of this make no conclusion, lest you say
Your queen and I are devils; yet, go on:
Th' offences we have made you do we'll answer;
If you first sinn'd with us, and that with us
You did continue fault, and that you slipp'd not   85
With any but with us.
   Leontes.   Is he won yet?
   Hermione. He'll stay, my lord.
   Leontes.   At my request he would not.
Hermione, my dearest, thou never spok'st
To better purpose.
   Hermione.   Never?
   Leontes.   Never, but once.
   Hermione. What! have I twice said well? when was't
     before?   90

---

68 **chang'd** : exchanged (either in words or perhaps in deeds, going
from one occupation to another) [*N*].   75 **hereditary** : by here-
dity [*N*].   80 **Grace to boot !** : Heaven help me! [*N*].   81 **Of this
. . . conclusion** : Do not follow this argument to a logical conclusion.

I prithee tell me; cram's with praise, and make's
As fat as tame things: one good deed, dying tongueless,
Slaughters a thousand waiting upon that.
Our praises are our wages: you may ride's
With one soft kiss a thousand furlongs ere   95
With spur we heat an acre. But to th' goal:
My last good deed was to entreat his stay:
What was my first? it has an elder sister,
Or I mistake you: O! would her name were Grace.
But once before I spoke to th' purpose? when?   100
Nay, let me have't; I long.
   Leontes.   Why, that was when
Three crabbed months had sour'd themselves to death,
Ere I could make thee open thy white hand
And clap thyself my love: then didst thou utter,
'I am yours for ever.'
   Hermione.   'Tis grace indeed.   105
Why, lo you now, I have spoke to th' purpose twice:
The one for ever earn'd a royal husband,
Th' other for some while a friend.
                    [*Giving her hand to* POLIXENES.
   Leontes. [*Aside.*] Too hot, too hot!
To mingle friendship far is mingling bloods.   110
I have *tremor cordis* on me: my heart dances;
But not for joy; not joy. This entertainment
May a free face put on, derive a liberty
From heartiness, from bounty, fertile bosom,
And well become the agent: 't may, I grant: 115
But to be paddling palms and pinching fingers,

92–93 **one . . . that**: praise withheld from one good deed will
prevent others from being done (**tongueless**: without praise).
95 **ere**: before.   96 **heat**: traverse quickly (cf. *heat* in racing,
e.g. 'dead heat').   **acre**: one furlong (as a measure of *length*).
goal: point (of our talk).   111 *tremor cordis*: palpitation.
113 **a free face**: an appearance of candour [*N*].   114 **fertile
bosom**: generosity.

As now they are, and making practis'd smiles,
As in a looking-glass; and then to sigh, as 'twere
The mort o' th' deer; O! that is entertainment
My bosom likes not, nor my brows. Mamillius,　　　120
Art thou my boy?
　　Mamillius.　　　Ay, my good lord.
　　Leontes.　　　　　　　　　　I' fecks?
Why, that's my bawcock. What! hast smutch'd thy nose?
They say it is a copy out of mine. Come, captain,
We must be neat; not neat, but cleanly, captain:
And yet the steer, the heifer, and the calf,　　　125
Are all call'd neat. Still virginalling
Upon his palm? How now, you wanton calf!
Art thou my calf?
　　Mamillius.　　　Yes, if you will, my lord.
　　Leontes. Thou want'st a rough pash and the shoots that
　　I have,
To be full like me: yet they say we are　　　130
Almost as like as eggs; women say so,
That will say anything: but were they false
As o'er-dy'd blacks, as wind, as waters, false
As dice are to be wish'd by one that fixes
No bourn 'twixt his and mine, yet were it true　　　135
To say this boy were like me. Come, sir page,
Look on me with your welkin eye: sweet villain!
Most dear'st! my collop! Can thy dam?—may't be?—
Affection! thy intention stabs the centre:
Thou dost make possible things not so held,　　　140

119 **mort:** death [N].　　121 **I' fecks?:** In faith?　　122
bawcock: fine fellow.　　126 **virginalling:** fingering, as on the
virginals (a keyboard instrument) [N].　　127 **wanton:** frisky [N].
129 **rough pash:** shaggy head.　　**shoots:** horns.　　133 **o'er-
dy'd blacks:** black clothes made rotten by too frequent dyeing.
135 **bourn:** boundary.　　137 **welkin:** sky-blue.　　138 **collop:**
literally, a slice of meat; a term of endearment, his son being a
portion of his flesh.　　139 **Affection:** sexual love [N].

Communicat'st with dreams;—how can this be?—
With what's unreal thou co-active art,
And fellow'st nothing: then, 'tis very credent
Thou mayst co-join with something; and thou dost,
And that beyond commission, and I find it,   145
And that to the infection of my brains
And hardening of my brows.

Polixenes.   What means Sicilia?

Hermione. He something seems unsettled.

Polixenes.   How, my lord!

Leontes. What cheer? how is't with you, best brother?

Hermione.   You look
As if you held a brow of much distraction: 150
Are you mov'd, my lord?

Leontes.   No, in good earnest.
How sometimes nature will betray its folly,
Its tenderness, and make itself a pastime
To harder bosoms! Looking on the lines
Of my boy's face, methoughts I did recoil   155
Twenty-three years, and saw myself unbreech'd,
In my green velvet coat, my dagger muzzled,
Lest it should bite its master, and so prove,
As ornaments oft does, too dangerous:
How like, methought, I then was to this kernel,   160
This squash, this gentleman. Mine honest friend,
Will you take eggs for money?

Mamillius.   No my lord, I'll fight.

Leontes. You will? why, happy man be's dole! My
    brother,
Are you so fond of your young prince as we
Do seem to be of ours?

Polixenes.   If at home, sir,   165

---

161 **squash :** a young pea-pod.   162 **take . . . money :** allow
yourself to be cheated [*N*].   163 **happy . . . dole ! :** may he have
good luck! (proverbial: dole = lot, destiny).

He's all my exercise, my mirth, my matter,
Now my sworn friend and then mine enemy;
My parasite, my soldier, statesman, all:
He makes a July's day short as December,
And with his varying childness cures in me   170
Thoughts that would thick my blood.
    Leontes.   So stands this squire
Offic'd with me. We two will walk, my lord,
And leave you to your graver steps. Hermione,
How thou lov'st us, show in our brother's welcome:
Let what is dear in Sicily be cheap: 175
Next to thyself and my young rover, he's
Apparent to my heart.
    Hermione.   If you would seek us,
We are yours i' th' garden: shall's attend you there?
    Leontes. To your own bents dispose you: you'll be found,
Be you beneath the sky.—[*Aside.*] I am angling now, 180
Though you perceive me not how I give line.
Go to, go to!
How she holds up the neb, the bill to him!
And arms her with the boldness of a wife
To her allowing husband!

                  [*Exeunt* POLIXENES *and* HERMIONE.
                Gone already!   185
Inch-thick, knee-deep, o'er head and ears a fork'd one!

---

166 **matter :** serious consideration (opposed to 'mirth').   168
parasite : one who lives at another's expense. (The young prince
sometimes played the part of a 'court parasite'.)   171 **thick my
blood :** make me sad. (Melancholy was thought to have this physio-
logical effect.)   171–2 **So ... me :** This boy is just the same to
me (with an allusion to the squire's service of the knight).   176
rover : disorderly fellow, robber; used here as a term of affection.
177 **Apparent to :** heir apparent to, having a claim upon.   183
the neb, the bill : the mouth. (Neb = face, nose, mouth; here presumably mouth, since it is the same as 'bill'. To neb = to kiss.)
185 **allowing :** approving.

Go play, boy, play; thy mother plays, and I
Play too, but so disgrac'd a part, whose issue
Will hiss me to my grave: contempt and clamour
Will be my knell. Go play, boy, play. There have
    been,   190
Or I am much deceiv'd, cuckolds ere now;
And many a man there is even at this present,
Now, while I speak this, holds his wife by th' arm,
That little thinks she has been sluic'd in 's absence,
And his pond fish'd by his next neighbour, by   195
Sir Smile, his neighbour: nay, there's comfort in 't,
Whiles other men have gates, and those gates open'd,
As mine, against their will. Should all despair
That have revolted wives the tenth of mankind
Would hang themselves. Physic for 't there's none;   200
It is a bawdy planet, that will strike
Where 'tis predominant; and 'tis powerful, think it,
From east, west, north, and south: be it concluded,
No barricado for a belly: know 't;
It will let in and out the enemy   205
With bag and baggage. Many a thousand on 's
Have the disease, and feel 't not. How now, boy!
   Mamillius. I am like you, they say.
   Leontes.   Why, that's some comfort.
What! Camillo there?
   Camillo. Ay, my good lord.   210
   Leontes. Go play, Mamillius; thou 'rt an honest man.
                           [*Exit* MAMILLIUS.
Camillo, this great sir will yet stay longer.
   Camillo. You had much ado to make his anchor hold:
When you cast out, it still came home.
   Leontes.   Didst note it?

   201 **It**: i.e. lust.   **strike**: blast (referring to the supposed effects
of the heavenly bodies).   202 **predominant**: in the ascendant.
214 **still ... home**: always failed to hold.

Camillo. He would not stay at your petitions; made 215
His business more material.

   Leontes.   Didst perceive it?
[*Aside.*] They're here with me already, whisp'ring, round-
      ing
'Sicilia is a so-forth'. 'Tis far gone,
When I shall gust it last. How came't, Camillo,
That he did stay?

   Camillo.   At the good queen's entreaty.   220
   Leontes. At the queen's, be't: 'good' should be pertinent;
But so it is, it is not. Was this taken
By any understanding pate but thine?
For thy conceit is soaking; will draw in
More than the common blocks: not noted, is't,   225
But of the finer natures? by some severals
Of head-piece extraordinary? lower messes
Perchance are to this business purblind? say.

   Camillo. Business, my lord! I think most understand
Bohemia stays here longer.

   Leontes.   Ha!
   Camillo.   Stays here longer.   230
   Leontes. Ay, but why?
   Camillo. To satisfy your highness and the entreaties
Of our most gracious mistress.

   Leontes.   Satisfy!
Th' entreaties of your mistress! satisfy!
Let that suffice. I have trusted thee, Camillo,   235
With all the nearest things to my heart, as well

---

216 **material :** important.   217 **rounding :** whispering secretly
[*N*].   218 **so-forth :** so-and-so (used to avoid the word 'cuckold',
which Leontes will not utter).   219 **gust :** taste (metaphorical
for 'find out about').   221 **pertinent :** applicable.   222 **so
it is :** in this instance.   **taken :** comprehended.   225 **blocks :**
heads [*N*].   226 **of :** by.   **severals :** individuals.   227
lower messes : inferiors [*N*].   228 **purblind :** wholly blind.
236 **as well :** as well as.

My chamber-councils, wherein, priest-like, thou
Hast cleans'd my bosom: I from thee departed
Thy penitent reform'd; but we have been
Deceiv'd in thy integrity, deceiv'd   240
In that which seems so.
  Camillo.   Be it forbid, my lord!
  Leontes. To bide upon't, thou art not honest; or,
If thou inclin'st that way, thou art a coward,
Which hoxes honesty behind, restraining
From course requir'd; or else thou must be counted   245
A servant grafted in my serious trust,
And therein negligent; or else a fool
That seest a game play'd home, the rich stake drawn,
And tak'st it all for jest.
  Camillo.   My gracious lord,
I may be negligent, foolish, and fearful;   250
In every one of these no man is free,
But that his negligence, his folly, fear,
Among the infinite doings of the world,
Sometime puts forth. In your affairs, my lord,
If ever I were wilful-negligent,   255
It was my folly; if industriously
I play'd the fool, it was my negligence,
Not weighing well the end; if ever fearful
To do a thing, where I the issue doubted,
Whereof the execution did cry out   260
Against the non-performance, 'twas a fear
Which oft infects the wisest: these, my lord,
Are such allow'd infirmities that honesty
Is never free of: but, beseech your Grace,

237 **chamber-councils** : deliberations on state affairs [*N*].   242
bide : insist.   244 **hoxes ... behind** : cuts the back sinews of
honesty [*N*].   246 **grafted ... trust** : grown into my complete
confidence.   248 **home** : to the end [*N*].   254 **puts forth** :
appears.   256 **industriously** : deliberately [*N*].

Be plainer with me; let me know my trespass   **265**
By its own visage; if I then deny it,
'Tis none of mine.

   Leontes.   Ha' not you seen, Camillo,—
But that's past doubt; you have, or your eyeglass
Is thicker than a cuckold's horn,—or heard,—
For to a vision so apparent rumour   **270**
Cannot be mute,—or thought,—for cogitation
Resides not in that man that does not think,—
My wife is slippery? If thou wilt confess,—
Or else be impudently negative,
To have nor eyes, nor ears, nor thought,—then say   **275**
My wife's a hobby-horse; deserves a name
As rank as any flax-wench that puts to
Before her troth-plight: say 't and justify 't.

   Camillo. I would not be a stander-by, to hear
My sovereign mistress clouded so, without   **280**
My present vengeance taken: 'shrew my heart,
You never spoke what did become you less
Than this; which to reiterate were sin
As deep as that, though true.

   Leontes.   Is whispering nothing?
Is leaning cheek to cheek? is meeting noses?   **285**
Kissing with inside lip? stopping the career
Of laughter with a sigh?—a note infallible
Of breaking honesty,—horsing foot on foot?
Skulking in corners? wishing clocks more swift?
Hours, minutes? noon, midnight? and all eyes   **290**
Blind with the pin and web but theirs, theirs only,

---

266 **By . . . visage** : without disguise, exactly.   268 **eyeglass** :
lens of the eye [*N*].   281 **present** : immediate.   **'shrew** : beshrew—
a mild expletive.   284 **as that, though true** : as adultery, even
if it were true.   286 **career** : a full gallop (used metaphorically).
288 **breaking honesty** : adultery.   291 **Blind** : i.e. wishing all
eyes to be blind.   **pin and web** : cataract.

That would unseen be wicked? is this nothing?
Why, then the world and all that's in't is nothing;
The covering sky is nothing; Bohemia nothing;
My wife is nothing; nor nothing have these nothings,   295
If this be nothing.
  Camillo.   Good my lord, be cur'd
Of this diseas'd opinion, and betimes;
For 'tis most dangerous.
  Leontes.   Say it be, 'tis true.
  Camillo. No, no, my lord.
  Leontes.   It is; you lie, you lie:
I say thou liest, Camillo, and I hate thee;   300
Pronounce thee a gross lout, a mindless slave,
Or else a hovering temporizer, that
Canst with thine eyes at once see good and evil,
Inclining to them both: were my wife's liver
Infected as her life, she would not live   305
The running of one glass.
  Camillo.   Who does infect her?
  Leontes. Why, he that wears her like her medal, hanging
About his neck, Bohemia: who, if I
Had servants true about me, that bare eyes
To see alike mine honour as their profits,   310
Their own particular thrifts, they would do that
Which should undo more doing: ay, and thou,
His cup-bearer,—whom I from meaner form
Have bench'd and rear'd to worship, who mayst see
Plainly, as heaven sees earth, and earth sees heaven,   315
How I am gall'd,—mightst bespice a cup,

---

302 **hovering temporizer** : wavering time-server.   306 **glass** :
hour-glass.   307 **like her medal** : like a miniature portrait
of herself.   311 **thrifts** : gains.   314 **bench'd . . . worship** :
dignified and raised to honour (the bench being a seat of honour in
contrast with the forms occupied by 'lower messes').   316 **gall'd** :
injured [*N*].

To give mine enemy a lasting wink;
Which draught to me were cordial.
  Camillo.   Sir, my lord,
I could do this, and that with no rash potion,
But with a ling'ring dram that should not work   320
Maliciously like poison: but I cannot
Believe this crack to be in my dread mistress,
So sovereignly being honourable.
I have lov'd thee,—
  Leontes.   Make that thy question, and go rot!
Dost think I am so muddy, so unsettled,   325
To appoint myself in this vexation;
Sully the purity and whiteness of my sheets,
Which to preserve is sleep; which being spotted
Is goads, thorns, nettles, tails of wasps?
Give scandal to the blood o' th' prince my son,   330
Who I do think is mine, and love as mine,
Without ripe moving to't? Would I do this?
Could man so blench?
  Camillo.   I must believe you, sir:
I do; and will fetch off Bohemia for't;
Provided that when he's remov'd, your highness   335
Will take again your queen as yours at first,
Even for your son's sake; and thereby for sealing
The injury of tongues in courts and kingdoms

---

317 **To give ... wink**: to close my enemy's eyes for ever.   318
cordial: medicinal.   319 **rash**: quick-working.   321 **Maliciously**: with obvious symptoms (so as to suggest 'malice aforethought').   323 **So ... honourable**: being so eminently honourable.   325 **so muddy, so unsettled**: so unreliable in mind [*N*]. **326 To appoint ... vexation**: to become convinced of such a troublesome situation.   332 **Without ... to't**: without sufficient cause.   333 **blench**: start aside (literally of a horse; metaphorically here of a swerving from the path of right conduct).   **334 fetch off**: kill (a euphemism: cf. the modern 'liquidate').   337 **thereby**: by means of that.   337–8 **for sealing ... tongues**: to stop gossip.

Known and allied to yours.

Leontes.   Thou dost advise me
Even so as I mine own course have set down: 340
I'll give no blemish to her honour, none.

Camillo. My lord,
Go then; and with a countenance as clear
As friendship wears at feasts, keep with Bohemia,
And with your queen. I am his cupbearer;   345
If from me he have wholesome beverage,
Account me not your servant.

Leontes.   This is all:
Do 't, and thou hast the one half of my heart;
Do 't not, thou split'st thine own.

Camillo.   I'll do 't, my lord.   349

Leontes. I will seem friendly, as thou hast advis'd me.

                                        [*Exit.*

Camillo. O miserable lady! But, for me,
What case stand I in? I must be the poisoner
Of good Polixenes; and my ground to do 't
Is the obedience to a master; one
Who, in rebellion with himself, will have   355
All that are his so too. To do this deed
Promotion follows. If I could find example
Of thousands that had struck anointed kings,
And flourish'd after, I'd not do 't; but since
Nor brass nor stone nor parchment bears not one,   360
Let villany itself forswear 't. I must
Forsake the court: to do 't, or no, is certain
To me a break-neck. Happy star reign now!
Here comes Bohemia.

                    Re-enter POLIXENES.

Polixenes.   This is strange: methinks

353 **ground to do't** : reason for doing it.   355 **with** : against
[*N*].   363 **a break-neck** : ruin.   **Happy . . . now!** : Good
fortune attend me! (i.e. in his meeting with Polixenes).

My favour here begins to warp. Not speak?—   365
Good day, Camillo.

  Camillo.   Hail, most royal sir!

  Polixenes. What is the news i' th' court?

  Camillo.   None rare, my lord.

  Polixenes. The king hath on him such a countenance
As he had lost some province and a region
Lov'd as he loves himself: even now I met him   370
With customary compliment, when he,
Wafting his eyes to th' contrary, and falling
A lip of much contempt, speeds from me and
So leaves me to consider what is breeding
That changes thus his manners.   375

  Camillo. I dare not know, my lord.

  Polixenes. How! dare not? do not? Do you know, and
    dare not?
Be intelligent to me: 'tis thereabouts;
For, to yourself, what you do know, you must,
And cannot say you dare not. Good Camillo,   380
Your chang'd complexions are to me a mirror
Which shows me mine chang'd too; for I must be
A party in this alteration, finding
Myself thus alter'd with 't.

  Camillo.   There is a sickness
Which puts some of us in distemper; but   385
I cannot name the disease, and it is caught
Of you that yet are well.

  Polixenes.   How caught of me?
Make me not sighted like the basilisk:
I have look'd on thousands, who have sped the better

---

365 **warp** : go awry.   367 **None rare** : Nothing special.   369
As : as if.   372 **Wafting . . . contrary** : looking the other way.
372–3 **falling . . . contempt** : dropping his lip contemptuously.
374 **what is breeding** : what is going to happen.   381 **complexions** : attitude [*N*].

By my regard, but kill'd none so. Camillo,—   390
As you are certainly a gentleman, thereto
Clerk-like experienc'd, which no less adorns
Our gentry than our parents' noble names,
In whose success we are gentle,—I beseech you,
If you know aught which does behove my knowledge 395
Thereof to be inform'd, imprison 't not
In ignorant concealment.
   Camillo.   I may not answer.
   Polixenes. A sickness caught of me, and yet I well?
I must be answer'd. Dost thou hear, Camillo;
I conjure thee, by all the parts of man   400
Which honour does acknowledge,—whereof the least
Is not this suit of mine,—that thou declare
What incidency thou dost guess of harm
Is creeping toward me; how far off, how near;
Which way to be prevented if to be;   405
If not, how best to bear it.
   Camillo.   Sir, I will tell you;
Since I am charg'd in honour and by him
That I think honourable. Therefore mark my counsel,
Which must be ev'n as swiftly followed as
I mean to utter it, or both yourself and me   410
Cry 'lost', and so good night!
   Polixenes.   On, good Camillo.
   Camillo. I am appointed him to murder you.
   Polixenes. By whom, Camillo?

---

392 **Clerk-like experienc'd** : having experience of learning [*N*].
393 **gentry** : high rank.   394 **success** : succession.   **gentle** :
noble.   395–7 **If you . . . concealment** : If you know anything that I ought to know about, do not conceal it and keep me
ignorant of it.   400 **conjure** : enjoin solemnly.   **parts** :
duties [*N*].   403 **incidency** : befalling, happening.   407 **in
honour** : on my honour.   411 **Cry** : proclaim (imperative mood).
good night ! : goodbye for ever!   412 **him** : by him, or as
the man.

Camillo. By the king.

Polixenes. For what?

Camillo. He thinks, nay, with all confidence he swears,
As he had seen 't or been an instrument   415
To vice you to 't, that you have touch'd his queen
Forbiddenly.

Polixenes. O, then my best blood turn
To an infected jelly, and my name
Be yok'd with his that did betray the Best!
Turn then my freshest reputation to   420
A savour, that may strike the dullest nostril
Where I arrive; and my approach be shunn'd,
Nay, hated too, worse than the great'st infection
That e'er was heard or read!

Camillo. Swear his thought over
By each particular star in heaven and   425
By all their influences, you may as well
Forbid the sea for to obey the moon
As or by oath remove or counsel shake
The fabric of his folly, whose foundation
Is pil'd upon his faith, and will continue   430
The standing of his body.

Polixenes. How should this grow?

Camillo. I know not: but I am sure 'tis safer to
Avoid what's grown than question how 'tis born.
If therefore you dare trust my honesty,
That lies enclosed in this trunk, which you   435
Shall bear along impawn'd, away to-night!
Your followers I will whisper to the business,
And will by twos and threes at several posterns

416 vice : screw [*N*].   **421 savour :** stink.   **424 Swear...over :**
outswear, over-swear, or 'swear down' what he thinks; protest by
oath that he is wrong.   **428 or ... or :** either . . . or.   **431
How . . . grow ? :** How could this suspicion arise ?   **435 trunk :**
body (Camillo's).   **436 impawn'd :** as a pledge of good faith.
438 posterns : back gates.

Clear them o' th' city. For myself, I'll put
My fortunes to your service, which are here   440
By this discovery lost. Be not uncertain;
For, by the honour of my parents, I
Have utt'red truth, which, if you seek to prove,
I dare not stand by; nor shall you be safer
Than one condemn'd by the king's own mouth,   445
Thereon his execution sworn.
   Polixenes.   I do believe thee:
I saw his heart in's face. Give me thy hand:
Be pilot to me and thy places shall
Still neighbour mine. My ships are ready and
My people did expect my hence departure   450
Two days ago. This jealousy
Is for a precious creature: as she's rare
Must it be great, and, as his person's mighty
Must it be violent, and, as he does conceive
He is dishonour'd by a man which ever   455
Profess'd to him, why, his revenges must
In that be made more bitter. Fear o'ershades me:
Good expedition be my friend, and comfort
The gracious queen, part of his theme, but nothing
Of his ill-ta'en suspicion! Come, Camillo;   460
I will respect thee as a father if
Thou bear'st my life off hence: let us avoid.
   Camillo. It is in mine authority to command
The keys of all the posterns: please your highness
To take the urgent hour. Come, sir, away!   465
                                     [Exeunt.

---

   441 discovery: disclosure.   **448–9 thy places ... mine**: your
position will always be near my own (i.e. you will have a high position
at court).   **456 Profess'd to him**: declared himself his friend.
458 expedition: speed [*N*].   **459–60 part ... suspicion**: who
has a place in his jealous thoughts, but who is not at all what he
misguidedly suspects [*N*].   **462 avoid**: depart.   **465 take
... hour**: act at once.

ACT II

Scene I

Enter HERMIONE, MAMILLIUS, *and* Ladies.

Hermione. Take the boy to you: he so troubles me,
'Tis past enduring.
    First Lady.   Come, my gracious lord,
Shall I be your playfellow?
    Mamillius.   No, I'll none of you.
    First Lady. Why, my sweet lord?
    Mamillius. You'll kiss me hard and speak to me as if 5
I were a baby still. I love you better.
    Second Lady. And why so, my lord?
    Mamillius.   Not for because
Your brows are blacker; yet black brows, they say,
Become some women best, so that there be not
Too much hair there, but in a semicircle,   10
Or a half-moon made with a pen.
    Second Lady.   Who taught' this?
    Mamillius. I learn'd it out of women's faces. Pray now,
What colour are your eyebrows?
    First Lady.   Blue, my lord.
    Mamillius. Nay, that's a mock: I have seen a lady's nose
That has been blue, but not her eyebrows.
    Second Lady.   Hark ye; 15
The queen your mother rounds apace: we shall
Present our services to a fine new prince
One of these days; and then you'd wanton with us,
If we would have you.

---

11 **taught' this :** taught you this. (The apostrophe shows that a word has been omitted, which for metrical reasons must be pronounced slightly or not at all.)   18 **wanton :** play.

First Lady.   She is spread of late
Into a goodly bulk: good time encounter her!   20
  Hermione. What wisdom stirs amongst you? Come sir,
    now
I am for you again: pray you, sit by us,
And tell's a tale.
  Mamillius.   Merry or sad shall 't be?
  Hermione. As merry as you will.
  Mamillius.   A sad tale 's best for winter.
I have one of sprites and goblins.
  Hermione.   Let's have that, good sir.
Come on, sit down: come on, and do your best   26
To fright me with your sprites; you're powerful at it.
  Mamillius. There was a man,—
  Hermione.   Nay, come, sit down; then on.
  Mamillius. Dwelt by a churchyard. I will tell it softly;
Yond crickets shall not hear it.   30
  Hermione.   Come on, then, and give 't me in mine ear.

          Enter LEONTES, ANTIGONUS, *and* Lords.

  Leontes. Was he met there? his train? Camillo with him?
  First Lord. Behind the tuft of pines I met them: never
Saw I men scour so on their way: I eyed them
Even to their ships.
  Leontes.   How blest am I   35
In my just censure, in my true opinion!
Alack, for lesser knowledge! How accurs'd
In being so blest! There may be in the cup
A spider steep'd, and one may drink, depart,
And yet partake no venom, for his knowledge   40

20 **good ... her!**: may she be safely delivered of her child!   21
What ... you?: What are you gossiping about?   22 **I am for you**:
I am ready for you.   30 **crickets**: tittering women (because they
make a noise like the chirping of crickets).   34 **scour**: go quickly.
36 **censure**: judgement, opinion.   37 **Alack ... knowledge!**:
If only I had known less!

Is not infected; but if one present
Th' abhorr'd ingredient to his eye, make known
How he hath drunk, he cracks his gorge, his sides,
With violent hefts. I have drunk, and seen the spider.
Camillo was his help in this, his pandar: 45
There is a plot against my life, my crown;
All 's true that is mistrusted: that false villain
Whom I employ'd was pre-employ'd by him:
He has discover'd my design, and I
Remain a pinch'd thing; yea, a very trick   50
For them to play at will. How came the posterns
So easily open?
   First Lord.   By his great authority;
Which often hath no less prevail'd than so
On your command.
   Leontes.   I know 't too well.
[*To* HERMIONE.] Give me the boy: I am glad you did not
   nurse him: 55
Though he does bear some signs of me, yet you
Have too much blood in him.
   Hermione.   What is this? sport?
   Leontes. Bear the boy hence; he shall not come about her;
Away with him!—[*Exit* MAMILLIUS, *attended.*] and let her
   sport herself
With that she 's big with; for 'tis Polixenes   60
Has made thee swell thus.
   Hermione.   But I'd say he had not,
And I'll be sworn you would believe my saying,
Howe'er you lean to th' nayward.

---

   43 gorge : throat [*N*].   **44 hefts :** vomiting (heavings).   **47
All 's . . . mistrusted :** Everything that I suspected is true.   **49
He :** i.e. Camillo. **discover'd :** revealed.   **50 pinch'd :** contracted,
narrowed [*N*].   **trick :** puppet.   **57 sport :** a joke.   **61
But I'd say :** I need only say [*N*].   **63 lean . . . nayward :** in-
cline towards denial.

Leontes.   You, my lords,
Look on her, mark her well; be but about
To say, 'she is a goodly lady', and   65
The justice of your hearts will thereto add
''Tis pity she's not honest, honourable':
Praise her but for this her without-door form,—
Which, on my faith, deserves high speech,—and straight
The shrug, the hum or ha, these petty brands   70
That calumny doth use,—O, I am out!—
That mercy does, for calumny will sear
Virtue itself: these shrugs, these hums and ha's,
When you have said 'she's goodly', come between,
Ere you can say 'she's honest'. But be't known,   75
From him that has most cause to grieve it should be,
She's an adulteress.
Hermione.   Should a villain say so,
The most replenish'd villain in the world,
He were as much more villain: you, my lord,
Do but mistake.
Leontes.   You have mistook, my lady,   80
Polixenes for Leontes. O thou thing
Which I'll not call a creature of thy place,
Lest barbarism, making me the precedent,
Should a like language use to all degrees,
And mannerly distinguishment leave out   85
Betwixt the prince and beggar: I have said
She's an adulteress; I have said with whom:
More, she's a traitor, and Camillo is
A federary with her, and one that knows
What she should shame to know herself   90
But with her most vile principal, that she's
A bed-swerver, even as bad as those

68 **without-door form :** external appearance.   89 **federary :**
confederate [*N*].   91 **But :** even.   **principal :** i.e. Polixenes.

That vulgars give bold'st titles; ay, and privy
To this their late escape.
  Hermione.   No, by my life,
Privy to none of this. How will this grieve you,   **95**
When you shall come to clearer knowledge, that
You thus have publish'd me! Gentle my lord,
You scarce can right me throughly then to say
You did mistake.
  Leontes.   No; if I mistake
In those foundations which I build upon,   **100**
The centre is not big enough to bear
A schoolboy's top. Away with her to prison!
He who shall speak for her is afar off guilty
But that he speaks.
  Hermione.   There's some ill planet reigns:
I must be patient till the heavens look   **105**
With an aspect more favourable. Good my lords,
I am not prone to weeping, as our sex
Commonly are; the want of which vain dew
Perchance shall dry your pities; but I have
That honourable grief lodg'd here which burns   **110**
Worse than tears drown. Beseech you all, my lords,
With thoughts so qualified as your charities
Shall best instruct you, measure me; and so
The king's will be perform'd!
  Leontes.   Shall I be heard?
  Hermione. Who is't that goes with me? Beseech your
    highness,   **115**
My women may be with me; for you see

---

   93 **That . . . titles :** that the common people give coarse names
to.   93–94 **privy To :** in the secret of.   94 **late :** recent.   97
Gentle my lord : My noble lord [*N*].   101 **centre :** the earth [*N*].
103 **afar off guilty :** guilty to some degree.   104 **But . . .**
speaks : only for speaking.   106 **aspect :** accent on second
syllable [*N*].

My plight requires it. Do not weep, good fools;
There is no cause: when you shall know your mistress
Has deserv'd prison, then abound in tears
As I come out: this action I now go on   120
Is for my better grace. Adieu, my lord:
I never wish'd to see you sorry; now
I trust I shall. My women, come; you have leave.
    Leontes. Go, do our bidding: hence!
                      [Exeunt Queen *guarded, and* Ladies.
    First Lord. Beseech your highness call the queen again.
    Antigonus. Be certain what you do, sir, lest your jus-
    tice   126
Prove violence: in the which three great ones suffer,
Yourself, your queen, your son.
    First Lord.   For her, my lord,
I dare my life lay down, and will do 't, sir,
Please you t' accept it,—that the queen is spotless   130
I' th' eyes of heaven and to you: I mean,
In this which you accuse her.
    Antigonus.   If it prove
She's otherwise, I'll keep my stables where
I lodge my wife; I'll go in couples with her;
Than when I feel and see her no further trust her;   135
For every inch of woman in the world,
Ay, every dram of woman's flesh is false,
If she be.
    Leontes. Hold your peaces!
    First Lord.   Good my lord,—
    Antigonus. It is for you we speak, not for ourselves.
You are abus'd, and by some putter-on   140
That will be damn'd for 't; would I knew the villain,

---

  117 **fools :** term of endearment. 126-7 **lest . . violence :** lest
your action turn out to be based not on justice but on anger.   132
In this ... her: in respect of the charge you bring against her.   140
abus'd: deceived.   **putter-on :** plotter.

I would land-damn him. Be she honour-flaw'd,—
I have three daughters; the eldest is eleven,
The second and the third, nine and some five;
If this prove true, they'll pay for 't: by mine honour,   145
I'll geld them all; fourteen they shall not see,
To bring false generations: they are co-heirs;
And I had rather glib myself than they
Should not produce fair issue.

   Leontes.   Cease! no more.
You smell this business with a sense as cold   150
As is a dead man's nose; but I do see 't and feel 't,
As you feel doing thus, and see withal
The instruments that feel.

   Antigonus.   If it be so,
We need no grave to bury honesty:
There's not a grain of it the face to sweeten   155
Of the whole dungy earth.

   Leontes.   What! lack I credit?

   First Lord. I had rather you did lack than I, my lord,
Upon this ground; and more it would content me
To have her honour true than your suspicion,
Be blam'd for 't how you might.

   Leontes.   Why, what need we   160
Commune with you of this, but rather follow
Our forceful instigation? Our prerogative
Calls not your counsels, but our natural goodness

---

142 **land-damn**: (perhaps a dialect word for) curse *N*].   144
some: about.   146 **geld**: render sexually incapable.   147 **To...
generations**: to have illegitimate children.   **co-heirs**: joint
heirs (i.e. they divide the inheritance among them).   148 **glib**:
geld.   154 **We ... honesty**: because there is none to bury.
156 **lack I credit?**: don't you believe me?   158 **ground**: matter.
160–2 **Why ... instigation?**: Why, what need have I to discuss
this matter with you? I might merely follow my own powerful impulse.   162–4 **Our ... this**: My position as king does not call
for your advice (i.e. renders it unnecessary) but I have confided in

Imparts this; which if you,—or stupified
Or seeming so in skill,—cannot or will not 165
Relish a truth like us, inform yourselves
We need no more of your advice: the matter,
The loss, the gain, the ord'ring on 't, is all
Properly ours.
 Antigonus. And I wish, my liege,
You had only in your silent judgment tried it, 170
Without more overture.
 Leontes.   How could that be?
Either thou art most ignorant by age,
Or thou wert born a fool. Camillo's flight,
Added to their familiarity,
Which was as gross as ever touch'd conjecture, 175
That lack'd sight only, nought for approbation
But only seeing, all other circumstances
Made up to th' deed, doth push on this proceeding:
Yet, for a greater confirmation,—
For in an act of this importance 'twere 180
Most piteous to be wild,—I have dispatch'd in post
To sacred Delphos, to Apollo's temple,
Cleomenes and Dion, whom you know
Of stuff'd sufficiency. Now, from the oracle
They will bring all; whose spiritual counsel had, 185
Shall stop or spur me. Have I done well?

you out of my goodness. **164–5 or stupified ... skill :** either
grown stupid or appearing so in cunning. **166 Relish :** appreciate.
169 Properly ours : exclusively mine. **171 overture :** publicity.
172 thou ... age : you have grown foolish. **175 as gross ...
conjecture :** as clear as ever conjecture reached to (i.e. as clear as
anything could be that relied on induction from circumstantial evidence and not on actual witnesses). **176 approbation :** proof.
178 push ... proceeding : compel me to go on with the matter.
181 wild : rash. **in post :** to travel with special speed. **184
stuff'd sufficiency :** more than adequate ability. **185 all :** i.e.
all we need to know.

First Lord. Well done, my lord.

Leontes. Though I am satisfied and need no more
Than what I know, yet shall the oracle
Give rest to th' minds of others, such as he   190
Whose ignorant credulity will not
Come up to th' truth. So have we thought it good
From our free person she should be confin'd,
Lest that the treachery of the two fled hence
Be left her to perform. Come, follow us: 195
We are to speak in public; for this business
Will raise us all.

Antigonus. [*Aside.*] To laughter, as I take it,
If the good truth were known.   [*Exeunt.*

Scene II

Enter PAULINA, *a* Gentleman *and* Attendants.

Paulina. The keeper of the prison, call to him;
Let him have knowledge who I am.—[*Exit* Gentleman.]
    Good lady,
No court in Europe is too good for thee;
What dost thou then in prison?

Re-enter Gentleman *with the* Gaoler.

                              Now, good sir,
You know me, do you not?

Gaoler.   For a worthy lady   5
And one who much I honour.

Paulina.   Pray you then,
Conduct me to the queen.

190–2 **such as he . . . truth :** either Antigonus or else, generally,
any who will not believe as Leontes does.   192 **So :** i.e. *because*
she is guilty, and *until* the oracle pronounces on the matter.   193
free : easily accessible, open to danger.   195 **perform :** carry out
(by murdering me).   197 **raise :** rouse, stir up or elevate [*N*].

Gaoler.   I may not, madam.
To the contrary I have express commandment.
  Paulina. Here's ado,
To lock up honesty and honour from   10
Th' access of gentle visitors! Is't lawful, pray you,
To see her women? any of them? Emilia?
  Gaoler. So please you, madam,
To put apart these your attendants, I
Shall bring Emilia forth.
  Paulina.   I pray now, call her.   15
Withdraw yourselves.   [*Exeunt* Attendants.
  Gaoler.   And madam,
I must be present at your conference.
  Paulina. Well, be't so, prithee.   [*Exit* Gaoler.
Here's such ado to make no stain a stain,
As passes colouring.

               Re-enter Gaoler, *with* EMILIA.

                    Dear gentlewoman,   20
How fares our gracious lady?
  Emilia. As well as one so great and so forlorn
May hold together. On her frights and griefs,—
Which never tender lady hath borne greater,—
She is something before her time deliver'd.   25
  Paulina. A boy?
  Emilia.   A daughter; and a goodly babe,
Lusty and like to live: the queen receives
Much comfort in't; says, 'My poor prisoner,
I am innocent as you.'
  Paulina.   I dare be sworn: 29
These dangerous unsafe lunes i' th' king, beshrew them!
He must be told on't, and he shall: the office
Becomes a woman best; I'll take't upon me.

---

11 **gentle** : noble.   20 **colouring** : dyeing [*N*].   23 **On** : In
consequence of.   30 **lunes** : fits of lunacy.   **beshrew** : curse.

If I prove honey-mouth'd, let my tongue blister,
And never to my red-look'd anger be
The trumpet any more. Pray you, Emilia,   35
Commend my best obedience to the queen:
If she dares trust me with her little babe,
I'll show't the king and undertake to be
Her advocate to th' loud'st. We do not know
How he may soften at the sight o' th' child: 40
The silence often of pure innocence
Persuades when speaking fails.
   Emilia.   Most worthy madam,
Your honour and your goodness is so evident
That your free undertaking cannot miss
A thriving issue: there is no lady living   45
So meet for this great errand. Please your ladyship
To visit the next room, I'll presently
Acquaint the queen of your most noble offer,
Who but to-day hammered of this design,
But durst not tempt a minister of honour,   50
Lest she should be denied.
   Paulina.   Tell her, Emilia,
I'll use that tongue I have: if wit flow from 't
As boldness from my bosom, let 't not be doubted
I shall do good.
   Emilia.   Now be you blest for it!
I'll to the queen. Please you, come something nearer. 55
   Gaoler. Madam, if 't please the queen to send the babe,
I know not what I shall incur to pass it,
Having no warrant.

---

44 free : spontaneous, freely offered.   **44–45 cannot ... issue :**
cannot but be successful.   **47 presently :** at once.   **49 hammered
of :** thought hard and repeatedly about.   **50 tempt :** make trial
of (i.e. try to get the aid of).   **minister of honour :** a servant of
high birth and position, as opposed to a mere hired domestic.   **52
wit :** intelligence, sense.   **57 what :** what punishment.   **to
pass it :** if I let it pass.

Paulina.   You need not fear it, sir:
The child was prisoner to the womb, and is
By law and process of great nature thence   60
Freed and enfranchis'd; not a party to
The anger of the king, nor guilty of,
If any be, the trespass of the queen.

Gaoler. I do believe it.

Paulina. Do not you fear: upon mine honour, I   65
Will stand betwixt you and danger.   [*Exeunt.*

Scene III

Enter LEONTES, ANTIGONUS, Lords, *and other*
Attendants.

Leontes. Nor night, nor day, no rest; it is but weakness
To bear the matter thus; mere weakness. If
The cause were not in being,—part o' th' cause,
She th' adulteress; for the harlot king
Is quite beyond mine arm, out of the blank   5
And level of my brain, plot-proof; but she
I can hook to me: say, that she were gone,
Given to the fire, a moiety of my rest
Might come to me again. Who's there?

First Attendant.   [*Advancing.*] My lord?

Leontes. How does the boy?

First Attendant.   He took good rest to-night; 10
'Tis hop'd his sickness is discharg'd.

61 **enfranchis'd** : freed [*N*].   63 **If any be** : i.e. if there be any
trespass.   4 **harlot** : lewd (used of either sex in Shakespeare).   5–6
out of . . . plot-proof : beyond the range of my planning, secure from
plots (in shooting, blank = the mark aimed at, the white spot in the
centre of the target; level = aim).   7 **hook to me** : catch, get
hold of (from the grappling-hook used in sea-fights).   8 **moiety** :
half.

Leontes.   To see his nobleness!
Conceiving the dishonour of his mother,
He straight declin'd, droop'd, took it deeply,
Fasten'd and fix'd the shame on't in himself,   15
Threw off his spirit, his appetite, his sleep,
And downright languish'd. Leave me solely: go,
See how he fares. [*Exit* Attendant.]—Fie, fie! no thought
    of him;
The very thought of my revenges that way
Recoil upon me: in himself too mighty,   20
And in his parties, his alliance; let him be
Until a time may serve: for present vengeance,
Take it on her. Camillo and Polixenes
Laugh at me; make their pastime at my sorrow:
They should not laugh, if I could reach them, nor   25
Shall she within my power.

           Enter PAULINA, *with a* Child.

First Lord.   You must not enter.
Paulina. Nay, rather, good my lords, be second to me:
Fear you his tyrannous passion more, alas,
Than the queen's life? a gracious, innocent soul,
More free than he is jealous.
Antigonus.   That's enough.   30
Second Attendant. Madam, he hath not slept tonight;
    commanded
None should come at him.
Paulina.   Not so hot, good sir;

12 **To see** : Imagine.   13 **Conceiving** : Understanding.   17
solely : alone.   18 **no thought of him** : let me not think of him
(Polixenes).   21 **parties** : allies (explained by 'his alliance').   27
be second to : support (cf. 'seconds' in boxing).   28–29 **Fear . . .
life?** : Are you more afraid *of* his unjust anger than you are afraid *for*
the life of the queen?   30 **More . . . jealous** : whose freedom from
the sin which is the ground of his jealousy is greater than that jealousy
itself.   32 **Not so hot** : Don't be so impatient.

I come to bring him sleep. 'Tis such as you,
That creep like shadows by him and do sigh
At each his needless heavings, such as you   35
Nourish the cause of his awaking: I
Do come with words as med'cinal as true,
Honest as either, to purge him of that humour
That presses him from sleep.

    Leontes.   What noise there, ho?

    Paulina. No noise, my lord; but needful conference   40
About some gossips for your highness.

    Leontes.   How!
Away with that audacious lady! Antigonus,
I charg'd thee that she should not come about me:
I knew she would.

    Antigonus.   I told her so, my lord,
On your displeasure's peril, and on mine,   45
She should not visit you.

    Leontes.   What! canst not rule her?

    Paulina. From all dishonesty he can: in this,
Unless he take the course that you have done,
Commit me for committing honour, trust it,
He shall not rule me.

    Antigonus.   La you now! you hear;   50
When she will take the rein I let her run;
But she'll not stumble.

    Paulina.   Good my liege, I come,
And I beseech you, hear me, who professes
Myself your loyal servant, your physician,
Your most obedient counsellor, yet that dares   55
Less appear so in comforting your evils

---

35 **heavings** : sighs.   **39 presses . . . sleep** : lies heavily on
him and prevents him from sleeping [*N*].   **41 gossips** : sponsors
at baptism.   **47 dishonesty** : dishonourable conduct (as often).
49 trust it : be quite sure.   **50 La you now !** : Look now!
(though 'la' is not etymologically connected with 'look').

Than such as most seem yours: I say, I come
From your good queen.

   Leontes.   Good queen!

   Paulina. Good queen, my lord, good queen; I say, good
     queen;

And would by combat make her good, so were I   60
A man, the worst about you.

   Leontes.   Force her hence.

   Paulina. Let him that makes but trifles of his eyes
First hand me: on mine own accord I'll off;
But first I'll do my errand. The good queen,
For she is good, hath brought you forth a daughter: 65
Here 'tis; commends it to your blessing.

                        [*Laying down the* Child.

   Leontes.   Out!
A mankind witch! Hence with her, out o' door:
A most intelligencing bawd!

   Paulina.   Not so;
I am as ignorant in that as you
In so entitling me, and no less honest   70
Than you are mad; which is enough, I'll warrant,
As this world goes, to pass for honest.

   Leontes.   Traitors!
Will you not push her out? Give her the bastard.
[*To* ANTIGONUS.] Thou dotard! thou art woman-tir'd, un-
     roosted
By thy dame Partlet here. Take up the bastard;   75
Take 't up, I say; give 't to thy crone.

---

60 **make** : prove (with a suggestion of 'making good' what I say
about her [*N*]).   61 **worst** : weakest.   63 **hand** : lay hands on.
67 **mankind** : mannish, violent.   68 **intelligencing** : acting as
go-between. (Leontes means that she had served Hermione and
Polixenes in this way.)   69–70 **I am ... me** : I am as ignorant of the
profession of bawd (go-between) as you are of me in giving me that
name.   74 **woman-tir'd** : hen-pecked (tire (French, *tirer*) = tear).
unroosted : driven from your perch [*N*].   76 **crone** : old woman.

Paulina.   For ever
Unvenerable be thy hands, if thou
Tak'st up the princess by that forced baseness
Which he has put upon 't!
   Leontes.   He dreads his wife.   79
   Paulina. So I would you did; then, 'twere past all doubt,
You'd call your children yours.
   Leontes.   A nest of traitors!
   Antigonus. I am none, by this good light.
   Paulina.   Nor I; nor any
But one that 's here, and that 's himself; for he
The sacred honour of himself, his queen's,
His hopeful son's, his babe's, betrays to slander,   85
Whose sting is sharper than the sword's; and will
   not,—
For, as the case now stands, it is a curse
He cannot be compell'd to 't,—once remove
The root of his opinion, which is rotten
As ever oak or stone was sound.
   Leontes.   A callat   90
Of boundless tongue, who late hath beat her husband
And now baits me! This brat is none of mine;
It is the issue of Polixenes:
Hence with it; and, together with the dam
Commit them to the fire!
   Paulina.   It is yours;   95
And, might we lay th' old proverb to your charge,
'So like you, 'tis the worse.' Behold, my lords,
Although the print be little, the whole matter
And copy of the father; eye, nose, lip,

---

   78 by . . . baseness : under that falsely used term of bastard.
88–89 once . . . opinion : just pull out the root of (i.e. eradicate or
get rid of) his opinion.   **90 callat :** scold, strumpet (both meanings
intended here).   **91 boundless :** limitless.   **94 dam :** mother
(used of animals; cf. II. i. 133–4).

The trick of's frown, his forehead, nay, the valley,   100
The pretty dimples of his chin and cheek, his smiles,
The very mould and frame of hand, nail, finger:
And thou, good goddess Nature, which hast made it
So like to him that got it, if thou hast
The ordering of the mind too, 'mongst all colours   105
No yellow in't; lest she suspect, as he does,
Her children not her husband's.

    Leontes.   A gross hag!
And, lozel, thou art worthy to be hang'd,
That wilt not stay her tongue.

    Antigonus.   Hang all the husbands
That cannot do that feat, you'll leave yourself   110
Hardly one subject.

    Leontes.   Once more, take her hence.

    Paulina. A most unworthy and unnatural lord
Can do no more.

    Leontes.   I'll ha' thee burn'd.

    Paulina.   I care not:
It is an heretic that makes the fire,
Not she which burns in't. I'll not call you tyrant;   115
But this most cruel usage of your queen,—
Not able to produce more accusation
Than your own weak-hing'd fancy,—something savours
Of tyranny, and will ignoble make you,
Yea, scandalous to the world.

    Leontes.   On your allegiance,   120
Out of the chamber with her! Were I a tyrant,
Where were her life? she durst not call me so
If she did know me one. Away with her!

    Paulina. I pray you do not push me; I'll be gone.   124
Look to your babe, my lord; 'tis yours: Jove send her

---

   100 **trick** : habitual expression.   **valley** : perhaps the cleft of
the chin.   106 **No yellow** : let there be no yellow (symbol of
jealousy).   108 **lozel** : scoundrel.

A better guiding spirit! What needs these hands?
You, that are thus so tender o'er his follies,
Will never do him good, not one of you.
So, so: farewell; we are gone.   [*Exit.*

   Leontes. Thou, traitor, hast set on thy wife to this.   130
My child! away with 't!—even thou, that hast
A heart so tender o'er it, take it hence
And see it instantly consum'd with fire:
Even thou and none but thou. Take it up straight:
Within this hour bring me word 'tis done,—   135
And by good testimony,—or I'll seize thy life,
With what thou else call'st thine. If thou refuse
And wilt encounter with my wrath, say so;
The bastard brains with these my proper hands
Shall I dash out. Go, take it to the fire;   140
For thou sett'st on thy wife.

   Antigonus.   I did not, sir:
These lords, my noble fellows, if they please,
Can clear me in 't.

   First Lord.   We can, my royal liege,
He is not guilty of her coming hither.

   Leontes. You're liars all.   145

   First Lord. Beseech your highness, give us better
    credit:
We have always truly serv'd you, and beseech'
So to esteem of us; and on our knees we beg,
As recompense of our dear services
Past and to come, that you do change this purpose,   150
Which being so horrible, so bloody, must
Lead on to some foul issue. We all kneel.

---

    126 **needs** : need is there of [*N*].   136 **seize** : take (a legal expression).   139 **proper** : own.   146 **give . . . credit** : have more belief in us.   147 **beseech'** : beseech you (cf. II. i. 11).   148 **So . . . us** : to understand that we have done so.   149 **dear** : devoted.   152 **issue** : result.

Leontes. I am a feather for each wind that blows.
Shall I live on to see this bastard kneel
And call me father? Better burn it now   155
Than curse it then. But, be it; let it live:
It shall not neither.—[*To* ANTIGONUS.] You, sir, come you
    hither;
You that have been so tenderly officious
With Lady Margery, your midwife there,
To save this bastard's life,—for 'tis a bastard,   160
So sure as this beard's grey,—what will you adventure
To save this brat's life?
    Antigonus.   Any thing, my lord,
That my ability may undergo,
And nobleness impose: at least, thus much:
I'll pawn the little blood which I have left,   165
To save the innocent: any thing possible.
    Leontes. It shall be possible. Swear by this sword
Thou wilt perform my bidding.
    Antigonus.   I will, my lord.
    Leontes. Mark and perform it,—seest thou!—for the fail
Of any point in't shall not only be   170
Death to thyself, but to thy lewd-tongu'd wife,
Whom for this time we pardon. We enjoin thee,
As thou art liegeman to us, that thou carry
This female bastard hence; and that thou bear it
To some remote and desert place quite out   175
Of our dominions; and that there thou leave it,
Without more mercy, to it own protection,
And favour of the climate. As by strange fortune
It came to us, I do in justice charge thee,

---

153 **feather . . . blows :** changed by each new influence brought
to bear upon me.   156 **be it :** be it so (Leontes relents momentarily).
157 **shall not :** i.e. shall not live. (Leontes hesitates between sparing
and killing the child, before deciding to leave its fate to chance.)
158 **officious :** fussily busy.   169 **fail :** failure.   177 **it :** its [N].

On thy soul's peril and thy body's torture,   180
That thou commend it strangely to some place,
Where chance may nurse or end it. Take it up.
  Antigonus. I swear to do this, though a present death
Had been more merciful. Come on, poor babe:
Some powerful spirit instruct the kites and ravens   185
To be thy nurses! Wolves and bears, they say,
Casting their savageness aside have done
Like offices of pity. Sir, be prosperous
In more than this deed does require! And blessing
Against this cruelty fight on thy side;   190
Poor thing, condemn'd to loss!

                      [*Exit with the* Child.
  Leontes.   No; I'll not rear
Another's issue.

Enter a Servant.

  Servant.   Please your highness, posts
From those you sent to th' oracle are come
An hour since: Cleomenes and Dion,
Being well arriv'd from Delphos, are both landed,   195
Hasting to th' court.
  First Lord.   So please you, sir, their speed
Hath been beyond accompt.
  Leontes.   Twenty-three days
They have been absent: 'tis good speed; foretells
The great Apollo suddenly will have
The truth of this appear. Prepare you, lords;   200
Summon a session, that we may arraign
Our most disloyal lady; for, as she hath

---

181 **strangely :** abroad (where it will be a stranger; with a
reference back to 'strange fortune' in line 178) [*N*].   188 **offices :**
services.   189 **blessing :** (God's) protection [*N*].   192 **posts :**
express messengers.   197 **accompt :** calculation.   201
session : trial.

Been publicly accus'd, so shall she have
A just and open trial. While she lives
My heart will be a burden to me. Leave me,   205
And think upon my bidding.   [*Exeunt.*

206 **bidding** : command.

ACT III

Scene I

Enter CLEOMENES *and* DION.

Cleomenes. The climate's delicate, the air most sweet,
Fertile the isle, the temple much surpassing
The common praise it bears.
   Dion.   I shall report,
For most it caught me, the celestial habits,—
Methinks I so should term them,—and the reverence   5
Of the grave wearers. O, the sacrifice!
How ceremonious, solemn, and unearthly
It was i' th' offering!
   Cleomenes.   But of all, the burst
And the ear-deaf'ning voice o' th' oracle,
Kin to Jove's thunder, so surpris'd my sense,   10
That I was nothing.
   Dion.   If th' event o' th' journey
Prove as successful to the queen,—O, be 't so!—
As it hath been to us rare, pleasant, speedy,
The time is worth the use on 't.
   Cleomenes.   Great Apollo
Turn all to th' best! These proclamations,   15
So forcing faults upon Hermione,
I little like.
   Dion.   The violent carriage of it
Will clear or end the business: when the oracle,

---

3 **common** : general, usual [*N*].   4 **caught** : struck [*N*].
celestial habits : sacred vestments (celestial = heavenly).   8
burst : breaking into speech.   11 **event** : result.   16 **forcing
faults** : i.e. accusing her of faults as if they were already established
against her.   17 **violent carriage** : rapid pushing-on.   18
clear or end : i.e. clear it up (favourably for Hermione) or end it (in
her condemnation).

Thus by Apollo's great divine seal'd up,
Shall the contents discover, something rare   20
Even then will rush to knowledge.—Go:—fresh horses!
And gracious be the issue!   [*Exeunt.*

Scene II

Enter LEONTES, *Lords, Officers.*

Leontes. This sessions, to our great grief we pronounce,
Even pushes 'gainst our heart: the party tried
The daughter of a king, our wife, and one
Of us too much belov'd. Let us be clear'd
Of being tyrannous, since we so openly   5
Proceed in justice, which shall have due course,
Even to the guilt or the purgation.
Produce the prisoner.
    Officer. It is his highness' pleasure that the queen
Appear in person here in court.   10

Silence.

Enter HERMIONE *guarded;* PAULINA *and*
Ladies *attending.*

Leontes. Read the indictment.
    *Officer. Hermione, queen to the worthy Leontes, King of
Sicilia, thou art here accused and arraigned of high treason,
in committing adultery with Polixenes, King of Bohemia,
and conspiring with Camillo to take away the life of our* 15
sovereign lord the king, thy royal husband: the pretence

19 **great divine :** chief priest.   20 **contents :** accent on second
syllable.   **discover :** reveal.   **rare :** remarkable (cf. l. 13).
1 **sessions :** trial (a collective plural with the same meaning as the
singular).   2 **pushes . . . heart :** causes me deep sorrow.   7
purgation : acquittal.   16 *pretence:* design, plot.

whereof being by circumstances partly laid open, thou,
Hermione, contrary to the faith and allegiance of a true
subject, didst counsel and aid them, for their better safety,
to fly away by night.   20

  Hermione. Since what I am to say must be but that
Which contradicts my accusation, and
The testimony on my part no other
But what comes from myself, it shall scarce boot me
To say 'Not guilty': mine integrity   25
Being counted falsehood, shall, as I express it,
Be so receiv'd. But thus: if powers divine
Behold our human actions, as they do,
I doubt not then but innocence shall make
False accusation blush, and tyranny   30
Tremble at patience. You, my lord, best know,—
Who least will seem to do so,—my past life
Hath been as continent, as chaste, as true,
As I am now unhappy; which is more
Than history can pattern, though devis'd   35
And play'd to take spectators. For behold me,
A fellow of the royal bed, which owe
A moiety of the throne, a great king's daughter,
The mother to a hopeful prince, here standing
To prate and talk for life and honour 'fore   40
Who please to come and hear. For life, I prize it
As I weigh grief, which I would spare: for honour,
'Tis a derivative from me to mine,
And only that I stand for. I appeal
To your own conscience, sir, before Polixenes   45
Came to your court, how I was in your grace,
How merited to be so; since he came,

  24 **boot :** help [*N*].   27 **But thus :** i.e. But, since I have to
speak, this is what I say.   35 **history :** story (of any kind; here
a stage play) [*N*].   37 **fellow . . . bed :** royal wife.   **owe :**
own, possess by right.   38 **moiety :** half.

With what encounter so uncurrent I
Have strain'd, t' appear thus: if one jot beyond
The bound of honour, or in act or will   50
That way inclining, harden'd be the hearts
Of all that hear me, and my near'st of kin
Cry fie upon my grave!
   Leontes.   I ne'er heard yet
That any of these bolder vices wanted
Less impudence to gainsay what they did   55
Than to perform it first.
   Hermione.   That's true enough;
Though 'tis a saying, sir, not due to me.
   Leontes. You will not own it.
   Hermione.   More than mistress of
Which comes to me in name of fault, I must not
At all acknowledge. For Polixenes,—   60
With whom I am accus'd,—I do confess
I lov'd him as in honour he requir'd,
With such a kind of love as might become
A lady like me; with a love even such,
So and no other, as yourself commanded: 65
Which not to have done, I think had been in me
Both disobedience and ingratitude
To you and toward your friend, whose love had spoke,
Even since it could speak, from an infant, freely
That it was yours. Now, for conspiracy,   70
I know not how it tastes, though it be dish'd
For me to try how: all I know of it
Is that Camillo was an honest man;
And why he left your court, the gods themselves,

---

48 **encounter** : behaviour [*N*].   **uncurrent** : (slightly) unusual.
49 **strain'd** : gone beyond (what is right).   **if one jot** : sc. I have
'strain'd'.   54 **wanted**: lacked [*N*].   55 **Less**: for 'more' [*N*].
gainsay: deny.   57 **due**: applicable.   58 **mistress**: owner,
possessor [*N*].   62 **requir'd**: justly deserved.   69 **freely** : openly.

Wotting no more than I, are ignorant.   75
  Leontes. You knew of his departure, as you know
What you have underta'en to do in's absence.
  Hermione. Sir,
You speak a language that I understand not:
My life stands in the level of your dreams,   80
Which I'll lay down.
  Leontes.   Your actions are my dreams:
You had a bastard by Polixenes,
And I but dream'd it. As you were past all shame,—
Those of your fact are so,—so past all truth:
Which to deny concerns more than avails; for as   85
Thy brat hath been cast out, like to itself,
No father owning it, —which is, indeed,
More criminal in thee than it,—so thou
Shalt feel our justice, in whose easiest passage
Look for no less than death.
  Hermione.   Sir, spare your threats: 90
The bug which you would fright me with I seek.
To me can life be no commodity:
The crown and comfort of my life, your favour,
I do give lost; for I do feel it gone,
But know not how it went. My second joy,   95
And first-fruits of my body, from his presence
I am barr'd, like one infectious. My third comfort,
Starr'd most unluckily, is from my breast,
The innocent milk in it most innocent mouth,
Hal'd out to murder: myself on every post   100

75 **Wotting** : if they know.   77 **What ... absence** : i.e. to murder
Leontes.   80 **level: range** [*N*].   84 **Those ... fact** : those guilty of
your sort of crime.   85 **concerns ... avails** : gives you more trouble
than any good it will do you.   86 **like to itself** : i.e. like the
outcast it is.   89 **passage** : course.   91 **bug** : bugbear, bogey,
imaginary terror.   92 **commodity** : advantage.   94 **give:**
account.   98 **Starr'd:** fated.   99 **it** : its (cf. II. iii. 177,
note).

Proclaim'd a strumpet: with immodest hatred
The child-bed privilege denied, which 'longs
To women of all fashion: lastly, hurried
Here to this place, i' th' open air, before
I have got strength of limit. Now, my liege,   105
Tell me what blessings I have here alive,
That I should fear to die? Therefore proceed.
But yet hear this; mistake me not; no life,—
I prize it not a straw,—but for mine honour,
Which I would free: if I shall be condemn'd   110
Upon surmises, all proofs sleeping else
But what your jealousies awake, I tell you
'Tis rigour and not law. Your honours all,
I do refer me to the oracle:
Apollo be my judge!

   First Lord.   This your request   115
Is altogether just: therefore, bring forth,
And in Apollo's name, his oracle.

                     [Exeunt certain Officers.

   Hermione. The Emperor of Russia was my father:
O! that he were alive, and here beholding
His daughter's trial; that he did but see   120
The flatness of my misery; yet with eyes
Of pity, not revenge!

       Re-enter Officers, *with* CLEOMENES *and* DION.

   Officer. You here shall swear upon this sword of justice,
That you, Cleomenes and Dion, have   124
Been both at Delphos, and from thence have brought
This seal'd-up oracle, by the hand deliver'd
Of great Apollo's priest, and that since then

---

101 **immodest :** immoderate, extreme.   103 **of all fashion :** of
all sorts.   105 **strength of limit :** strength through resting the
correct length of time ('limit' = 'prescribed period of time' is found
only in Shakespeare).   121 **flatness :** completeness (as in 'that's
flat!'—with perhaps the added sense of lowness as in 'low spirits').

You have not dar'd to break the holy seal,
Nor read the secrets in 't.

Cleomenes.   }   All this we swear.
Dion.   }

Leontes. Break up the seals, and read.   130

Officer. *Hermione is chaste; Polixenes blameless; Camillo a*
true subject; Leontes a jealous tyrant; his innocent babe truly
begotten; and the king shall live without an heir if that which
is lost be not found!

Lords. Now blessed be the great Apollo!

Hermione.   Praised!   135

Leontes. Hast thou read truth?

Officer.   Ay, my lord; even so
As it is here set down.

Leontes. There is no truth at all i' th' oracle:
The sessions shall proceed: this is mere falsehood.

Enter a Servant.

Servant. My lord the king, the king!

Leontes.   What is the business?

Servant. O sir! I shall be hated to report it: 141
The prince your son, with mere conceit and fear
Of the queen's speed, is gone.

Leontes.   How! gone?

Servant.   Is dead.

Leontes. Apollo's angry; and the heavens themselves
Do strike at my injustice.   [HERMIONE *swoons.*
                     How now, there?   145

Paulina. This news is mortal to the queen:— look down,
And see what death is doing.

Leontes.   Take her hence:
Her heart is but o'ercharg'd; she will recover:
I have too much believ'd mine own suspicion:

141 **to report** : for reporting.   142 **conceit** : thought.   143
speed : fortune (i.e. the outcome of the trial).

Beseech you, tenderly apply to her   150
Some remedies for life.—

           [*Exeunt* PAULINA, *and* Ladies, *with* HERMIONE.

          Apollo, pardon
My great profaneness 'gainst thine oracle!
I'll reconcile me to Polixenes,
New woo my queen, recall the good Camillo,
Whom I proclaim a man of truth, of mercy;   155
For, being transported by my jealousies
To bloody thoughts and to revenge, I chose
Camillo for the minister to poison
My friend Polixenes: which had been done,
But that the good mind of Camillo tardied   160
My swift command; though I with death and with
Reward did threaten and encourage him,
Not doing it, and being done: he, most humane
And fill'd with honour, to my kingly guest
Unclasp'd my practice, quit his fortunes here,   165
Which you knew great, and to the hazard
Of all incertainties himself commended,
No richer than his honour: how he glisters
Through my rust! and how his piety
Does my deeds make the blacker!

           Re-enter PAULINA.

  Paulina.   Woe the while!   170
O, cut my lace, lest my heart, cracking it,
Break too!

  First Lord. What fit is this, good lady?

  Paulina. What studied torments, tyrant, hast for me?
What wheels? racks? fires? What flaying? boiling
In leads, or oils? what old or newer torture   175

160 **tardied :** delayed carrying out.   165 **Unclasp'd :** revealed
(as in opening a book with metal clasps).   **practice :** treachery,
plot.   168 **No . . . honour :** i.e. all he took away with him was
his honour.   173 **studied :** carefully thought out.

Must I receive, whose every word deserves
To taste of thy most worst? Thy tyranny,
Together working with thy jealousies,
Fancies too weak for boys, too green and idle
For girls of nine, O! think what they have done,   180
And then run mad indeed, stark mad; for all
Thy by-gone fooleries were but spices of it.
That thou betray'dst Polixenes, 'twas nothing;
That did but show thee of a fool, inconstant
And damnable ingrateful; nor was't much   185
Thou wouldst have poison'd good Camillo's honour
To have him kill a king; poor trespasses,
More monstrous standing by: whereof I reckon
The casting forth to crows thy baby daughter
To be or none or little; though a devil   190
Would have shed water out of fire ere done't:
Nor is't directly laid to thee, the death
Of the young prince, whose honourable thoughts,—
Thoughts high for one so tender,—cleft the heart
That could conceive a gross and foolish sire   195
Blemish'd his gracious dam: this is not, no,
Laid to thy answer: but the last,—O lords!
When I have said, cry, 'woe!'—the queen, the queen,
The sweet'st, dear'st creature's dead, and vengeance for't
Not dropp'd down yet.
  First Lord.   The higher powers forbid!   200
  Paulina. I say she's dead; I'll swear't: if word nor oath
Prevail not, go and see: if you can bring

179 **green**: childish, simple-minded.   182 **spices**: small
samples.   184 **of a fool**: as a fool (i.e. an inconstant and . . . sort
of fool).   185 **damnable**: damnably.   187 **To have him**: by
making him [*N*].   187–8 **poor . . . by**: poor sins beside the more
outrageous ones to follow.   191 **ere done't**: before he would
have done it.   194 **cleft**: split, broke.   195 **conceive**: understand that.   197 **to thy answer**: to your charge (as an indictment
for you to answer).   198 **said**: said it, spoken.

Tincture or lustre in her lip, her eye,
Heat outwardly, or breath within, I'll serve you
As I would do the gods. But, O thou tyrant!   205
Do not repent these things, for they are heavier
Than all thy woes can stir; therefore betake thee
To nothing but despair. A thousand knees
Ten thousand years together, naked, fasting,
Upon a barren mountain, and still winter   210
In storm perpetual, could not move the gods
To look that way thou wert.

   Leontes.   Go on, go on;
Thou canst not speak too much; I have deserv'd
All tongues to talk their bitterest.

   First Lord.   Say no more;
Howe'er the business goes, you have made fault   215
I' th' boldness of your speech.

   Paulina.   I am sorry for 't:
All faults I make, when I shall come to know them,
I do repent. Alas! I have show'd too much
The rashness of a woman: he is touch'd   219
To th' noble heart. What's gone and what's past help
Should be past grief: do not receive affliction
At my petition; I beseech you, rather
Let me be punish'd, that have minded you
Of what you should forget. Now, good my liege,
Sir, royal sir, forgive a foolish woman: 225
The love I bore your queen,—lo, fool again!—
I'll speak of her no more, nor of your children;
I'll not remember you of my own lord,
Who is lost too: take your patience to you,

---

   203 Tincture : colour.   **207 Than . . . stir :** than all thy penitential acts (such as are specified in the lines following) could move
(i.e. atone for).   **210 still :** always.   **215 you :** Paulina.   **228
remember :** remind.   **229 take . . . you :** bear your affliction
patiently.

And I'll say nothing.

Leontes.   Thou didst speak but well,   230
When most the truth, which I receive much better
Than to be pitied of thee. Prithee, bring me
To the dead bodies of my queen and son:
One grave shall be for both: upon them shall
The causes of their death appear, unto   235
Our shame perpetual. Once a day I'll visit
The chapel where they lie, and tears shed there
Shall be my recreation: so long as nature
Will bear up with this exercise, so long
I daily vow to use it. Come and lead me   240
To these sorrows.   [*Exeunt.*

Scene III

Enter ANTIGONUS, *with the* Child; *and a* Mariner.

Antigonus. Thou art perfect, then, our ship hath touch'd upon
The deserts of Bohemia?

Mariner.   Ay, my lord; and fear
We have landed in ill time: the skies look grimly
And threaten present blusters. In my conscience,
The heavens with that we have in hand are angry,   5
And frown upon's.

Antigonus. Their sacred wills be done! Go, get aboard;
Look to thy bark: I'll not be long before
I call upon thee.

Mariner.   Make your best haste, and go not
Too far i' th' land: 'tis like to be loud weather;   10

238 **recreation**: pastime *and* means of restoration [*N*].   238–
9 **so long ... exercise**: i.e. as long as he lives.   1 **perfect**:
certain.   4 **present**: imminent.   5 **that ... hand**: the
abandoning of the child.   10 **loud**: rough.

Besides, this place is famous for the creatures
Of prey that keep upon 't.

   Antigonus.   Go thou away:
I'll follow instantly.

   Mariner.   I am glad at heart
To be so rid o' th' business.   [*Exit.*

   Antigonus.   Come, poor babe:
I have heard, but not believ'd, the spirits o' th' dead   15
May walk again: if such thing be, thy mother
Appear'd to me last night, for ne'er was dream
So like a waking. To me comes a creature,
Sometimes her head on one side, some another;
I never saw a vessel of like sorrow,   20
So fill'd, and so becoming: in pure white robes,
Like very sanctity, she did approach
My cabin where I lay; thrice bow'd before me,
And, gasping to begin some speech, her eyes
Became two spouts: the fury spent, anon   25
Did this break from her: 'Good Antigonus,
Since fate, against thy better disposition,
Hath made thy person for the thrower-out
Of my poor babe, according to thine oath,
Places remote enough are in Bohemia,   30
There weep and leave it crying; and, for the babe
Is counted lost for ever, Perdita,
I prithee, call 't: for this ungentle business,
Put on thee by my lord, thou ne'er shalt see
Thy wife Paulina more': and so, with shrieks,   35
She melted into air. Affrighted much,
I did in time collect myself, and thought

---

   12 keep : live.   **20–21 vessel . . . becoming :** a creature so
sorrowful and in whom sorrow was so beautiful [*N*].   **23 cabin :**
berth.   **28 made thy person :** chosen thee.   **32 Perdita**
means 'the lost one' (past participle of Latin *perdere* = lose).   **33
ungentle :** ignoble.

This was so and no slumber. Dreams are toys;
Yet for this once, yea, superstitiously,
I will be squar'd by this. I do believe   40
Hermione hath suffer'd death; and that
Apollo would, this being indeed the issue
Of King Polixenes, it should here be laid,
Either for life or death, upon the earth
Of its right father. Blossom, speed thee well!   45
                              [*Laying down* Child.
There lie; and there thy character: there these;
                              [*Laying down a bundle.*
Which may, if fortune please, both breed thee, pretty,
And still rest thine. The storm begins: poor wretch!
That for thy mother's fault art thus expos'd
To loss and what may follow. Weep I cannot,   50
But my heart bleeds, and most accurs'd am I
To be by oath enjoin'd to this. Farewell!
The day frowns more and more: thou'rt like to have
A lullaby too rough. I never saw
The heavens so dim by day. A savage clamour!   55
Well may I get aboard! This is the chase:
I am gone for ever.   [*Exit, pursued by a bear.*

Enter a Shepherd.

Shepherd. I would there were no age between ten and
three-and-twenty, or that youth would sleep out the

38 **This . . . so :** that this was real.   **toys :** trifles (and
therefore to be disregarded).   39 **superstitiously :** over scru-
pulously, too precisely.   40 **squar'd :** directed (in my actions).
45 **Blossom :** alluding to the child's beauty and fragility.   46
character : i.e. the written account by which Perdita was afterwards
made known to Leontes.   **these :** i.e. the box containing gold and
jewels, later found by the Shepherd.   47–48 **breed . . . thine :**
provide for your upbringing, pretty one, and still remain yours (i.e.
some will be left over).   50 **loss . . . follow :** i.e. abandonment
and possible death.

rest; for there is nothing in the between but getting 60
wenches with child, wronging the ancientry, stealing,
fighting. Hark you now! Would any but these boiled
brains of nineteen and two-and-twenty hunt this
weather? They have scar'd away two of my best sheep;
which I fear the wolf will sooner find than the master: 65
if anywhere I have them, 'tis by the sea-side, browsing
of ivy. Good luck, an't be thy will! what have we here?
Mercy on's, a barne; a very pretty barne! A boy or a
child, I wonder? A pretty one; a very pretty one;
sure some scape: though I am not bookish, yet I can 70
read waiting-gentlewoman in the scape. This has
been some stair-work, some trunk-work, some behind-
door-work; they were warmer that got this than the
poor thing is here. I'll take it up for pity; yet I'll
tarry till my son come; he halloed but even now. Whoa, 75
ho, hoa!

Enter Clown.

Clown. Hilloa, loa!

Shepherd. What! art so near? If thou'lt see a thing to
talk on when thou art dead and rotten, come hither. What
ail'st thou, man? 80

Clown. I have seen two such sights by sea and by land!
but I am not to say it is a sea, for it is now the sky: betwixt the firmament and it you cannot thrust a bodkin's
point.

Shepherd. Why, boy, how is it? 85

---

60 **the rest**: i.e. the interval between ten and twenty-three. 61
ancientry: older people. 62–63 **boiled brains**: hotheads, madmen.
67 **Good . . . will!**: May this be a lucky chance, if it be thy (i.e.
God's) will! 68 **barne**: bairn, infant [*N*]. 69 **child**: girl
[*N*]. 70 **scape**: 'slip' (i.e. a fall from chastity: cf. escapade).
72 **trunk-work**: secret work by means of a trunk (in which a lover
could be concealed). 83 **bodkin**: needle.

Clown. I would you did but see how it chafes, how it rages, how it takes up the shore! but that's not to the point. O! the most piteous cry of the poor souls; sometimes to see 'em, and not to see 'em; now the ship boring the moon with her mainmast, and anon swallowed 90 with yest and froth, as you'd thrust a cork into a hogshead. And then for the land-service: to see how the bear tore out his shoulderbone; how he cried to me for help and said his name was Antigonus, a nobleman. But to make an end of the ship: to see how the sea 95 flap-dragon'd it: but, first, how the poor souls roared, and the sea mock'd them; and how the poor gentleman roared, and the bear mock'd him, both roaring louder than the sea or weather.

Shepherd. Name of mercy! when was this, boy? 100

Clown. Now, now; I have not wink'd since I saw these sights: the men are not yet cold under water, nor the bear half din'd on the gentleman: he's at it now.

Shepherd. Would I had been by, to have help'd the old man! 105

Clown. I would you had been by the ship side, to have help'd her: there your charity would have lack'd footing.

Shepherd. Heavy matters! heavy matters! but look thee here, boy. Now bless thyself: thou mett'st with things dying, I with things new born. Here's a sight 110 for thee; look thee, a bearing-cloth for a squire's child! Look thee here: take up, take up, boy; open't. So, let's see: it was told me, I should be rich by the

---

86 **chafes** : is angry.   87 **takes up** : rebukes *and* swallows up (a pun).   91–92 **hogshead** : barrel.   92 **land-service** : military service (as opposed to naval service—hence Antigonus as opposed to the sailors) *and* service as at table (Antigonus being 'served' to the bear).   96 **flap-dragon'd** : swallowed [*N*].   109 **bless thyself** : make the Sign of the Cross [*N*].   111 **bearing-cloth** : mantle used to cover a child when carrying it to church for baptism.

fairies: this is some changeling.—Open 't. What's within,
boy?   115

Clown. You're a made old man: if the sins of your youth
are forgiven you, you're well to live. Gold! all gold!

Shepherd. This is fairy gold, boy, and 'twill prove so: up
with 't, keep it close: home, home, the next way. We are
lucky, boy; and to be so still, requires nothing but secrecy.
Let my sheep go. Come, good boy, the next way home.

Clown. Go you the next way with your findings. I'll go
see if the bear be gone from the gentleman, and how much
he hath eaten; they are never curst but when they are
hungry. If there be any of him left, I'll bury it.   125

Shepherd. That's a good deed. If thou mayst discern
by that which is left of him what he is, fetch me to th' sight
of him.

Clown. Marry, will I; and you shall help to put him i' th'
ground.   130

Shepherd. 'Tis a lucky day, boy, and we'll do good deeds
on 't.   [*Exeunt.*

---

116 **made** : successful [*N*].   117 **well to live** : well to do.
118 **prove** : turn out to be.   119 **close** : secret [*N*].   **next** :
nearest.   124 **curst** : bad-tempered.

ACT IV

Scene I

Enter Time, *the Chorus.*

Time. **I,** that please some, try all, both joy and terror
Of good and bad, that makes and unfolds error,
Now take upon me, in the name of Time,
To use my wings. Impute it not a crime
To me or my swift passage, that I slide   5
O'er sixteen years, and leave the growth untried
Of that wide gap; since it is in my power
To o'erthrow law, and in one self-born hour
To plant and o'erwhelm custom. Let me pass
The same I am, ere ancient'st order was   10
Or what is now receiv'd: I witness to
The times that brought them in; so shall I do
To th' freshest things now reigning, and make stale
The glistering of this present, as my tale
Now seems to it. Your patience this allowing,   15
I turn my glass and give my scene such growing
As you had slept between. Leontes leaving,—
Th' effects of his fond jealousies so grieving,
That he shuts up himself,—imagine me,
Gentle spectators, that I now may be   20
In fair Bohemia; and remember well,
I mention'd a son o' th' king's, which Florizel

3 **in the name** : i.e. under the name. (The audience must be told
who he is.)   6 **untried** : undescribed [*N*].   8 **self-born** :
begotten by me (Shakespeare regards the Hours as daughters of
Time) [*N*].   14 **glistering** : shining (here implying newness)
[*N*].   15 **seems** : i.e. seems stale.   **Your . . . allowing** : If
you will permit me this liberty.   16 **my glass** : i.e. the hour-glass
which the emblematic figure of Time always carries.   17 **As** : as if.

I now name to you: and with speed so pace
To speak of Perdita, now grown in grace
Equal with wond'ring: what of her ensues   25
I list not prophesy; but let Time's news
Be known when 'tis brought forth. A shepherd's daughter
And what to her adheres, which follows after,
Is th' argument of Time. Of this allow,
If ever you have spent time worse ere now: 30
If never, yet that Time himself doth say
He wishes earnestly you never may.   [*Exit.*

Scene II

Enter POLIXENES *and* CAMILLO.

Polixenes. I pray thee, good Camillo, be no more
importunate: 'tis a sickness denying thee anything; a
death to grant this.

Camillo. It is fifteen years since I saw my country:
though I have for the most part been aired abroad, I   5
desire to lay my bones there. Besides, the penitent
king, my master, hath sent for me; to whose feeling
sorrows I might be some allay, or I o'erween to think
so, which is another spur to my departure.

Polixenes. As thou lov'st me, Camillo, wipe not out   10
the rest of thy services by leaving me now. The need I
have of thee thine own goodness hath made: better not

---

23 **pace :** move forward in an orderly fashion.   25 **Equal with
wond'ring :** i.e. she has increased in grace just as much as the
wonder of others at her grace has increased.   26 **list :** care.   28
adheres : pertains.   29 **argument :** subject.   **Of this allow :**
Approve of this.   1–3 **I pray . . . this:** Please do not ask me
again: it hurts me to have to refuse you anything, but to lose you
would be worse still.   5 **been aired abroad :** breathed foreign
air, lived abroad.   7 **feeling :** deeply felt.   8 **allay :** solace.
o'erween : am bold enough, presumptuous enough.

to have had thee than thus to want thee. Thou, having
made me businesses which none without thee can sufficiently manage, must either stay to execute them 15
thyself or take away with thee the very services thou
hast done; which if I have not enough considered,—
as too much I cannot,—to be more thankful to thee
shall be my study, and my profit therein, the heaping
friendships. Of that fatal country, Sicilia, prithee speak 20
no more, whose very naming punishes me with the
remembrance of that penitent, as thou call'st him, and
reconciled king, my brother; whose loss of his most
precious queen and children are even now to be afresh
lamented. Say to me, when saw'st thou the Prince 25
Florizel, my son? Kings are no less unhappy, their
issue not being gracious, than they are in losing them
when they have approved their virtues.

Camillo. Sir, it is three days since I saw the prince.
What his happier affairs may be, are to me unknown; 30
but I have missingly noted he is of late much retired
from court, and is less frequent to his princely exercises
than formerly he hath appeared.

Polixenes. I have considered so much, Camillo, and
with some care; so far, that I have eyes under my ser- 35
vice which look upon his removedness; from whom I
have this intelligence, that he is seldom from the
house of a most homely shepherd; a man, they say, that
from very nothing, and beyond the imagination of his
neighbours, is grown into an unspeakable estate. 40

Camillo. I have heard, sir, of such a man, who hath a

---

13 **want** : lack.   19–20 **the heaping friendships** : the increase of friendship.   28 **approved** : proved.   30
happier : i.e. than the 'princely exercises' referred to below.   31
missingly : with regret.   35–36 **eyes ... removedness** : servants in my employ who are investigating his absences.   37 **from** :
away from.   40 **unspeakable** : huge.

daughter of most rare note: the report of her is extended
more than can be thought to begin from such a cottage.

Polixenes. That's likewise part of my intelligence;
but, I fear, the angle that plucks our son thither. Thou 45
shalt accompany us to the place; where we will, not
appearing what we are, have some question with the
shepherd; from whose simplicity I think it not uneasy
to get the cause of my son's resort thither. Prithee, be
my present partner in the business, and lay aside the 50
thoughts of Sicilia.

Camillo. I willingly obey your command.

Polixenes. My best Camillo!—We must disguise ourselves.

[*Exeunt.*

Scene III

Enter AUTOLYCUS, *singing.*

> When daffodils begin to peer,
>   With heigh! the doxy over the dale,
> Why, then comes in the sweet o' the year;
>   For the red blood reigns in the winter's pale.   4
>
> The white sheet bleaching on the hedge,
>   With heigh! the sweet birds, O how they sing!
> Doth set my pugging tooth on edge;
>   For a quart of ale is a dish for a king.   8
>
> The lark, that tirra-lyra chants,
>   With heigh! with heigh! the thrush and the jay,
> Are summer songs for me and my aunts,
>   While we lie tumbling in the hay.   12

42–43 **the report ... cottage :** she is much more widely known
than you would expect for one in such a lowly position.   45
angle : baited hook (of a fishing-rod) [*N*].   47 **question :** conversation.   48 **uneasy :** difficult.   1 **peer :** appear (not the
same word as peer = to look closely).   2 **doxy :** woman beggar.
3 **the sweet :** the best part.   7 **pugging :** thievish [*N*].   11
aunts : women of loose morals.

I have serv'd Prince Florizel, and in my time wore three-
pile; but now I am out of service:

> But shall I go mourn for that, my dear? 15
> The pale moon shines by night;
> And when I wander here and there,
> I then do most go right.
>
> If tinkers may have leave to live,
> And bear the sow-skin budget, 20
> Then my account I well may give,
> And in the stocks avouch it.

My traffic is sheets; when the kite builds, look to lesser
linen. My father nam'd me Autolycus; who being, as
I am, litter'd under Mercury, was likewise a snapper- 25
up of unconsidered trifles. With die and drab I pur-
chas'd this caparison, and my revenue is the silly cheat.
Gallows and knock are too powerful on the highway:
beating and hanging are terrors to me: for the life to
come, I sleep out the thought of it. A prize! a prize! 30

Enter Clown.

Clown. Let me see: every 'leven wether tods; every tod
yields pound and odd shilling: fifteen hundred shorn, what
comes the wool to?

Autolycus. [*Aside.*] If the springe hold, the cock's mine.

Clown. I cannot do 't without counters. Let me see; 35
what am I to buy for our sheep-shearing feast? Three

13–14 **three-pile** : the best velvet. 20 **budget** : wallet, pouch [N].
26–27 **With die . . . caparison** : Dice and women have brought me
to these rags. 27 **silly cheat** : petty theft (thieves' jargon). 28
knock : beating [N]. 31 **every . . . tods** : Every eleven sheep
yield a tod (i.e. 28 lb.) of wool. 34 **springe** : trap. **cock** :
woodcock (proverbially regarded as foolish). 35 **counters** :
imitation coins used for calculation.

pound of sugar; five pound of currants; rice,—what
will this sister of mine do with rice? But my father
hath made her mistress of the feast, and she lays it on.
She hath made me four-and-twenty nosegays for the   40
shearers, three-man song-men all, and very good ones;
but they are most of them means and bases: but one
puritan amongst them, and he sings psalms to hornpipes. I must have saffron to colour the warden pies;
mace; dates, none,—that's out of my note: nutmegs,   45
seven; a race or two of ginger,—but that I may beg;
four pound of prunes, and as many of raisins o' th' sun.

Autolycus. O! that ever I was born!

[Grovelling on the ground.

Clown. I' th' name of me!   49

Autolycus. O! help me, help me! pluck but off these rags,
and then death, death!

Clown. Alack, poor soul! thou hast need of more rags
to lay on thee, rather than have these off.

Autolycus. O, sir! the loathsomeness of them offend me
more than the stripes I have received, which are mighty
ones and millions.   56

Clown. Alas, poor man! a million of beating may come to
a great matter.

Autolycus. I am robb'd, sir, and beaten; my money and
apparel ta'en from me, and these detestable things put
upon me.   61

Clown. What, by a horseman or a footman?

---

39 **lays it on :** is extravagant.   41 **three-man song-men :**
singers of (lively) songs in three parts.   42 **means :** tenors.
44 **saffron :** a herb producing a strong but harmless yellow dye.
warden pies : pies made of warden pears (so called because first
grown at the Abbey of Warden in Berkshire).   45 **mace :** a herb.
out of my note : not my concern (i.e. not among the things he
must remember to get. He has not a written 'note').   46 **race :**
root.   47 **raisins o' th' sun :** sun-dried, as distinct from oven-
dried, raisins.

Autolycus. A footman, sweet sir, a footman. 63

Clown. Indeed, he should be a footman, by the garments he hath left with thee: if this be a horseman's coat, it hath seen very hot service. Lend me thy hand, I'll help thee: come, lend me thy hand. [*Helping him up.*

Autolycus. O! good sir, tenderly, O!

Clown. Alas, poor soul! 69

Autolycus. O! good sir; softly, good sir! I fear, sir, my shoulder-blade is out.

Clown. How now! canst stand?

Autolycus. Softly, dear sir; [*Picks his pocket.*] good sir, softly. You ha' done me a charitable office.

Clown. Dost lack any money? I have a little money for thee. 76

Autolycus. No, good sweet sir: no, I beseech you, sir. I have a kinsman not past three-quarters of a mile hence, unto whom I was going: I shall there have money, or anything I want: offer me no money, I pray you! That kills my heart. 81

Clown. What manner of fellow was he that robb'd you?

Autolycus. A fellow, sir, that I have known to go about with troll-my-dames: I knew him once a servant of the prince. I cannot tell, good sir, for which of his virtues it was, but he was certainly whipp'd out of the court. 86

Clown. His vices, you would say: there's no virtue whipp'd out of the court: they cherish it, to make it stay there, and yet it will no more but abide. 89

Autolycus. Vices, I would say, sir. I know this man well: he hath been since an ape-bearer; then a process-server,

---

83–84 **go about with troll-my-dames** : carry round with him a game for ladies (also called 'troll-madam' and played by 'trolling' balls through hoops set on a board—cf. bagatelle). 89 **no more but abide** : only just stay [*N*]. 91 **ape-bearer** : a showman who travelled about with performing monkeys. **process-server** : the same as **bailiff** (l. 92), an officer who serves writs or summonses.

a bailiff; then he compass'd a motion of the Prodigal
Son, and married a tinker's wife within a mile where
my land and living lies; and having flown over many
knavish professions, he settled only in rogue: some 95
call him Autolycus.

Clown. Out upon him! Prig, for my life, prig: he haunts
wakes, fairs, and bear-baitings.

Autolycus. Very true, sir; he, sir, he: that's the rogue
that put me into this apparel.   100

Clown. Not a more cowardly rogue in all Bohemia: if
you had but look'd big and spit at him, he'd have run.

Autolycus. I must confess to you, sir, I am no fighter: I
am false of heart that way, and that he knew, I warrant
him.   105

Clown. How do you now?

Autolycus. Sweet sir, much better than I was: I can
stand and walk. I will even take my leave of you, and pace
softly towards my kinsman's.

Clown. Shall I bring thee on the way?   110

Autolycus. No, good-fac'd sir; no, sweet sir.

Clown. Then fare thee well: I must go buy spices for our
sheep-shearing.

Autolycus. Prosper you, sweet sir!—[*Exit* Clown.]
Your purse is not hot enough to purchase your spice. 115
I'll be with you at your sheep-shearing too. If I make
not this cheat bring out another, and the shearers prove
sheep, let me be unroll'd, and my name put in the book
of virtue.

---

92 **compass'd a motion :** acquired a puppet-show.   94 **land
and living :** landed property (a high-falutin' term used to impress
the Clown).   **flown over :** passed quickly through.   97
Prig : Thief.   108–9 **pace softly :** walk quietly.   115 **hot :**
full (with a play on the word, for spices are 'hot').   117 **cheat :**
trick.   **bring out :** lead to. (He now knows about the sheep-
shearing.)   118 **unroll'd :** i.e. his name removed from the
fraternity of vagabonds (see note on ll. 1–12).

Jog on, jog on, the footpath way,   120
    And merrily hent the stile-a:
A merry heart goes all the day,
    Your sad tires in a mile-a.   [*Exit.*

Scene IV

Enter FLORIZEL *and* PERDITA.

Florizel. These your unusual weeds to each part of you
Does give a life: no shepherdess, but Flora
Peering in April's front. This your sheep-shearing
Is as a meeting of the petty gods,
And you the queen on 't.
   Perdita.   Sir, my gracious lord,   5
To chide at your extremes it not becomes me:
O! pardon, that I name them. Your high self,
The gracious mark o' th' land, you have obscur'd
With a swain's wearing, and me, poor lowly maid,
Most goddess-like prank'd up. But that our feasts   10
In every mess have folly, and the feeders
Digest it with a custom, I should blush
To see you so attired,—sworn, I think,
To show myself a glass.
   Florizel.   I bless the time
When my good falcon made her flight across   15
Thy father's ground.
   Perdita.   Now, Jove afford you cause!
To me the difference forges dread; your greatness

121 **hent**: take hold of (or perhaps 'take' in the sense of 'vault').
3 **Peering . . . front**: appearing at the beginning of April (cf. IV. iii.
1).   4 **petty gods**: lesser gods (the classical *Di minores*).   **6**
extremes: extravagances (i.e. of behaviour, in providing costumes
which she thinks inappropriate).   8 **mark**: object of notice
(landmark to guide them or mark at which they aim).   10 **prank'd**:
dressed conspicuously.   11 **mess**: dish [*N*].   17 **difference**:
i.e. in our rank.

Hath not been us'd to fear. Even now I tremble
To think your father, by some accident,
Should pass this way as you did. O, the Fates!   20
How would he look, to see his work, so noble,
Vilely bound up? What would he say? Or how
Should I, in these my borrowed flaunts, behold
The sternness of his presence?
 Florizel.   Apprehend
Nothing but jollity. The gods themselves,   25
Humbling their deities to love, have taken
The shapes of beasts upon them: Jupiter
Became a bull, and bellow'd; the green Neptune
A ram, and bleated; and the fire-rob'd god,
Golden Apollo, a poor humble swain,   30
As I seem now. Their transformations
Were never for a piece of beauty rarer,
Nor in a way so chaste, since my desires
Run not before mine honour, nor my lusts
Burn hotter than my faith.
 Perdita.   O! but, sir,   35
Your resolution cannot hold, when 'tis
Oppos'd, as it must be, by th' power of the king.
One of these two must be necessities,
Which then will speak, that you must change this pur-
  pose,
Or I my life.
 Florizel. Thou dearest Perdita,   40
With these forc'd thoughts, I prithee, darken not
The mirth o' th' feast: or I'll be thine, my fair,
Or not my father's; for I cannot be
Mine own, nor anything to any, if
I be not thine: to this I am most constant,   45

 23 in these ... flaunts: i.e. flaunting in these garments which
imply a rank not truly mine [*N*]. **32 for ... rarer**: for the sake of
a more beautiful woman. **41 forc'd**: far-fetched.

Though destiny say no. Be merry, gentle;
Strangle such thoughts as these with any thing
That you behold the while. Your guests are coming:
Lift up your countenance, as it were the day
Of celebration of that nuptial which   50
We two have sworn shall come.
  Perdita.   O lady Fortune,
Stand you auspicious!
  Florizel.   See, your guests approach:
Address yourself to entertain them sprightly,
And let's be red with mirth.   54

Enter Shepherd, *with* POLIXENES *and* CAMILLO *disguised*;
      Clown, MOPSA, DORCAS, *and others.*

  Shepherd. Fie, daughter! when my old wife liv'd, upon
This day she was both pantler, butler, cook;   56
Both dame and servant; welcom'd all, serv'd all,
Would sing her song and dance her turn; now here,
At upper end o' th' table, now i' th' middle;
On his shoulder, and his; her face o' fire   60
With labour, and the thing she took to quench it
She would to each one sip. You are retired,
As if you were a feasted one and not
The hostess of the meeting: pray you, bid
These unknown friends to's welcome; for it is   65
A way to make us better friends, more known.
Come, quench your blushes and present yourself
That which you are, mistress o' th' feast: come on,
And bid us welcome to your sheep-shearing,
As your good flock shall prosper.

46 **gentle** : i.e. gentle one.   47–48 **with any . . . while** : i.e.
with the things that you see at the present time (at the feast).   54
red : flushed.   56 **pantler** : servant in charge of the pantry.
57 **dame** : mistress.   60 **On his . . . his** : i.e. dancing; or, perhaps, at his shoulder . . ., to serve them.   65 **to's** : goes with 'unknown', not 'welcome'.   66 **more known** : better acquainted.

Perdita.   [*To* POLIXENES.] Sir, welcome: 70
It is my father's will I should take on me
The hostess-ship o' th' day:— [*To* CAMILLO.] You're wel-
    come, sir.
Give me those flowers there, Dorcas. Reverend sirs,
For you there's rosemary and rue; these keep
Seeming and savour all the winter long: 75
Grace and remembrance be to you both,
And welcome to our shearing!
    Polixenes.   Shepherdess,—
A fair one are you,—well you fit our ages
With flowers of winter.
    Perdita.   Sir, the year growing ancient,
Not yet on summer's death, nor on the birth   80
Of trembling winter, the fairest flower o' th' season
Are our carnations, and streak'd gillyvors,
Which some call nature's bastards: of that kind
Our rustic garden's barren, and I care not
To get slips of them.
    Polixenes.   Wherefore, gentle maiden,   85
Do you neglect them?
    Perdita.   For I have heard it said
There is an art which in their piedness shares
With great creating nature.
    Polixenes.   Say there be;
Yet nature is made better by no mean
But nature makes that mean: so, over that art,   90
Which you say adds to nature, is an art
That nature makes. You see, sweet maid, we marry
A gentler scion to the wildest stock,
And make conceive a bark of baser kind

---

74 **rosemary and rue** : herbs [*N*].   75 **Seeming and savour** :
appearance and scent.   82 **gillyvors** : gillyflowers [*N*].   85 **slips** :
cuttings.   86 **For** : Because.   87 **piedness** : variegation (referring to
the 'streaks': cf. l. 82).   89 **mean** : means.   93 **scion** : offspring.

By bud of nobler race: this is an art   95
Which does mend nature, change it rather, but
The art itself is nature.

Perdita.   So it is.

Polixenes. Then make your garden rich in gillyvors,
And do not call them bastards.

Perdita.   I'll not put
The dibble in earth to set one slip of them;   100
No more than, were I painted, I would wish
This youth should say, 'twere well, and only therefore
Desire to breed by me. Here's flowers for you;
Hot lavender, mints, savory, marjoram;
The marigold, that goes to bed with' sun,   105
And with him rises weeping: these are flowers
Of middle summer, and I think they are given
To men of middle age. Y'are very welcome.

Camillo. I should leave grazing, were I of your flock,
And only live by gazing.

Perdita.   Out, alas!   110
You'd be so lean, that blasts of January
Would blow you through and through. Now, my fair'st
          friend,
I would I had some flowers o' th' spring that might
Become your time of day; and yours, and yours,
That wear upon your virgin branches yet   115
Your maidenheads growing: O Proserpina!
For the flowers now that frighted thou let'st fall
From Dis's waggon! daffodils,
That come before the swallow dares, and take

100 **dibble** : a gardening tool.   101 **painted** : i.e. with cos-
metics.   104 **Hot** : aromatic ? [*N*]   **mints** : plural, because there
are several varieties.   **savory** : a herb.   105 **with'** : with
the (cf. II. i. 11 and II. iii. 147).   112 **friend** : lover (i.e. Florizel).
116 **maidenheads** : maidenhood, virginity (of either sex) [*N*].
118 **waggon** : chariot [*N*].   119 **take** : bewitch.

The winds of March with beauty; violets dim,   120
But sweeter than the lids of Juno's eyes
Or Cytherea's breath; pale primroses,
That die unmarried, ere they can behold
Bright Phœbus in his strength, a malady
Most incident to maids; bold oxlips and   125
The crown imperial; lilies of all kinds,
The flower-de-luce being one. O! these I lack
To make you garlands of, and my sweet friend,
To strew him o'er and o'er!

   Florizel.   What! like a corse?   129
   Perdita. No, like a bank for love to lie and play on;
Not like a corse; or if,—not to be buried,
But quick and in mine arms. Come, take your flowers:
Methinks I play as I have seen them do
In Whitsun pastorals: sure this robe of mine
Does change my disposition.

   Florizel.   What you do   135
Still betters what is done. When you speak, sweet,
I'd have you do it ever: when you sing,
I'd have you buy and sell so; so give alms;
Pray so; and, for the ord'ring your affairs,
To sing them too: when you do dance, I wish you   140
A wave o' th' sea, that you might ever do
Nothing but that; move still, still so,
And own no other function: each your doing,
So singular in each particular,
Crowns what you are doing in the present deeds,   145
That all your acts are queens.

122 accent Cytheréa's [*N*].   129 **corse** : corpse.   132 **quick :**
alive.   133 **play** : act (as queen) [*N*].   135-6 **What . . . done :**
What you are doing (at any time) is (i.e. seems) always better than
what you have been doing before.   139 **ord'ring . . . affairs :**
running the house.   142 **still** : always.   143 **own . . . function :**
do nothing else.   143-6 **each . . . queens** : everything you do
(so unique in each detail) makes appear best whatever you are

Perdita.   O Doricles!
Your praises are too large: but that your youth,
And the true blood which peeps fairly through 't,
Do plainly give you out an unstain'd shepherd,
With wisdom I might fear, my Doricles,   150
You woo'd me the false way.
　Florizel.   I think you have
As little skill to fear as I have purpose
To put you to't. But, come; our dance, I pray.
Your hand, my Perdita: so turtles pair
That never mean to part.
　Perdita.   I'll swear for 'em.   155
　Polixenes. This is the prettiest low-born lass that ever
Ran on the green-sward: nothing she does or seems
But smacks of something greater than herself,
Too noble for this place.
　Camillo.   He tells her something
That makes her blood look out. Good sooth, she is   160
The queen of curds and cream.
　Clown.   Come on, strike up.
　Dorcas. Mopsa must be your mistress: marry, garlic,
To mend her kissing with.
　Mopsa.   Now, in good time!
　Clown. Not a word, a word: we stand upon our
　　manners.   164

doing at the moment, so that all your acts are supreme [*N*].   146
Doricles : see l. 167.   150–1 i.e. I should have good reason to
fear you were (now) trying to seduce me by flattery.   151–3 **I
think . . . to 't :** I think you have as little ability to be afraid of me,
as I have purpose to give you cause for fear [*N*].   154 **turtles :**
turtle doves (symbolic of love and constancy).   158 **smacks of :**
tastes of, suggests.   160 **look out :** appear. (She is blushing : cf.
l. 148.)   161 **strike up :** to the band.   162 **mistress :** here
'partner' for the dance, which would include kissing in some of
the figures.   **marry :** an exclamation [*N*].   163 **in good time :**
what (will you say) next ?   164 **we . . . manners :** we must be
well-behaved.

Come, strike up. [*Music. Here a dance of Shepherds and*
Shepherdesses.

Polixenes. Pray, good shepherd, what fair swain is this
Which dances with your daughter?

Shepherd. They call him Doricles, and boasts himself
To have a worthy feeding; but I have it
Upon his own report and I believe it: 170
He looks like sooth. He says he loves my daughter:
I think so too; for never gaz'd the moon
Upon the water as he'll stand and read
As 'twere my daughter's eyes; and, to be plain,
I think there is not half a kiss to choose   175
Who loves another best.

Polixenes.   She dances featly.

Shepherd. So she does any thing, though I report it
That should be silent. If young Doricles
Do light upon her, she shall bring him that
Which he not dreams of.   180

Enter Servant.

Servant. O master! if you did but hear the pedlar at
the door, you would never dance again after a tabor and
pipe; no, the bagpipe could not move you. He sings
several tunes faster than you'll tell money; he utters
them as he had eaten ballads and all men's ears grew to 185
his tunes.

Clown. He could never come better: he shall come
in: I love a ballad but even too well, if it be doleful

---

168 **boasts**: i.e. he boasts [*N*].   169 **worthy feeding**: a
good-sized pasturage.   176 **another**: the other.   **featly**:
lightly, nimbly, ably. (It is in the last, most general, sense that the
Shepherd understands the word.)   179–80 **that . . . of**: i.e.
Perdita's wealth, which the Shepherd has hoarded.   182 **after**:
to the accompaniment of.   184 **tell**: count.   187 **better**: i.e.
at a better time.

matter merrily set down, or a very pleasant thing indeed
and sung lamentably.   190

Servant. He hath songs for man or woman, of all sizes;
no milliner can so fit his customers with gloves: he has
the prettiest love-songs for maids; so without bawdry,
which is strange; with such delicate burthens of dildos
and fadings, 'jump her and thump her'; and where 195
some stretch-mouth'd rascal would, as it were, mean
mischief and break a foul gap into the matter, he makes
the maid to answer, 'Whoop, do me no harm, good
man'; puts him off, slights him with 'Whoop, do me
no harm, good man'.   200

Polixenes. This is a brave fellow.

Clown. Believe me, thou talkest of an admirable
conceited fellow. Has he any unbraided wares?

Servant. He hath ribbons of all the colours i' th' rain-
bow; points more than all the lawyers in Bohemia can 205
learnedly handle, though they come to him by th' gross;
inkles, caddisses, cambrics, lawns: why, he sings 'em
over, as they were gods or goddesses. You would think
a smock were a she-angel, he so chants to the sleeve-
hand and the work about the square on't.   210

Clown. Prithee, bring him in, and let him approach
singing.

189 **pleasant** : cheerful [*N*].   194 **burthens** : refrains.   **dildos
and fadings**: obscure words used in the refrains of songs of the
time [*N*].   196 **stretch-mouth'd** : lewd.   197 **break ...
matter** : insert an indecent parenthesis ('patter' spoken between
parts of the song).   202–3 **admirable conceited** : very clever.
203 **unbraided** : unfaded, new.   205 **points** : laces with metal
tags (with a pun on 'points' of an argument).   207 **inkles** :
tapes.   **caddisses** : caddis ribbons (caddis = worsted yarn)
from which garters, &c., were made.   **cambrics, lawns** :
kinds of fine linen from which ruffles, sleeves, &c., were made.   209
smock : shift, chemise.   **chants to** : sings the praises of.   **sleeve-
hand** : cuff.   210 **square** : the part covering the breast.

Perdita. Forewarn him that he use no scurrilous words
in 's tunes.   [*Exit* Servant.

Clown. You have of these pedlars, that have more in
them than you'd think, sister.   216

Perdita. Ay, good brother, or go about to think.

Enter AUTOLYCUS, *singing.*

> Lawn as white as driven snow;
> Cypress black as e'er was crow;
> Gloves as sweet as damask roses;   220
> Masks for faces and for noses;
> Bugle-bracelet, necklace-amber,
> Perfume for a lady's chamber;
> Golden quoifs and stomachers,
> For my lads to give their dears;   225
> Pins and poking-sticks of steel;
> What maids lack from head to heel:
> Come buy of me, come; come buy, come buy;
> Buy, lads, or else your lasses cry:
> Come buy.   230

Clown. If I were not in love with Mopsa, thou shouldst
take no money of me; but being enthrall'd as I am, it will
also be the bondage of certain ribbons and gloves.

Mopsa. I was promis'd them against the feast; but they
come not too late now.   235

---

217 **go about** : intend.   219 **cypress** : crape (probably derived
from Cyprus, where it was either made or exported to the West).
220 **sweet** : i.e. because scented.   221 **Masks ... noses** : i.e. to
cover all or part of the face (to protect the complexion or conceal
identity).   222 **Bugle-bracelet** : bracelet of glass beads,
usually black.   **necklace-amber** : amber for necklaces.   224
quoifs : tight-fitting caps.   **stomachers** : ornamental garments
worn behind the lacing of the bodice.   226 **poking-sticks** : used,
when heated, for ironing the pleats of starched ruffs.   232
enthrall'd : made a slave.   232–3 **it will ... gloves** : it will
also oblige me to buy . . .   234 **against** : in preparation for, in
time for.

Dorcas. He hath promis'd you more than that, or there be liars.

Mopsa. He hath paid you all he promis'd you: may be he has paid you more, which will shame you to give him again.   240

Clown. Is there no manners left among maids? will they wear their plackets where they should bear their faces? Is there not milking-time? when you are going to bed? or kill-hole? to whistle off these secrets, but you must be tittle-tattling before all our guests? 'Tis 245 well they are whisp'ring: clamour your tongues, and not a word more.

Mopsa. I have done. Come, you promis'd me a tawdry lace and a pair of sweet gloves.

Clown. Have I not told thee how I was cozen'd by the way, and lost all my money?   251

Autolycus. And indeed, sir, there are cozeners abroad; therefore it behoves men to be wary.

Clown. Fear not thou, man, thou shalt lose nothing here.

Autolycus. I hope so, sir; for I have about me many parcels of charge.   256

Clown. What hast here? ballads?

Mopsa. Pray now, buy some: I love a ballad in print, a life, for then we are sure they are true.

Autolycus. Here's one to a very doleful tune, how a usurer's wife was brought to bed of twenty money-bags at a burden; and how she long'd to eat adders' heads and toads carbonado'd.   263

Mopsa. Is it true, think you?

242 **plackets** : petticoats.   244 **kill-hole** : kiln-hole, a small building containing a furnace for drying grain, making malt, &c., and convenient for gossiping.   246 **clamour** : silence [*N*].   248–9 **tawdry lace** : a silk tie (*or* necklace) [*N*].   249 **sweet** : scented. 250 **cozen'd** : cheated.   256 **parcels of charge** : items of value. 259 **a life** : on my life.   263 **carbonado'd** : slashed, cut up for cooking.

Autolycus. Very true, and but a month old.   265

Dorcas. Bless me from marrying a usurer!

Autolycus. Here's the midwife's name to't, one Mistress Taleporter, and five or six honest wives that were present. Why should I carry lies abroad?

Mopsa. Pray you now, buy it.   270

Clown. Come on, lay it by: and let's first see moe ballads; we'll buy the other things anon.

Autolycus. Here's another ballad of a fish that appeared upon the coast on Wednesday the fourscore of April, forty thousand fathom above water, and sung 275 this ballad against the hard hearts of maids: it was thought she was a woman and was turn'd into a cold fish for she would not exchange flesh with one that lov'd her. The ballad is very pitiful and as true.

Dorcas. Is it true too, think you?   280

Autolycus. Five justices' hands at it, and witnesses more than my pack will hold.

Clown. Lay it by too: another.

Autolycus. This is a merry ballad, but a very pretty one.

Mopsa. Let's have some merry ones.   285

Autolycus. Why, this is a passing merry one, and goes to the tune of 'Two maids wooing a man': there's scarce a maid westward but she sings it: 'tis in request, I can tell you.

Mopsa. We can both sing it: if thou'lt bear a part thou shalt hear; 'tis in three parts.   291

Dorcas. We had the tune on't a month ago.

Autolycus. I can bear my part; you must know 'tis my occupation: have at it with you.

　　　　Get you hence, for I must go,   295
　　　　Where it fits not you to know.

266 **Bless me :** (God) protect me.　　267 **to't :** to vouch for it.
271 **lay it by :** put it aside (because he intends to buy it).　　281
hands : signatures.

Dorcas.	Whither?
Mopsa.	O! whither?
Dorcas.	Whither?
Mopsa.	It becomes thy oath full well, 300
	Thou to me thy secrets tell.
Dorcas.	Me too: let me go thither.
Mopsa.	Or thou goest to th' grange or mill.
Dorcas.	If to either, thou dost ill.
Autolycus.	Neither. 305
Dorcas.	What, neither?
Autolycus.	Neither.
Dorcas.	Thou hast sworn my love to be.
Mopsa.	Thou hast sworn it more to me:
	Then whither goest? say whither? 310

Clown. We'll have this song out anon by ourselves my
father and the gentlemen are in sad talk, and we'll not
trouble them: come, bring away thy pack after me.
Wenches, I'll buy for you both. Pedlar, let's have the first
choice. Follow me, girls.   315

[*Exit with* DORCAS *and* MOPSA.

Autolycus. And you shall pay well for 'em.

Will you buy any tape, or lace for your cape,
    My dainty duck, my dear-a?
Any silk, any thread, any toys for your head,
    Of the new'st and fin'st, fin'st wear-a?   320
Come to the pedlar, money's a meddler,
That doth utter all men's ware-a.   [*Exit.*

Re-enter Servant.

Servant. Master, there is three carters, three shepherds, three neat-herds, three swine-herds, that have

303 **Or** : Either.   **grange** : large farm-house.   312 **sad** :
serious.   317 **lace** : probably tape for tying the cape.   318
duck : darling.   319 **toys** : ornaments.   321 **meddler** : inter-
mediary, means of exchange.   322 **utter** : put on the market.

made themselves all men of hair; they call themselves 325
Saltiers; and they have a dance which the wenches say
is a gallimaufry of gambols, because they are not in't;
but they themselves are o' th' mind,—if it be not too
rough for some that know little but bowling,— it will
please plentifully.   330

Shepherd. Away! we'll none on't: here has been too much
homely foolery already. I know, sir, we weary you.

Polixenes. You weary those that refresh us: pray, let's
see these four threes of herdsmen.   334

Servant. One three of them, by their own report, sir, hath
danc'd before the king; and not the worst of the three but
jumps twelve foot and a half by th' squier.

Shepherd. Leave your prating: since these good men are
pleas'd, let them come in: but quickly now.

Servant. Why, they stay at door, sir.   340

      [*Lets in herdsmen. Here a dance of twelve Satyrs.*

Polixenes. [*To* Shepherd.] O, father! you'll know more of
    that hereafter.

[*To* CAMILLO.] Is it not too far gone? 'Tis time to part them:
He's simple and tells much. [*To* FLORIZEL.] How now, fair
    shepherd!
Your heart is full of something that does take
Your mind from feasting. Sooth, when I was young, 345
And handed love as you do, I was wont
To load my she with knacks: I would have ransack'd
The pedlar's silken treasury and have pour'd it
To her acceptance; you have let him go

    327 gallimaufry: medley.   **328 are o' th' mind**: are under
the impression (that).   **329 bowling**: bowls is here regarded as a
quiet and grave pursuit.   **333 You . . . us**: You are not annoying us but you *are* annoying those who want to entertain us (by
refusing to see their performance).   **336 not the worst . . . but**:
even the worst.   **337 squier**: foot-rule.   **346 handed**: had to
do with, was concerned with.   **347 knacks**: knick-knacks, small
presents.   **348 silken treasury**: collection of silks.

And nothing marted with him. If your lass   350
Interpretation should abuse and call this
Your lack of love or bounty, you were straited
For a reply, at least if you make a care
Of happy holding her.
   Florizel.   Old sir, I know
She prizes not such trifles as these are.   355
The gifts she looks from me are pack'd and lock'd
Up in my heart, which I have given already,
But not deliver'd. O! hear me breathe my life
Before this ancient sir, whom, it should seem,
Hath sometime lov'd: I take thy hand; this hand,   360
As soft as dove's down, and as white as it,
Or Ethiopian's tooth, or the fann'd snow that's bolted
By th' northern blasts twice o'er.
   Polixenes.   What follows this?
How prettily th' young swain seems to wash
The hand was fair before! I have put you out;   365
But to your protestation: let me hear
What you profess.
   Florizel.   Do, and be witness to't.
   Polixenes. And this my neighbour too?
   Florizel.   And he, and more
Than he, and men, the earth, the heavens, and all;
That, were I crown'd the most imperial monarch,   370
Thereof most worthy, were I the fairest youth
That ever made eye swerve, had force and knowledge

---

350 marted: marketed.   **351 Interpretation...abuse**: should misinterpret, misunderstand.   **352 straited**: in straits, difficulties.   **353-4 if you . . . her**: if you want to keep her happy.
356 looks: looks for, expects.   **358 breathe my life**: make vows of lifelong love [N].   **362 bolted**: sifted (like flour).   **365 was**: i.e. which was [N].   **put you out**: put you off your speech.   **371 Thereof . . . worthy**: i.e. most worthy of being so crowned.   **372 made . . . swerve**: made people follow him with their looks. **force**: strength.

More than was ever man's, I would not prize them
Without her love; for her employ them all,
Commend them and condemn them to her service   375
Or to their own perdition.
   Polixenes.   Fairly offer'd.
   Camillo. This shows a sound affection.
   Shepherd.   But, my daughter,
Say you the like to him?
   Perdita.   I cannot speak
So well, nothing so well; no, nor mean better:
By th' pattern of mine own thoughts I cut out   380
The purity of his.
   Shepherd.   Take hands; a bargain;
And, friends unknown, you shall bear witness to 't:
I give my daughter to him, and will make
Her portion equal his.
   Florizel.   O! that must be
I' th' virtue of your daughter: one being dead,   385
I shall have more than you can dream of yet;
Enough then for your wonder. But, come on;
Contract us 'fore these witnesses.
   Shepherd.   Come, your hand;
And, daughter, yours.
   Polixenes.   Soft, swain, awhile, beseech you.
Have you a father?
   Florizel.   I have; but what of him?   390
   Polixenes. Knows he of this?
   Florizel.   He neither does nor shall.
   Polixenes. Methinks a father
Is, at the nuptial of his son, a guest
That best becomes the table. Pray you, once more,
Is not your father grown incapable   395

---

380 **cut out** : fashion, design [*N*].   385 **one** : i.e. my father.
386 **yet** : at present.   387 **then** : i.e. at my father's death, when
you will know my rank.   389 **Soft** : 'Go easy'.

Of reasonable affairs? is he not stupid
With age and alt'ring rheums? can he speak? hear?
Know man from man? dispute his own estate?
Lies he not bed-rid? and again does nothing
But what he did being childish?

Florizel.   No, good sir: **400**
He has his health and ampler strength indeed
Than most have of his age.

Polixenes.   By my white beard,
You offer him, if this be so, a wrong
Something unfilial. Reason my son
Should choose himself a wife, but as good reason   **405**
The father,—all whose joy is nothing else
But fair posterity,—should hold some counsel
In such a business.

Florizel.   I yield all this;
But for some other reasons, my grave sir,
Which 'tis not fit you know, I not acquaint   **410**
My father of this business.

Polixenes.   Let him know't.

Florizel. He shall not.

Polixenes.   Prithee, let him.

Florizel.   No, he must not.

Shepherd. Let him, my son: he shall not need to grieve
At knowing of thy choice.

Florizel.   Come, come, he mustnot.
Mark our contract.

Polixenes.   Mark your divorce, young sir,   **415**
         [*Discovering himself.*

397 alt'ring rheums : weakening chills.   **398 dispute . . .
estate :** discuss his financial affairs.   **400 being childish :** when
a child. ('Is he in his second childhood?')   **404 Something :**
somewhat.   **Reason my son :** It is reasonable that my son.
('My son' has not slipped out unguardedly : Polixenes speaks as of
a hypothetical case.)   **408 yield :** grant.   **410 I not acquaint : I**
am not telling.   *SD **Discovering himself :*** i.e. Removing his disguise.

Whom son I dare not call: thou art too base
To be acknowledg'd: thou a sceptre's heir,
That thus affects a sheep-hook! Thou old traitor,
I am sorry that by hanging thee I can
But shorten thy life one week. And thou, fresh piece   420
Of excellent witchcraft, who of force must know
The royal fool thou cop'st with,—
   Shepherd.   O, my heart!
   Polixenes. I'll have thy beauty scratch'd with briers, and
     made
More homely than thy state. For thee, fond boy,
If I may ever know thou dost but sigh   425
That thou no more shalt see this knack,—as never
I mean thou shalt,—we'll bar thee from succession;
Not hold thee of our blood, no, not our kin,
Farre than Deucalion off: mark thou my words:
Follow us to the court. Thou, churl, for this time,   430
Though full of our displeasure, yet we free thee
From the dead blow of it. And you, enchantment,—
Worthy enough a herdsman; yea, him too,
That makes himself, but for our honour therein,
Unworthy thee,—if ever henceforth thou   435
These rural latches to his entrance open,
Or hoop his body more with thy embraces,
I will devise a death as cruel for thee
As thou art tender to 't.   [*Exit*.
   Perdita.   Even here undone!
I was not much afeard; for once or twice   440
I was about to speak and tell him plainly,

---

   421 of force : perforce, necessarily.   **422 cop'st with :** hast to
do with.   **424 state :** social position [*N*].   **fond :** foolish.
426 knack : toy trifle.   **429 Farre :** farther (the old comparative)
[*N*].   **430 churl :** i.e. the Shepherd (Polixenes has relented since
ll. 418–20).   **432 dead blow :** death-dealing blow [*N*].   **436
latches :** i.e. of her door.   **439 tender to 't :** too delicate for it.

The self-same sun that shines upon his court
Hides not his visage from our cottage, but
Looks on alike. Will't please you, sir, be gone?
I told you what would come of this: beseech you,   445
Of your own state take care: this dream of mine—
Being now awake, I'll queen it no inch further,
But milk my ewes and weep.

Camillo.   Why, how now, father!
Speak, ere thou diest.

Shepherd.   I cannot speak, nor think,
Nor dare to know that which I know. O sir!   450
You have undone a man of fourscore three,
That thought to fill his grave in quiet, yea,
To die upon the bed my father died,
To lie close by his honest bones: but now
Some hangman must put on my shroud and lay me   455
Where no priest shovels in dust. O cursed wretch!
That knew'st this was the prince, and wouldst adventure
To mingle faith with him. Undone! undone!
If I might die within this hour, I have liv'd
To die when I desire.   [*Exit.*

Florizel.   Why look you so upon me?   460
I am but sorry, not afeard; delay'd,
But nothing alt'red. What I was, I am:
More straining on for plucking back; not following
My leash unwillingly.

Camillo.   Gracious my lord,
You know your father's temper: at this time   465
He will allow no speech, which I do guess
You do not purpose to him; and as hardly

---

444 **Looks on alike :** Looks on (all ?) impartially [*N*].   446
state : position (as heir; cf. l. 427).   458 **mingle faith :** exchange
vows.   460 **you :** Perdita (?).   463-4 **not following . . .
unwillingly :** i.e. not going, against my will, in the direction Polixenes wants me.

Will he endure your sight as yet, I fear:
Then, till the fury of his highness settle,
Come not before him.

  Florizel.   I not purpose it.   470
I think, Camillo?

  Camillo.   Even he, my lord.

  Perdita. How often have I told you 'twould be thus!
How often said my dignity would last
But till 'twere known!

  Florizel.   It cannot fail but by
The violation of my faith; and then   475
Let nature crush the sides o' th' earth together
And mar the seeds within! Lift up thy looks:
From my succession wipe me, father; I
Am heir to my affection.

  Camillo.   Be advis'd.

  Florizel. I am; and by my fancy: if my reason 480
Will thereto be obedient, I have reason;
If not, my senses, better pleas'd with madness,
Do bid it welcome.

  Camillo.   This is desperate, sir.

  Florizel. So call it; but it does fulfil my vow,
I needs must think it honesty. Camillo,   485
Not for Bohemia, nor the pomp that may
Be thereat glean'd for all the sun sees or
The close earth wombs or the profound seas hides
In unknown fathoms, will I break my oath
To this my fair belov'd. Therefore, I pray you, 490
As you have ever been my father's honour'd friend,
When he shall miss me,—as, in faith, I mean not

---

 469 his highness : his (offended) sense of dignity (cf. l. 525) [*N*].
473 dignity : honourable position (as your intended bride). **478–**
9 I willingly give up the throne for my love (cf. l. 427). **484**
but it does fulfil : if only it fulfils. **487 thereat :** there. **488**
hides : a form of the third person plural.

To see him any more,—cast your good counsels
Upon his passion: let myself and fortune
Tug for the time to come. This you may know   495
And so deliver, I am put to sea
With her whom here I cannot hold on shore;
And most opportune to our need, I have
A vessel rides fast by, but not prepar'd
For this design. What course I mean to hold   500
Shall nothing benefit your knowledge, nor
Concern me the reporting.

  Camillo.   O my lord!
I would your spirit were easier for advice,
Or stronger for your need.

  Florizel.   Hark, Perdita. [*Takes her aside.*
[*To* CAMILLO.] I'll hear you by and by.

  Camillo.   He's irremovable,
Resolv'd for flight. Now were I happy if   506
His going I could frame to serve my turn,
Save him from danger, do him love and honour,
Purchase the sight again of dear Sicilia
And that unhappy king, my master, whom   510
I so much thirst to see.

  Florizel.   Now, good Camillo,
I am so fraught with curious business that
I leave out ceremony.

  Camillo.   Sir, I think
You have heard of my poor services, i' th' love
That I have borne your father?

493–4 **cast . . . passion**: use good advice to quieten his anger
(metaphor from casting water on a fire).   494–5 **let . . . come**:
I must resolutely face the chances of the future (tug = fight).
496 **deliver**: report.   497 **whom . . . hold**: whose love I cannot
keep.   498 **opportune**: accented on the second syllable.   501–
2 **Shall . . . reporting**: will do you no good to know, nor need I
trouble to tell you.   503 **easier for**: more amenable to.   511–
13 **Now . . . ceremony**: Florizel apologizes for speaking aside.

Florizel.   Very nobly   515
Have you deserv'd: it is my father's music
To speak your deeds, not little of his care
To have them recompens'd as thought on.
    Camillo.   Well, my lord,
If you may please to think I love the king
And through him what's nearest to him, which is   520
Your gracious self, embrace but my direction,
If your more ponderous and settled project
May suffer alteration. On mine honour
I'll point you where you shall have such receiving
As shall become your highness; where you may   525
Enjoy your mistress,—from the whom, I see,
There's no disjunction to be made, but by,
As, heavens forfend! your ruin,—marry her;
And with my best endeavours in your absence
Your discontenting father strive to qualify,   530
And bring him up to liking.
    Florizel.   How, Camillo,
May this, almost a miracle, be done?
That I may call thee something more than man,
And, after that trust to thee.
    Camillo.   Have you thought on
A place whereto you'll go?
    Florizel.   Not any yet: 535
But as th' unthought-on accident is guilty
To what we wildly do, so we profess

518 **recompens'd . . . on :** rewarded as fully as they are remembered.   519 **If . . . think :** a polite form.   521 **embrace . . . direction :** only submit to my guidance.   522–3 **If . . . alteration :** If your very important and fixed plan will allow of alteration [*N*].   527 **disjunction :** separation.   529–31 **And . . . liking :** and to the best of my ability I'll [understood from l. 524] endeavour, during your absence, to moderate your discontented father and win his approval for you [*N*].   534 **after that :** as such.   536–9 i.e. But as the unexpected happening (Polixenes' interference) is the cause of

Ourselves to be the slaves of chance and flies
Of every wind that blows.
  Camillo.   Then list to me:
This follows, if you will not change your purpose   540
But undergo this flight; make for Sicilia,
And there present yourself and your fair princess,—
For so, I see, she must be,—'fore Leontes;
She shall be habited as it becomes
The partner of your bed. Methinks I see   545
Leontes opening his free arms and weeping
His welcomes forth; asks thee, the son, forgiveness
As 'twere i' th' father's person; kisses the hands
Of your fresh princess; o'er and o'er divides him
'Twixt his unkindness and his kindness: th' one   550
He chides to hell, and bids the other grow
Faster than thought or time.
  Florizel.   Worthy Camillo,
What colour for my visitation shall I
Hold up before him?
  Camillo.   Sent by the king your father
To greet him and to give him comforts. Sir,   555
The manner of your bearing towards him, with
What you as from your father shall deliver,
Things known betwixt us three, I'll write you down:
The which shall point you forth at every sitting
What you must say; that he shall not perceive   560

our unpremeditated action, so we admit we are leaving everything
to chance and will go whatever way circumstances direct us (like
flies before the wind).   **544 habited** : dressed.   **546 free** : gracious,
bounteous.   **548 As 'twere . . . person** : as if you were your
father.   **549 fresh** : young and lovely [*N*].   **553 colour** :
excuse.   **554 Hold up** : present.   **555 comforts** : i.e. reassur-
ances of forgiveness and friendship.   **557 deliver** : say
[*N*].   **559 point you forth** : indicate, show you.   **sitting** :
session (of the King in Council) or perhaps, more generally, inter-
view.

But that you have your father's bosom there
And speak his very heart.

   Florizel.   I am bound to you.
There is some sap in this.

   Camillo.   A course more promising
Than a wild dedication of yourselves
To unpath'd waters, undream'd shores, most certain   565
To miseries enough: no hope to help you,
But as you shake off one to take another;
Nothing so certain as your anchors, who
Do their best office, if they can but stay you
Where you'll be loath to be. Besides, you know   570
Prosperity's the very bond of love,
Whose fresh complexion and whose heart together
Affliction alters.

   Perdita.   One of these is true:
I think affliction may subdue the cheek,
But not take in the mind.

   Camillo.   Yea, say you so?   575
There shall not at your father's house these seven years
Be born another such.

   Florizel.   My good Camillo,
She is as forward of her breeding as
She is i' th' rear 'our birth.

   Camillo.   I cannot say 'tis pity
She lacks instructions, for she seems a mistress   580
To most that teach.

   Perdita.   Your pardon, sir; for this
I'll blush you thanks.

   Florizel.   My prettiest Perdita!

---

   561 bosom : intimate thoughts.   **563 sap** : prospect of growth,
hope of a good outcome.   **564 wild dedication** : thoughtless
handing-over.   **567 one** : one misery.   **575 take in** : conquer
[*N*].   **576 these seven years** : in a long time, ever.   **579**
'our : of our [*N*].   **581 To** : compared with.

But O! the thorns we stand upon. Camillo,
Preserver of my father, now of me,
The med'cine of our house, how shall we do?   585
We are not furnish'd like Bohemia's son,
Nor shall appear in Sicilia.

   Camillo.   My lord,
Fear none of this: I think you know my fortunes
Do all lie there: it shall be so my care
To have you royally appointed as if   590
The scene you play were mine. For instance, sir,
That you may know you shall not want, one word.

                             [They talk aside.

Enter AUTOLYCUS.

   Autolycus. Ha, ha! what a fool Honesty is! and Trust,
his sworn brother, a very simple gentleman! I have sold
all my trumpery: not a counterfeit stone, not a ribbon, 595
glass, pomander, brooch, table-book, ballad, knife, tape,
glove, shoe-tie, bracelet, horn-ring, to keep my pack
from fasting: they throng who should buy first, as if
my trinkets had been hallowed and brought a bene-
diction to the buyer: by which means I saw whose purse 600
was best in picture; and what I saw, to my good use
I remem'red. My clown—who wants but something
to be a reasonable man,—grew so in love with the
wenches' song that he would not stir his pettitoes till

---

   587 Nor ... appear : i.e. appear so.   **588–9 my fortunes ...
there :** my property is all there.   **590 royally appointed :**
equipped like royalty.   **596 pomander :** scent ball, worn round
the neck.   **table-book :** note-book.   **597 horn-ring :** presumably a finger-ring of horn.   **598 from fasting :** i.e. he has
sold everything and there is nothing to feed his pack with, to put
into it.   **599 hallowed :** blessed (like sacred images, &c.).   **601
best in picture :** perhaps 'best in appearance', i.e. fullest-looking,
with possibly a play on picking = stealing.   **604 pettitoes :** pig's
trotters (i.e. the Clown's feet).

he had both tune and words; which so drew the rest 605
of the herd to me that all their other senses stuck in
ears: you might have pinch'd a placket, it was sense-
less; 'twas nothing to geld a codpiece of a purse; I would
have fil'd keys off that hung in chains: no hearing, no
feeling, but my sir's song, and admiring the nothing of 610
it; so that, in this time of lethargy I pick'd and cut most
of their festival purses; and had not the old man come
in with a hubbub against his daughter and the king's
son, and scar'd my choughs from the chaff, I had not
left a purse alive in the whole army.　　　　　　615

[CAMILLO, FLORIZEL, *and* PERDITA *come forward.*

Camillo.　Nay, but my letters, by this means being there
So soon as you arrive, shall clear that doubt.

Florizel.　And those that you'll procure from King
　Leontes—

Camillo.　Shall satisfy your father.

Perdita.　　　　　　　　　　Happy be you!
All that you speak shows fair.

Camillo. [*Seeing* AUTOLYCUS.] Who have we here? 620
We'll make an instrument of this: omit
Nothing may give us aid.

Autolycus. [*Aside.*] If they have overheard me now, why,
hanging.

Camillo.　How now, good fellow! Why shakest thou so?
Fear not, man; here's no harm intended to thee.　626

Autolycus.　I am a poor fellow, sir.

Camillo.　Why, be so still; here's nobody will steal

606–7 stuck in ears: went to their ears, became hearing, so that
they had no sense but that [*N*].　　　**607 pinch'd a placket**: stolen
a petticoat.　　　**608 geld . . . purse**: cut off a purse from the
front of a man's hose.　　　**610 my sir's**: i.e. the Clown's (ironic).
nothing: nonsense (with a pun on 'noting').　　　**614 choughs**:
jackdaws. (The rustics swoop on the ballads like birds on the chaff
separated from the corn.)　　　**622 Nothing may**: nothing that
may.

that from thee; yet, for the outside of thy poverty we
must make an exchange; therefore, discase thee in- 630
stantly,—thou must think, there's a necessity in 't,—
and change garments with this gentleman: though the
pennyworth on his side be the worst, yet hold thee,
there's some boot.

Autolycus. I am a poor fellow, sir.—[*Aside.*] I know ye
well enough.   636

Camillo. Nay, prithee, dispatch: the gentleman is half
flayed already.

Autolycus. Are you in earnest, sir? [*Aside.*] I smell the
trick on 't.   640

Florizel. Dispatch, I prithee.

Autolycus. Indeed, I have had earnest; but I cannot with
conscience take it.

Camillo. Unbuckle, unbuckle.—

          [FLORIZEL *and* AUTOLYCUS *exchange garments.*
Fortunate mistress,—let my prophecy   645
Come home to ye!—you must retire yourself
Into some covert: take your sweetheart's hat
And pluck it o'er your brows; muffle your face;
Dismantle you, and, as you can, disliken
The truth of your own seeming; that you may,—   650
For I do fear eyes over,—to shipboard
Get undescried.

Perdita.   I see the play so lies
That I must bear a part.

630 **discase :** undress.   632–3 **though ... worst :** though he gets
the worst of the exchange.   634 **boot :** advantage, gain. (Camillo
gives him money.)   639–40 **I smell ... on 't :** I see through
your scheme.   641 **Dispatch :** Hurry.   642 **earnest :** a first
instalment (i.e. the money given by Camillo at l. 634).   645–6 **let
my ... ye :** i.e. may you be indeed fortunate!   647 **covert :**
thicket.   649–50 **as you ... seeming :** make yourself as unlike
your true appearance as you can.   651 **eyes over :** probably
'watching eyes' (of Polixenes' spies) [*N*].

Camillo. No remedy.
Have you done there?
　　Florizel. Should I now meet my father
He would not call me son.
　　Camillo. Nay, you shall have no hat.
　　　　　　　　　　　　[*Giving it to* PERDITA.
Come, lady, come. Farewell, my friend.
　　Autolycus. Adieu, sir.　656
　　Florizel. O Perdita, what have we twain forgot!
Pray you, a word. 　[*They converse apart.*
　　Camillo. [*Aside.*] What I do next shall be to tell the king
Of this escape, and whither they are bound; 　660
Wherein my hope is I shall so prevail
To force him after: in whose company
I shall review Sicilia, for whose sight
I have a woman's longing.
　　Florizel. Fortune speed us!
Thus we set on, Camillo, to th' sea-side. 　665
　　Camillo. The swifter speed the better.

　　　　[*Exeunt* FLORIZEL, PERDITA, *and* CAMILLO.

Autolycus. I understand the business; I hear it. To
have an open ear, a quick eye, and a nimble hand, is
necessary for a cut-purse: a good nose is requisite also,
to smell out work for th' other senses. I see this is the 670
time that the unjust man doth thrive. What an exchange had this been without boot! what a boot is here
with this exchange! Sure, the gods do this year connive
at us, and we may do anything extempore. The prince
himself is about a piece of iniquity; stealing away from 675
his father with his clog at his heels. If I thought it
were a piece of honesty to acquaint the king withal,

663 **review** : see again.　　672 **boot** : see l. 634.　　674 **extempore** : without previous planning.　　675 **about** : engaged in.
676 **clog** : wench (literally, encumbrance).

I would not do 't: I hold it the more knavery to conceal it, and therein am I constant to my profession.   679

Re-enter Clown *and* Shepherd.

Aside, aside: here is more matter for a hot brain. Every lane's end, every shop, church, session, hanging, yields a careful man work.

Clown. See, see, what a man you are now! There is no other way but to tell the king she's a changeling and none of your flesh and blood.   685

Shepherd. Nay, but hear me.

Clown. Nay, but hear me.

Shepherd. Go to, then.

Clown. She being none of your flesh and blood, your flesh and blood has not offended the king; and so your 690 flesh and blood is not to be punish'd by him. Show those things you found about her; those secret things, all but what she has with her: this being done, let the law go whistle: I warrant you.   694

Shepherd. I will tell the king all, every word, yea, and his son's pranks too; who, I may say, is no honest man neither to his father nor to me, to go about to make me the king's brother-in-law.

Clown. Indeed, brother-in-law was the furthest off you could have been to him, and then your blood had been the dearer by I know how much an ounce.   701

Autolycus. [*Aside.*] Very wisely, puppies!

Shepherd. Well, let us to the king: there is that in this fardel will make him scratch his beard.

Autolycus. [*Aside.*] I know not what impediment this complaint may be to the flight of my master.   706

680 **Aside:** Let me step aside.   **hot:** busy.   682 **careful:** industrious (ironic).   684 **changeling:** see III. iii. 114, note. 688 **Go to:** usually deprecatory but here = go on.   693–4 **let ... whistle:** you need not worry about the law.   704 **fardel:** bundle.   706 **my master:** i.e. Florizel.

Clown. Pray heartily he be at' palace.

Autolycus. [*Aside.*] Though I am not naturally honest, I am so sometimes by chance: let me pocket up my pedlar's excrement. [*Takes off his false beard.*] How now, rustics! whither are you bound?   711

Shepherd. To th' palace, an it like your worship.

Autolycus. Your affairs there, what, with whom, the condition of that fardel, the place of your dwelling, your names, your ages, of what having, breeding, and anything that is fitting to be known, discover.   716

Clown. We are but plain fellows, sir.

Autolycus. A lie; you are rough and hairy. Let me have no lying; it becomes none but tradesmen, and they often give us soldiers the lie; but we pay them for 720 it with stamped coin, not stabbing steel; therefore they do not give us the lie.

Clown. Your worship had like to have given us one, if you had not taken yourself with the manner.

Shepherd. Are you a courtier, an 't like you, sir?   725

Autolycus. Whether it like me or no, I am a courtier. Seest thou not the air of the court in these enfoldings? hath not my gait in it the measure of the court? receives not thy nose court-odour from me? reflect I not on thy baseness court-contempt? Think'st thou, for 730 that I insinuate, or toaze from thee thy business, I am therefore no courtier? I am courtier, cap-a-pe, and one that will either push on or pluck back thy business there: whereupon I command thee to open thy affair.

---

707 **at' palace :** at the palace (cf. IV. iv. 105 &c.).   710
excrement : beard [*N*].   712 **an . . . worship :** if you please, sir.   715 **having :** property.   716 **discover :** show, tell.   728
measure : stately walk (literally, dance).   731 **insinuate :** cajole, wheedle.   **toaze :** literally, comb out; hence, find out by questioning.   732 **cap-a-pe :** top to toe.   733 **push . . . back :** help or hinder.   734 **open :** disclose.

Shepherd. My business, sir, is to the king.   735
Antolycus. What advocate hast thou to him?
Shepherd. I know not, an't like you.
Clown. Advocate's the court-word for a pheasant: say
you have none.   739
Shepherd. None, sir; I have no pheasant, cock nor hen.
Autolycus. How blessed are we that are not simple men!
Yet nature might have made me as these are,
Therefore I'll not disdain.
Clown. This cannot be but a great courtier.
Shepherd. His garments are rich, but he wears them not
handsomely.   746
Clown. He seems to be the more noble in being fantastical:
a great man, I'll warrant; I know by the picking on's
teeth.
Autolycus. The fardel there? what's i' th' fardel? Where-
fore that box?   751
Shepherd. Sir, there lies such secrets in this fardel and box
which none must know but the king; and which he shall
know within this hour if I may come to th' speech of him.
Autolycus. Age, thou hast lost thy labour.   755
Shepherd. Why, sir?
Autolycus. The king is not at the palace; he is gone
aboard a new ship to purge melancholy and air himself: for,
if thou be'st capable of things serious, thou must know the
king is full of grief.   760
Shepherd. So 'tis said, sir, about his son, that should have
married a shepherd's daughter.
Autolycus. If that shepherd be not in handfast, let him
fly: the curses he shall have, the tortures he shall feel, will
break the back of man, the heart of monster.   765

747 **fantastical**: eccentric.   758 **purge melancholy**: rid
himself of the melancholy humour [*N*].   761 **should have**:
was to have.   763 **in handfast**: held fast (i.e. in prison), under
arrest.

Clown. Think you so, sir?

Autolycus. Not he alone shall suffer what wit can make
heavy and vengeance bitter; but those that are germane to him, though remov'd fifty times, shall all come
under the hangman: which though it be great pity, 770
yet it is necessary. An old sheep-whistling rogue, a
ram-tender, to offer to have his daughter come into
grace! Some say he shall be ston'd; but that death is
too soft for him, say I: draw our throne into a sheep
cote! all deaths are too few, the sharpest too easy.   775

Clown. Has the old man e'er a son, sir, do you hear,
an 't like you, sir?

Autolycus. He has a son, who shall be flay'd alive;
then 'nointed over with honey, set on the head of a
wasp's nest; then stand till he be three quarters and a 780
dram dead; then recover'd again with aqua-vitae or
some other hot infusion; then, raw as he is, and in the
hottest day prognostication proclaims, shall he be set
against a brickwall, the sun looking with a southward
eye upon him, where he is to behold him with flies 785
blown to death. But what talk we of these traitorly
rascals, whose miseries are to be smil'd at, their offences being so capital? Tell me,—for you seem to be
honest plain men,—what you have to the king: being
something gently consider'd, I'll bring you where he is 790
abroad, tender your persons to his presence, whisper
him in your behalfs; and if it be in man besides the
king to effect your suits, here is man shall do it.

Clown. He seems to be of great authority: close with

767 **wit** : ingenuity.   768 **germane** : related.   773 **grace** :
reputation, dignity.   781 **aqua-vitae** : spirits.   783 **prognostication** : the weather forecast of the almanac.   785 **he** : i.e.
the sun.   788 **capital** : deserving death.   789 **what you have
to** : what is your business with.   790 **gently consider'd** : treated
as a gentleman (a euphemism: he means 'bribed').   794 **close** :
make an agreement.

him, give him gold; and though authority be a stubborn 795
bear, yet he is oft led by the nose with gold. Show the
inside of your purse to the outside of his hand, and
no more ado. Remember, 'ston'd', and 'flay'd alive'!

Shepherd. An't please you, sir, to undertake the business
for us, here is that gold I have: I'll make it as much more
and leave this young man in pawn till I bring it you. 801

Autolycus. After I have done what I promised?

Shepherd. Ay, sir.

Autolycus. Well, give me the moiety. Are you a party in
this business? 805

Clown. In some sort, sir: but though my case be a pitiful
one, I hope I shall not be flay'd out of it.

Autolycus. O! that's the case of the shepherd's son: hang
him, he'll be made an example.

Clown. Comfort, good comfort! we must to the king 810
and show our strange sights: he must know 'tis none of
your daughter nor my sister; we are gone else. Sir, I
will give you as much as this old man does when the
business is performed; and remain, as he says, your
pawn till it be brought you. 815

Autolycus. I will trust you. Walk before toward the sea-
side; go on the right hand; I will but look upon the hedge
and follow you.

Clown. We are bless'd in this man, as I may say, even
bless'd. 820

Shepherd. Let's before as he bids us. He was provided to
do us good.

[*Exeunt* Shepherd *and* Clown.

Autolycus. If I had a mind to be honest I see Fortune
would not suffer me: she drops booties in my mouth.
I am courted now with a double occasion, gold, and a 825

---

801 **in pawn :** as security, hostage.   804 **moiety :** half.   806
case : situation *and* skin (a pun).   812 **gone :** done for.   824
booties : spoils, plunder.   825 **occasion :** opportunity.

means to do the prince my master good; which who
knows how that may turn back to my advancement?
I will bring these two moles, these blind ones, aboard
him: if he think it fit to shore them again, and that the
complaint they have to the king concerns him nothing, 830
let him call me rogue for being so far officious; for I am
proof against that title and what shame else belongs to
't. To him will I present them: there may be matter
in it.   [*Exit.*

827 **turn back** : turn out.   833 **matter** : profit.

ACT V

Scene I

Enter LEONTES, CLEOMENES, DION, PAULINA, *and others.*

Cleomenes. Sir, you have done enough, and have per-
form'd
A saint-like sorrow: no fault could you make
Which you have not redeem'd; indeed, paid down
More penitence than done trespass. At the last,
Do as the heavens have done, forget your evil;   5
With them forgive yourself.

Leontes.   Whilst I remember
Her and her virtues, I cannot forget
My blemishes in them, and so still think of
The wrong I did myself; which was so much,
That heirless it hath made my kingdom, and   10
Destroy'd the sweet'st companion that e'er man
Bred his hopes out of.

Paulina.   True, too true, my lord;
If one by one you wedded all the world,
Or from the all that are took something good,
To make a perfect woman, she you kill'd   15
Would be unparallel'd.

Leontes.   I think so. Kill'd!
She I kill'd! I did so; but thou strik'st me
Sorely to say I did: it is as bitter
Upon thy tongue as in my thought. Now, good now,
Say so but seldom.

---

8 **in them** : i.e. in relation to them.   11–12 **that ... of** : that
ever gave a man hopes for a happy future.   14 **from ... are** :
from each woman alive.   19 **good now** : I implore you (an entreaty, which cannot be explained literally).

Cleomenes.　　　　Not at all, good lady:　　　20
You might have spoken a thousand things that would
Have done the time more benefit, and grac'd
Your kindness better.
　Paulina.　　　　You are one of those
Would have him wed again.
　Dion.　　　　　　If you would not so,
You pity not the state, nor the remembrance　　25
Of his most sovereign name; consider little
What dangers, by his highness' fail of issue,
May drop upon his kingdom and devour
Incertain lookers-on. What were more holy
Than to rejoice the former queen is well?　　30
What holier than for royalty's repair,
For present comfort, and for future good,
To bless the bed of majesty again
With a sweet fellow to 't?
　Paulina.　　　　There is none worthy,
Respecting her that's gone. Besides, the gods　　35
Will have fulfill'd their secret purposes;
For has not the divine Apollo said,
Is 't not the tenour of his oracle,
That King Leontes shall not have an heir
Till his lost child be found? which that it shall,　　40
Is all as monstrous to our human reason
As my Antigonus to break his grave
And come again to me; who, on my life,
Did perish with the infant. 'Tis your counsel
My lord should to the heavens be contrary,　　45

22 **done . . . benefit**: been more valuable at this time.　　25–26
remembrance . . . name: handing down of his name (and dynasty).
(So 'royalty's repair', l. 31.)　　26 **consider**: i.e. you consider.
29 **Incertain lookers-on**: i.e. those who play no active part in political affairs and are doubtful about the future.　　35 **Respecting**:
in comparison with.　　36 **Will**: must.　　41 **Is all as monstrous**:
seems quite as unnatural.

Oppose against their wills.—[*To* LEONTES.] Care not for issue;
The crown will find an heir: great Alexander
Left his to th' worthiest, so his successor
Was like to be the best.
    Leontes.   Good Paulina,
Who hast the memory of Hermione,   50
I know, in honour; O! that ever I
Had squar'd me to thy counsel! then, even now,
I might have look'd upon my queen's full eyes,
Have taken treasure from her lips,—
    Paulina.   And left them
More rich, for what they yielded.
    Leontes.   Thou speak'st truth. 55
No more such wives; therefore, no wife: one worse,
And better us'd, would make her sainted spirit
Again possess her corpse and on this stage,—
Where we offenders now appear,—soul-vex'd,
Begin, 'And why to me?'
    Paulina.   Had she such power, 60
She had just cause.
    Leontes.   She had; and would incense me
To murder her I married.
    Paulina.   I should so:
Were I the ghost that walk'd, I'd bid you mark
Her eye, and tell me for what dull part in 't
You chose her; then I'd shriek, that even your ears 65
Should rift to hear me; and the words that follow'd
Should be 'Remember mine'.
    Leontes.   Stars, stars!
And all eyes else dead coals. Fear thou no wife;
I'll have no wife, Paulina.
    Paulina.   Will you swear
Never to marry but by my free leave?   70

---

52 **squar'd . . . to** : been guided by.   53 **full eyes** : i.e. not
hollow.   66 **rift** : split.   67 **mine** : i.e. my eyes.

Leontes. Never, Paulina: so be bless'd my spirit!

Paulina. Then, good my lords, bear witness to his oath.

Cleomenes. You tempt him over much.

Paulina.   Unless another,
As like Hermione as is her picture,
Affront his eye.

Cleomenes.   Good madam,—

Paulina.   I have done.   75
Yet, if my lord will marry,—if you will, sir,
No remedy, but you will,—give me the office
To choose you a queen: she shall not be so young
As was your former; but she shall be such
As, walk'd your first queen's ghost, it should take joy 80
To see her in your arms.

Leontes.   My true Paulina,
We shall not marry till thou bidd'st us.

Paulina.   That
Shall be when your first queen's again in breath;
Never till then.   84

Enter a Gentleman.

Gentleman. One that gives out himself Prince Florizel,
Son of Polixenes, with his princess,—she
The fairest I have yet beheld,—desires access
To your high presence.

Leontes.   What with him? he comes not
Like to his father's greatness; his approach,
So out of circumstance and sudden, tells us   90
'Tis not a visitation fram'd, but forc'd
By need and accident. What train?

Gentleman.   But few,
And those but mean.

73 **tempt** : try, test.   75 **Affront** : confront.   77 **No remedy...
will** : if you really must.   89 **Like to** : in a manner appropriate to.
90 **out of circumstance** : i.e. without the usual ceremonious accompaniments of a royal journey.   91 **fram'd** : previously arranged.

Leontes. His princess, say you, with him?

Gentleman. Ay, the most peerless piece of earth, I think,
That e'er the sun shone bright on.

Paulina. O Hermione! 95
As every present time doth boast itself
Above a better gone, so must thy grave
Give way to what's seen now. Sir, you yourself
Have said and writ so,—but your writing now
Is colder than that theme,—'She had not been, 100
Nor was not to be equall'd'; thus your verse
Flow'd with her beauty once: 'tis shrewdly ebb'd
To say you have seen a better.

Gentleman. Pardon, madam:
The one I have almost forgot—your pardon—
The other, when she has obtain'd your eye, 105
Will have your tongue too. This is a creature,
Would she begin a sect, might quench the zeal
Of all professors else, make proselytes
Of who she but bid follow.

Paulina. How! not women? 109

Gentleman. Women will love her, that she is a woman
More worth than any man; men, that she is
The rarest of all women.

Leontes. Go, Cleomenes;
Yourself, assisted with your honour'd friends,
Bring them to our embracement. Still 'tis strange,

[*Exeunt* CLEOMENES, Lords, *and* Gentleman.

He thus should steal upon us.

Paulina. Had our prince— 115
Jewel of children—seen this hour, he had pair'd

96–97 **As every . . . gone :** As the present time always declares
itself to be superior to a really better time in the past. 97 **thy
grave :** i.e. what thy grave holds. 106 **tongue :** praise. 108
professors : believers. 113 **assisted with :** accompanied by.
115 **our prince :** Mamillius.

Well with this lord: there was not full a month
Between their births.

   Leontes. Prithee, no more: cease! thou know'st
He dies to me again when talk'd of: sure,   120
When I shall see this gentleman, thy speeches
Will bring me to consider that which may
Unfurnish me of reason. They are come.

Re-enter CLEOMENES, *with* FLORIZEL, PERDITA, *and others.*

Your mother was most true to wedlock, prince;
For she did print your royal father off,   125
Conceiving you. Were I but twenty-one,
Your father's image is so hit in you,
His very air, that I should call you brother,
As I did him; and speak of something wildly
By us perform'd before. Most dearly welcome!   130
And your fair princess,—goddess! O, alas!
I lost a couple, that 'twixt heaven and earth
Might thus have stood begetting wonder as
You, gracious couple, do: and then I lost—
All mine own folly—the society,   135
Amity too, of your brave father, whom,
Though bearing misery, I desire my life
Once more to look on him.

   Florizel.   By his command
Have I here touch'd Sicilia; and from him
Give you all greetings that a king, at friend,   140
Can send his brother: and, but infirmity,—
Which waits upon worn times,—hath something seiz'd

125 **print . . . off** : i.e. make a copy of him.   127 **hit** : accurately copied, 'hit off' (cf. a 'striking' likeness. The metaphor is from
a stamp or seal).   129–30 **something . . . before** : some mad
deed that we had done earlier.   140 **at friend** : in friendship.
141 **but** : but that, were it not that.   142 **waits . . . times** :
attends old age.   142–43 **hath . . . ability** : has somewhat seized
upon (i.e. arrested; metaphorical for diminished) the power he

His wish'd ability, he had himself
The land and waters 'twixt your throne and his
Measur'd to look upon you, whom he loves—   145
He bade me say so—more than all the sceptres
And those that bear them living.

 Leontes.   O, my brother!—
Good gentleman,—the wrongs I have done thee stir
Afresh within me, and these thy offices,
So rarely kind, are as interpreters   150
Of my behind-hand slackness! Welcome hither,
As is the spring to th' earth. And hath he too
Expos'd this paragon to th' fearful usage—
At least ungentle—of the dreadful Neptune,
To greet a man not worth her pains, much less   155
Th' adventure of her person?

 Florizel.   Good my lord,
She came from Libya.

 Leontes.   Where the war-like Smalus,
That noble honour'd lord, is fear'd and lov'd?

 Florizel. Most royal sir, from thence; from him, whose
  daughter
His tears proclaim'd his, parting with her: thence—   160
A prosperous south-wind friendly—we have cross'd,
To execute the charge my father gave me
For visiting your highness: my best train
I have from your Sicilian shores dismiss'd;
Who for Bohemia bend, to signify   165
Not only my success in Libya, sir,
But my arrival and my wife's, in safety
Here where we are.

desired to have. **149 offices :** gracious acts. **150–1 interpreters ... slackness :** i.e. they show how slack I have been in my
'offices' towards him. **156 adventure :** risk. **159–60 from
him ... her :** from him who, when he parted from her, showed by
his tears that she was his daughter. **165 bend :** bend their way, are
bound.

Leontes.   The blessed gods
Purge all infection from our air whilst you
Do climate here! You have a holy father,   170
A graceful gentleman; against whose person,
So sacred as it is, I have done sin:
For which the heavens, taking angry note,
Have left me issueless; and your father's bless'd—
As he from heaven merits it—with you,   175
Worthy his goodness. What might I have been,
Might I a son and daughter now have look'd on,
Such goodly things as you!

Enter a Lord.

Lord.   Most noble sir,
That which I shall report will bear no credit,
Were not the proof so nigh. Please you, great sir,   180
Bohemia greets you from himself by me;
Desires you to attach his son, who has—
His dignity and duty both cast off—
Fled from his father, from his hopes, and with
A shepherd's daughter.
Leontes.   Where's Bohemia? speak.   185
Lord. Here in your city; I now came from him:
I speak amazedly, and it becomes
My marvel and my message. To your court
Whiles he was hast'ning,—in the chase it seems
Of this fair couple,—meets he on the way   190
The father of this seeming lady and
Her brother, having both their country quitted
With this young prince.
Florizel.   Camillo has betray'd me;

171 **graceful**: virtuous (full of the effects of grace).   182
attach: arrest.   183 **dignity**: rank, position.   187 **it**: my
amazement, confusion.

Whose honour and whose honesty till now
Endur'd all weathers.

Lord.   Lay 't so to his charge: 195
He 's with the king your father.

Leontes.   Who? Camillo?

Lord. Camillo, sir: I spake with him, who now
Has these poor men in question. Never saw I
Wretches so quake: they kneel, they kiss the earth,
Forswear themselves as often as they speak: 200
Bohemia stops his ears, and threatens them
With divers deaths in death.

Perdita.   O my poor father!
The heaven sets spies upon us, will not have
Our contract celebrated.

Leontes.   You are married?

Florizel. We are not, sir, nor are we like to be;   205
The stars, I see, will kiss the valleys first:
The odds for high and low 's alike.

Leontes.   My lord,
Is this the daughter of a king?

Florizel.   She is,
When once she is my wife.

Leontes. That 'once', I see, by your good father's
          speed,   210
Will come on very slowly. I am sorry,
Most sorry, you have broken from his liking
Where you were tied in duty; and as sorry
Your choice is not so rich in worth as beauty,
That you might well enjoy her.

Florizel.   Dear, look up: 215

---

195 **Lay 't . . . charge :** You may rightly accuse him of that.
198 **Has . . . question :** is questioning them.   200 **Forswear :**
contradict.   202 **With . . . death :** with different (unpleasant)
kinds of death when they come to execution.   212 **liking :** affection.   214 **worth :** rank.

Though Fortune, visible an enemy,
Should chase us with my father, power no jot
Hath she to change our loves. Beseech you, sir,
Remember since you ow'd no more to time
Than I do now; with thought of such affections,   220
Step forth mine advocate; at your request
My father will grant precious things as trifles.
   Leontes. Would he do so, I'd beg your precious mistress,
Which he counts but a trifle.
   Paulina.   Sir, my liege,
Your eye hath too much youth in 't: not a month   225
'Fore your queen died, she was more worth such gazes
Than what you look on now.
   Leontes.   I thought of her,
Even in these looks I made. [*To* FLORIZEL.] But your
   petition
Is yet unanswer'd. I will to your father:
Your honour not o'erthrown by your desires,   230
I am friend to them and you; upon which errand
I now go toward him. Therefore follow me,
And mark what way I make: come, good my lord.
                            [*Exeunt.*

   216 **Fortune, visible an enemy :** the goddess Fortune become
visible as an enemy (i.e. clearly showing herself hostile).   219–
20 **since . . . now :** when you were no older than I am now.   220
such affections : i.e. as Leontes must have had in the past and
Florizel has for Perdita now.   233 **way :** progress (with Polixenes).

Scene II

Enter AUTOLYCUS *and a* Gentleman.

Autolycus. Beseech you, sir, were you present at this relation?

Gentleman. I was by at the opening of the fardel, heard the old shepherd deliver the manner how he found it: whereupon, after a little amazedness, we were all com- 5
manded out of the chamber; only this methought I heard the shepherd say, he found the child.

Autolycus. I would most gladly know the issue of it.

Gentleman. I make a broken delivery of the business; but the changes I perceived in the king and Camillo 10
were very notes of admiration: they seem'd almost, with staring on one another, to tear the cases of their eyes; there was speech in their dumbness, language in their very gesture; they look'd as they had heard of a world ransom'd, or one destroyed: a notable passion 15
of wonder appeared in them; but the wisest beholder, that knew no more but seeing, could not say if th' importance were joy or sorrow; but in the extremity of the one it must needs be.

Enter another Gentleman.

Here comes a gentleman that haply knows more. The 20
news, Rogero?

Second Gentleman. Nothing but bonfires: the oracle is fulfill'd; the king's daughter is found: such a deal of wonder is broken out within this hour that ballad-makers cannot be able to express it. 25

2 **relation :** narrative, i.e. the story of Perdita's being found by the Shepherd. 5 **after . . . amazedness :** after the King had recovered from his first shock of surprise. 9 **broken delivery :** disjointed account. 15 **passion :** feeling [*N*]. 17 **importance :** import, significance.

Enter another Gentleman.

Here comes the lady Paulina's steward: he can deliver you more. How goes it now, sir? this news which is call'd true is so like an old tale, that the verity of it is in strong suspicion: has the king found his heir?

Third Gentleman. Most true, if ever truth were preg- 30
nant by circumstance: that which you hear you'll swear you see, there is such unity in the proofs. The mantle of Queen Hermione's, her jewel about the neck of it, the letters of Antigonus found with it, which they know to be his character; the majesty of the creature in resem- 35
blance of the mother, the affection of nobleness which nature shows above her breeding, and many other evi-
dences proclaim her with all certainty to be the king's daughter. Did you see the meeting of the two kings?

Second Gentleman. No. 40

Third Gentleman. Then have you lost a sight which was to be seen, cannot be spoken of. There might you have beheld one joy crown another, so and in such manner that it seem'd sorrow wept to take leave of them, for their joy waded in tears. There was casting 45
up of eyes, holding up of hands, with countenance of such distraction that they were to be known by gar-
ment, not by favour. Our king, being ready to leap out of himself for joy of his found daughter, as if that joy were now become a loss, cries, 'O, thy mother, 50
thy mother!' then asks Bohemia forgiveness; then

30–31 **pregnant**: clear.   31 **circumstance**: circumstantial evidence.   31–32 **that which ... see**: i.e. the evidence of the witnesses is as good as if you had been present at the events they tell of (because it is borne out by the 'proofs' mentioned afterwards). 35 **character**: handwriting.   36 **affection**: quality, disposition. 37 **breeding**: upbringing (cf. IV. iv. 578, note).   46 **countenance**: a plural, or perhaps abstract, 'demeanour'.   47 **were to be known**: could be recognized only.   48 **favour**: appearance, features.

embraces his son-in-law; then again worries he his
daughter with clipping her; now he thanks the old
shepherd, which stands by like a weather-bitten conduit
of many kings' reigns. I never heard of such another 55
encounter, which lames report to follow it and undoes
description to do it.

Second Gentleman. What, pray you, became of **Antigonus**
that carried hence the child?

Third Gentleman. Like an old tale still, which will 60
have matter to rehearse, though credit be asleep and
not an ear open. He was torn to pieces with a bear:
this avouches the shepherd's son, who has not only his
innocence—which seems much—to justify him, but a
handkerchief and rings of his that Paulina knows. 65

First Gentleman. What became of his bark and his
followers?

Third Gentleman. Wrack'd, the same instant of their
master's death, and in the view of the shepherd: so
that all the instruments which aided to expose the 70
child were even then lost when it was found. But, O!
the noble combat that 'twixt joy and sorrow was fought
in Paulina. She had one eye declin'd for the loss of her
husband, another elevated that the oracle was fulfill'd:
she lifted the princess from the earth, and so locks her 75
in embracing, as if she would pin her to her heart that
she might no more be in danger of losing.

First Gentleman. The dignity of this act was worth the
audience of kings and princes, for by such was it acted.

53 **clipping** : embracing.   54 **weather-bitten** : weather-worn.
conduit : fountain in the form of a statue [*N*].   56 **lames
report** : makes report limp after it (is impossible to recount fully).
56-57 **undoes . . . it** : baffles description to tell of it.   61 **matter
to rehearse** : something to talk about.   **credit** : belief.   64
innocence . . much : i.e. he was very simple-minded.   70 **instruments which** : agents who.   76-77 **that she . . . losing** :
'she' is Perdita; 'losing' = being lost.

Third Gentleman. One of the prettiest touches of all, 80
and that which angl'd for mine eyes,—caught the
water though not the fish,—was when at the relation
of the queen's death,—with the manner how she came
to 't bravely confess'd and lamented by the king,—how
attentiveness wounded his daughter; till, from one 85
sign of dolour to another, she did, with an 'alas!' I
would fain say, bleed tears, for I am sure my heart
wept blood. Who was most marble there changed
colour; some swooned, all sorrowed: if all the world
could have seen 't, the woe had been universal.   90

First Gentleman. Are they returned to the court?

Third Gentleman. No; the princess hearing of her
mother's statue, which is in the keeping of Paulina—
a piece many years in doing, and now newly perform'd
by that rare Italian master, Julio Romano, who, had he 95
himself eternity and could put breath into his work,
would beguile Nature of her custom, so perfectly he is
her ape: he so near to Hermione hath done Hermione
that they say one would speak to her and stand in
hope of answer: thither with all greediness of affection 100
are they gone, and there they intend to sup.

Second Gentleman. I thought she had some great
matter there in hand, for she hath privately, twice or
thrice a day, ever since the death of Hermione, visited
that removed house. Shall we thither and with our 105
company piece the rejoicing?

First Gentleman. Who would be thence that has the
benefit of access? every wink of an eye some new grace will
be born: our absence makes us unthrifty to our knowledge.
Let 's along.   110

[*Exeunt* Gentlemen.

94 **perform'd** : completed.   98 **ape** : mimic (like a monkey) [*N*].
105 **removed** : remote [*N*].   106 **piece** : augment, help to make up.
109 **unthrifty ... knowledge** : not industrious enough in collecting
information (i.e. we'll be missing the news).

Autolycus. Now, had I not the dash of my former life
in me, would preferment drop on my head. I brought
the old man and his son aboard the prince; told him
I heard them talk of a fardel and I know not what; but
he at that time, overfond of the shepherd's daughter,— 115
so he then took her to be,—who began to be much sea-
sick, and himself little better, extremity of weather
continuing, this mystery remained undiscover'd. But
'tis all one to me; for had I been the finder out of this
secret, it would not have relish'd among my other dis- 120
credits.

               [*Enter* Shepherd *and* Clown.]
Here come those I have done good to against my will,
and already appearing in the blossoms of their fortune.

Shepherd. Come, boy; I am past moe children, but
thy sons and daughters will be all gentlemen born.   125

Clown. You are well met, sir. You denied to fight
with me this other day, because I was no gentleman
born: see you these clothes? say you see them not and
think me still no gentleman born: you were best say
these robes are not gentleman born. Give me the lie, 130
do, and try whether I am not now gentleman born.

Autolycus. I know you are now, sir, a gentleman born.

Clown. Ay, and have been so any time these four
hours.

Shepherd. And so have I, boy.   135

Clown. So you have: but I was a gentleman born
before my father; for the king's son took me by the hand
and call'd me brother; and then the two kings call'd
father brother; and then the prince my brother and
the princess my sister call'd my father father; and so 140

---

111 **dash:** a slight admixture of something inferior (a witty
understatement on the part of Autolycus).   120–1 **relish'd . . .
discredits:** pleased among the things counted against me (i.e. made
me acceptable in spite of the things. . .).   124 **moe:** more.

we wept: and there was the first gentleman-like tears
that ever we shed.

Shepherd. We may live, son, to shed many more.

Clown. Ay; or else 'twere hard luck, being in so preposterous estate as we are.   145

Autolycus. I humbly beseech you, sir, to pardon me all
the faults I have committed to your worship, and to give
me your good report to the prince my master.

Shepherd. Prithee, son, do; for we must be gentle, now we
are gentlemen.   150

Clown. Thou wilt amend thy life?

Autolycus. Ay, an it like your good worship.

Clown. Give me thy hand: I will swear to the prince thou
art as honest a true fellow as any is in Bohemia.

Shepherd. You may say it, but not swear it.   155

Clown. Not swear it, now I am a gentleman? Let boors
and franklins say it, I'll swear it.

Shepherd. How if it be false, son?

Clown. If it be ne'er so false, a true gentleman may
swear it in the behalf of his friend; and I'll swear to the   160
prince thou art a tall fellow of thy hands and that thou
wilt not be drunk; but I know thou art no tall fellow of
thy hands and that thou wilt be drunk: but I'll swear
it, and I would thou wouldst be a tall fellow of thy hands.

Autolycus. I will prove so, sir, to my power.   165

Clown. Ay, by any means prove a tall fellow: if I do
not wonder how thou dar'st venture to be drunk, not
being a tall fellow, trust me not. Hark! the kings and
the princes, our kindred, are going to see the queen's
picture. Come, follow us: we'll be thy good masters.   170

                                                          [*Exeunt.*

144–5 **preposterous** : the Clown's mistake for 'prosperous'.   157
franklins : yeomen.   161 **a tall . . . hands** : courageous in
using thy hands (i.e. to handle his weapons), a 'tough guy'.   170
picture : in this instance, for 'painted statue'.

Scene III

Enter LEONTES, POLIXENES, FLORIZEL, PERDITA, CAMILLO,
PAULINA, Lords, *and* Attendants.

Leontes. O grave and good Paulina, the great comfort
That I have had of thee!
Paulina.   What, sovereign sir,
I did not well, I meant well. All my services
You have paid home; but that you have vouchsaf'd,
With your crown'd brother and these your contracted   5
Heirs of your kingdoms, my poor house to visit,
It is a surplus of your grace, which never
My life may last to answer.
Leontes.   O Paulina!
We honour you with trouble: but we came
To see the statue of our queen: your gallery   10
Have we pass'd through, not without much content
In many singularities, but we saw not
That which my daughter came to look upon,
The statue of her mother.
Paulina.   As she liv'd peerless,
So her dead likeness, I do well believe,   15
Excels whatever yet you look'd upon
Or hand of man hath done; therefore I keep it
Lovely, apart. But here it is: prepare
To see the life as lively mock'd as ever
Still sleep mock'd death: behold! and say 'tis well. 20
            [PAULINA *draws back a curtain, and discovers*
                        HERMIONE *as a statue.*

4 paid home : amply repaid.   **7-8 It ... answer** : i.e. the
visit is a greater honour than she can ever repay.   **9 honour ...
trouble** : i.e. the royal visit is an honour but also a trouble.   **12
singularities** : remarkable objects, rarities.   **19-20 life ...
death** : life imitated as closely as ever sleep imitated death ('life',
'lively' : pun).

I like your silence: it the more shows off
Your wonder; but yet speak; first you, my liege.
Comes it not something near?

Leontes.   Her natural posture!
Chide me, dear stone, that I may say, indeed
Thou art Hermione; or rather, thou art she   25
In thy not chiding, for she was as tender
As infancy and grace. But yet, Paulina,
Hermione was not so much wrinkled; nothing
So aged as this seems.

Polixenes.   O! not by much.

Paulina. So much the more our carver's excellence;   30
Which lets go by some sixteen years and makes her
As she liv'd now.

Leontes.   As now she might have done,
So much to my good comfort, as it is
Now piercing to my soul. O! thus she stood,
Even with such life of majesty,—warm life,   35
As now it coldly stands,—when first I woo'd her.
I am asham'd: does not the stone rebuke me
For being more stone than it? O, royal piece!
There's magic in thy majesty, which has
My evils conjur'd to remembrance, and   40
From thy admiring daughter took the spirits,
Standing like stone with thee.

Perdita.   And give me leave,
And do not say 'tis superstition, that
I kneel and then implore her blessing. Lady,
Dear queen, that ended when I but began,   45
Give me that hand of yours to kiss.

Paulina.   O, patience!

---

23 **near :** i.e. near the original.   32 **As :** as if.   33–34 **as it
is ... soul :** as it (the lifelike statue) now causes me penitential grief.
38 **more stone :** i.e. stony-hearted (in his previous treatment of
Hermione).   41 **admiring :** wondering [*N*].

The statue is but newly fix'd, the colour's
Not dry.
  Camillo. My lord, your sorrow was too sore laid on,
Which sixteen winters cannot blow away,   50
So many summers dry: scarce any joy
Did ever so long live; no sorrow
But kill'd itself much sooner.
  Polixenes.   Dear my brother,
Let him that was the cause of this have power
To take off so much grief from you as he   55
Will piece up in himself.
  Paulina.   Indeed, my lord,
If I had thought the sight of my poor image
Would thus have wrought you,—for the stone is
    mine,—
I'd not have show'd it.
  Leontes.   Do not draw the curtain.   59
  Paulina. No longer shall you gaze on't, lest your fancy
May think anon it moves.
  Leontes.   Let be, let be!
Would I were dead, but that, methinks, already—
What was he that did make it? See, my lord,
Would you not deem it breath'd, and that those
    veins
Did verily bear blood?
  Polixenes.   Masterly done: 65
The very life seems warm upon her lip.
  Leontes. The fixure of her eye has motion in't,
As we are mock'd with art.

47 **fix'd** : refers to the colouring, which has just been made fast or
permanent.   49 **too . . . laid on** : too deeply felt (continuing the
paint image).   56 **piece up** : increase [*N*].   58 **wrought** : moved
(cf. 'worked up').   63 **What . . .?** : What sort of person?
(—a magician?)   67–68 **The fixure. . . art** : The eye is fixed
in such a way that it appears to move, for so we are beguiled by
art [*N*].

Paulina.   I'll draw the curtain;
My lord's almost so far transported that
He'll think anon it lives.
    Leontes.   O sweet Paulina!   70
Make me to think so twenty years together:
No settled senses of the world can match
The pleasure of that madness. Let 't alone.
    Paulina. I am sorry, sir, I have thus far stirr'd you: but
I could afflict you further.
    Leontes.   Do, Paulina;   75
For this affliction has a taste as sweet
As any cordial comfort. Still, methinks,
There is an air comes from her: what fine chisel
Could ever yet cut breath? Let no man mock me,
For I will kiss her.
    Paulina.   Good my lord, forbear.   80
The ruddiness upon her lip is wet:
You'll mar it if you kiss it; stain your own
With oily painting. Shall I draw the curtain?
    Leontes. No, not these twenty years.
    Perdita.   So long could I
Stand by, a looker-on.
    Paulina.   Either forbear,   85
Quit presently the chapel, or resolve you
For more amazement. If you can behold it,
I'll make the statue move indeed, descend,
And take you by the hand; but then you'll think,—
Which I protest against,—I am assisted   90
By wicked powers.
    Leontes.   What you can make her do,
I am content to look on: what to speak,

---

69 **transported** : carried away by emotion.   72 **settled . . .
world** : sanity as the world regards it.   77 **cordial** : medicinal.
85 **forbear** : here = 'keep aloof' from what is to happen.   86
presently : at once.

I am content to hear; for 'tis as easy
To make her speak as move.
    Paulina.   It is requir'd
You do awake your faith. Then, all stand still;   95
On: those that think it is unlawful business
I am about, let them depart.
    Leontes.   Proceed:
No foot shall stir.
    Paulina.   Music, awake her: strike!   [*Music.*
'Tis time; descend; be stone no more: approach;
Strike all that look upon with marvel. Come;   100
I'll fill your grave up: stir; nay, come away;
Bequeath to death your numbness, for from him
Dear life redeems you. You perceive she stirs:
                      [HERMIONE *comes down.*
Start not; her actions shall be holy as
You hear my spell is lawful: do not shun her   105
Until you see her die again, for then
You kill her double. Nay, present your hand:
When she was young you woo'd her; now in age
Is she become the suitor?
    Leontes. [*Embracing her.*] O! she's warm.
If this be magic, let it be an art   110
Lawful as eating.
    Polixenes.   She embraces him.
    Camillo. She hangs about his neck:
If she pertain to life let her speak too.
    Polixenes. Ay; and make it manifest where she has liv'd,
Or how stol'n from the dead.
    Paulina.   That she is living,   115
Were it but told you, should be hooted at
Like an old tale; but it appears she lives,

---

100 **look upon :** look on.   106 **then :** if you do (shun her
before she die).   107 **double :** a second time.   117 **appears :**
is manifest that.

Though yet she speak not. Mark a little while.
Please you to interpose, fair madam: kneel
And pray your mother's blessing. Turn, good lady;   120
Our Perdita is found.
                    [*Presenting* PERDITA, *who kneels to* HERMIONE.
  Hermione.   You gods, look down,
And from your sacred vials pour your graces
Upon my daughter's head! Tell me, mine own,
Where hast thou been preserv'd? where liv'd? how found
Thy father's court? for thou shalt hear that I,   125
Knowing by Paulina that the oracle
Gave hope thou wast in being, have preserv'd
Myself to see the issue.
  Paulina.   There's time enough for that;
Lest they desire upon this push to trouble
Your joys with like relation. Go together,   130
You precious winners all: your exultation
Partake to every one. I, an old turtle,
Will wing me to some wither'd bough, and there
My mate, that's never to be found again,
Lament till I am lost.
  Leontes.   O! peace, Paulina!   135
Thou shouldst a husband take by my consent,
As I by thine a wife: this is a match,
And made between's by vows. Thou hast found mine;
But how, is to be question'd; for I saw her,
As I thought dead, and have in vain said many   140
A prayer upon her grave. I'll not seek far,—
For him, I partly know his mind,—to find thee
An honourable husband. Come, Camillo,
And take her by the hand: whose worth and honesty

---

  128 **issue :** outcome.   129 **upon this push :** at this juncture.
130 **with . . . relation :** i.e. by telling their stories also.   132
Partake to : share with.   **turtle :** dove [*N*].   135 **am lost :**
die (balancing 'found' in l. 134).   144 **whose:** refers to Camillo.

Is richly noted, and here justified   145
By us, a pair of kings. Let's from this place.
What! look upon my brother: both your pardons,
That e'er I put between your holy looks
My ill suspicion. This' your son-in-law,
And son unto the king,—whom heavens directing,   150
Is troth-plight to your daughter. Good Paulina,
Lead us from hence, where we may leisurely
Each one demand and answer to his part
Perform'd in this wide gap of time since first
We were dissever'd: hastily lead away.   155

                                                    [*Exeunt.*

145 richly noted : widely known.   **justified** : vouched for [*N*].
147 What! : (to Hermione).   **149 This'** : This is. (The apostrophe
is not in F, but it seems a likely emendation.)   **150 heavens
directing** : by God's guidance [*N*].   **151 troth-plight** :
engaged (cf. IV. iv. 415, note).   **153–4 to his ... Perform'd** :
about the part he played [*N*].

NOTES

s.d. = stage direction.

F = the first Folio.

Furness = Horace Howard Furness in his *New Variorum* edition of *The Winter's Tale*, fifth edition, Philadelphia, 1898.

Moorman = F. W. Moorman in his *Arden* edition of *The Winter's Tale*, London, 1912.

Wilson = John Dover Wilson in the *New Cambridge* edition of *The Winter's Tale* (ed. Sir Arthur Quiller-Couch and John Dover Wilson), Cambridge, 1931.

All other references to critics and commentators by name are confined to such passages as may be found cited in the *New Variorum* edition.

References to other plays follow the line-numbering of the one-volume Shakespeare in the Oxford Standard Authors series.

ACT I, Scene I

The opening situation is introduced, before we meet the chief characters, by a Bohemian and a Sicilian lord in conversation. The scene is highly ironic: the friendship which 'must branch' is to be broken, the young prince's death is to disappoint the people's hopes. Note also the *wit* which treats serious matters lightly, a mark of sophistication.

s.d. In this edition we omit the notes of location which earlier editors have added at the head of each scene. They are not to be found in F. In a play of Shakespeare, if it is important for us to know where the characters are, we shall be told in the dialogue : if it is not important, we had better not think about it. To place this scene, as has been the custom, in an 'Antechamber' and the next in 'A Room of State' would call for a change of scenery. At the Globe, with no scenery and no front curtain, the acting was continuous, and we lose the flow and the point of Shakespeare's stagecraft if we interfere with the pattern of rapid contrasts made by the coming and going of the characters.

13–15. We will . . . us. This is *wit*: it is not seriously intended to administer drugs, but the speaker wishes to convey a polite depreciation of his own country. Though the prose of this scene has been called colloquial, its diction is somewhat inflated in the courtly manner, and there is 'euphuistic' balance, e.g. 'praise' —'accuse'.

21. **[train'd** for 'trained' and similar elisions are taken from F. In the prose as well as the verse they indicate pronunciation and influence rhythm. An unelided '-ed' or '-est' should be pronounced as a distinct syllable.**]**

26. **hath :** an old form of third person plural, the reading of F. (Later editions altered unnecessarily to 'have'.)

28–30. **shook . . . winds.** It has been suggested that this image derives from 'a device, common in the title pages of old books, of two hands extended from opposite clouds, and joined as in token of friendship over a wide waste of country'. 'Hands across the sea' is an even more frequent notion and applies more aptly to the situation of Leontes and Polixenes and the symbolic use of the sea in this play (see III. iii. 81–99, note). For *vast = sea*, cf. *Pericles*, III. i. 1 : Thou god of this great vast.

32. **malice or matter :** heavily ironical. Leontes will soon have the malice, and the matter will be the innocent friendship of Hermione and Polixenes.

36–41. The wit is complicated. Camillo says that the aged and infirm want to go on living in order to see Mamillius grow up. He intends to praise Mamillius but has chosen a poor means of doing so, as Archidamus hints by asking if they would otherwise be content to die. This quibbling movement from courtly praise to experienced moralizing on the common human tendency to cling to life aptly closes a short scene which sets the tone of Sicilian sophistication.

ACT I, Scene II

Leontes becomes jealous of Polixenes and schemes to have him put to death. Camillo reveals the plot and plans escape. Religious images and references throughout draw attention to the prevailing theme of sin, which is exemplified in Leontes' jealousy. We move from prose to verse with the introduction of the main characters.

1. A shepherd figures in the King of Bohemia's opening words, distinguishing him and his kingdom from urbanized Sicilia and pointing forward to the partly symbolic shepherd who becomes Perdita's foster-father. More immediately the reference relates to the religious imagery of the lambs in l. 67 below.

3–9. time . . . it. A further nine months of saying thank you would not repay his host, so Polixenes asks that the thanks he now expresses may, like a nought at the end of a row of figures, multiply all the thanks he has said before. This *conceit* is typical of 'metaphysical wit' (see Introduction, p. 20).

11–14. The sentence is elliptical. 'My fears raise questions in me as to what may be happening while I am away—fears lest cold winds should be blowing at home (i.e. lest conditions should be bad, perhaps through treasonable talk or disturbances), to make me say that this uneasiness was only too well grounded.'

23–26. My affairs . . . trouble. 'If you prevent my going home, your kindness will only hurt me, while I shall be an inconvenience to you.' Note the forceful metaphors 'drag' and 'whip' as well as the continued distortion of word-order.

27. Ellipsis and distorted word-order pass to Leontes. They are so frequent in this play as to suggest that the writer is wrestling with a meaning beyond what the dialogue obviously states. There will be no comment on these features of style in future, unless they have some special significance.

28–29. 'I had not intended to speak until he had sworn not to stay'—and so my triumph in persuading him would have been the greater. Or perhaps: 'I thought I should get no opportunity to speak until . . .'—playful reproof of Leontes. Line 29 is metrically regular if 'You had' is pronounced 'You'd'.

37. with distaffs : used in spinning, and hence a woman's weapon. Cf. modern jokes about the rolling-pin. It is appropriate that the women should thwack him home to satisfy his paternal longing for his son.

44. [lady she : usually taken as adjective and noun, meaning *well-born woman*. But perhaps 'she' is redundant, as in 'The skipping king, he ambled up and down' (*1 Henry IV*, III. ii. 60).]

47–56. Hermione rallies Polixenes for his weak oath 'verily'. In this scene alone we see her as she must have been before Leontes brought tragedy into her life, gay and witty, a great lady who is still a lively young woman. Her deeper qualities will be revealed by the terrible test to which she will soon be subjected.

52–53. [Force me . . . guest. Perhaps there should be a question mark after 'guest'. Otherwise 'Force me' must have the sense of 'If you force me'.]

53–54. Prisoners, whether guilty or innocent, had to pay a fee on liberation. If Polixenes had to pay money, he would save his thanks.

67–75. These lines introduce the general theme of innocence and sin. The lamb is a favourite symbol of innocence, originally no doubt from its appearance (the white fleece suggesting purity; its gambolling, freedom from care); later, from its use in Old Testament sacrifices and from the parallel drawn between Our Lord and the Passover lamb. Sin is associated with sexual maturity, the strengthening of the animal 'spirits' by the increase of 'blood'. (Phrases such as 'young blood', 'hot blood', are constantly associated with deeds of anger and lust.) Polixenes' implication that sex is necessarily sinful (see ll. 76–80) is not truly Christian nor is it Shakespeare's belief, as we see from the treatment of Perdita later and from the response, here, of the good Hermione. It is, however, dramatically a fitting prelude to Leontes' jealousy.

70. Some editors insert 'no,' before 'nor', and others adopt other emendations, to make this a 'regular' blank verse line. But Shakespeare's regularity is not arithmetical. Although he usually has ten syllables to the line, the fundamental principle of his verse is *time*, not number. Here the medial pause at 'ill-doing' takes up the time of half a foot, like a 'rest' in music.

74–75. the imposition . . . ours. The eighteenth-century scholar Theobald took this to mean 'except for original sin', but the nineteenth-century Furness and others following him take it as meaning that even original sin was cleared away because of the boys' innocence, a notion which Shakespeare and his contemporaries would hardly entertain. Yet Furness's suggestion seems more acceptable linguistically, and Polixenes is not theologically correct in another matter (see previous note) and may be wrong here too. We may, however, accept Furness's interpretation and take it as a witty hyperbole (or exaggeration). Polixenes does not literally mean that their original sin would have been done away, but merely uses a powerful *fiction* to stress their childish innocence. Such fictional exaggerations are common enough, e.g. 'You could have knocked me down with a feather.'

80. The theme of sin is followed by the theme of grace. Both are lightly introduced, in witty conversation, but they will have their effect on a perceptive audience.

86. Is . . . yet? Leontes must have stepped aside for a while. Wilson, who believes that the king was jealous before the scene opens, thinks it 'more than probable' that on coming up he heard Hermione's last few words, which, without what went before, would seem like an admission of guilt. But a matter of such importance is not left to mere 'business' on the Elizabethan stage: Shakespeare would have made it quite clear to us by giving Leontes some reference, in ordinary dialogue or aside, to what he had over-heard of Hermione's speech. The dialogue does in fact suggest that it was Hermione's success in persuading Polixenes to stay, and not anything she said, that caused his sudden uprush of jealousy. There is no textual support for the notion that Leontes was already jealous; and a sudden, inexplicable jealousy is quite acceptable both psychologically and in relation to the play's 'inner meaning' (see Introduction, pp. 33 ff.).

87. At . . . not. Possibly the first intimation of jealousy. The actor playing Leontes might show bitterness behind the apparently loving dialogue that follows.

91–101. The images used by the unsuspecting Hermione as well as the jealous Leontes have ominous overtones for the audience. The 'cramming' of domestic animals is for 'slaughter', and the latter word is used, though in another connexion, in the following line. Note also the sour crab-apples of l. 102.

99. Grace. Hermione hopes that the elder sister of her good deed was called Grace. The metaphor involves a pun on *grace* as a name and as a term in theology: she hopes that her first good deed was inspired by divine grace (and so was truly good). Commentators have ignored this quip, which keeps the underlying notions of innocence, sin, and grace before the audience.

104. clap. At an engagement the couple struck the palms of their hands together to signify agreement. The gesture is still found among the French peasantry on striking a bargain.

105. 'Tis grace indeed : a further pun, this time on the theological meaning of *grace* (a free gift of divine power) and the social meaning (the *graciousness* of her consenting to marry).

The word 'grace' is used with differing meanings and degrees of religious significance throughout the play: see II. i. 120–1 (and note); III. i. 22; III. ii. 46, 196; IV. i. 24; IV. iv. 8, 773; V. i. 171; V. ii. 108; V. iii. 7, 27, 121–3 (and note). For interpretation, see Introduction, pp. 38–39.

111–12. my heart . . . joy. See Psalm xxviii, v. 8 (Book of Common Prayer): 'The Lord is my strength, and my shield; my heart hath trusted in him, and I am helped: therefore *my heart danceth for joy*, and in my song will I praise him.' This allusion depends on dramatic convention: the pagan Leontes could not know the Psalms. Beginning the phrase in italics, he checks and corrects himself: his palpitation is not for joy. And, as the audience may note, his heart dances not through faith but lack of faith. Leontes' speech in his jealousy is more broken and elliptical than usual; it expresses agitation, confusion, and nervous tension.

112–15. **This entertainment . . . agent :** i.e. this behaviour (of Hermione to Polixenes: she has just offered him her hand in friendship) may have an appearance of candour (and) derive its freedom from good feeling, kindness, generosity, and so be quite correct in the person so acting.

116–19. Leontes in his jealousy distorts the polite behaviour of Hermione and Polixenes, which he can see as he speaks, into a wholly imaginary picture of lovers' dalliance.

119. **The mort . . . deer :** usually the sound on the hunting horn announcing the kill, but here surely the deep, sobbing sighs of the dying animal—*mort* being used literally. To give a literal significance to what is ordinarily understood figuratively is a form of wit. The pun *deer-dear* suggests that Hermione is the prey and has been won by Polixenes.

120. **my brows.** The reference is to the popular jest according to which the cuckold is said to wear horns.

123–36. Leontes is assailed with a doubt as to whether he is really the father of Mamillius but comforts himself in the thought of their resemblance.

124–8. 'Neat' means *clean* but also *cattle*. Leontes is still thinking of horns and so retreats from the word, then asserts it again, for the calf is 'neat' and has no horns. The sexual theme is punningly present in 'virginalling' (virgin) and 'wanton' (*frisky* but also *a loose woman*).

139–47. A difficult passage, expressing the speaker's disturbed mind. It follows from 'Can thy dam ?—may 't be ? ' Is it possible that the gracious Hermione can be an adultress ? Paraphrase: 'Sexual love, your intensity penetrates, like a dagger, to the heart's core. You make possible what is thought impossible, you hold communication with dreams (i.e. a real person may love a figure in a dream)— how can this happen ?—you have (sexual) intercourse with something that does not exist, becoming the companion of what is really nothing : then, it is easy to believe that you can have intercourse with *something* ; and you do, and that beyond what is lawful, and I discover it, so that my brain is unsettled and I find myself a cuckold.'

149. Many editors give this line to Polixenes, but there is no reason

to desert F: Leontes here and in the following speech is trying to dissemble.

155. [**methoughts**: a variant of *methought*, perhaps formed on analogy with *methinks*.]

156. **Twenty-three years**: making Leontes about thirty.

159. [**does**. Singular for plural is frequent in Shakespeare.]

162. **take ... money**: proverbial, of unknown origin. Eggs used to be very cheap, and so it means to accept something comparatively worthless, hence to be imposed on. Leontes thinks of himself as imposed on by Hermione.

173–5. **Hermione ... cheap.** These lines have an obvious double meaning.

178. [**shall's**: *shall us*, for *shall we*.]

179–80. This polite speech again has a secondary meaning: 'Do what you like; you'll be found out.'

180–1. **I am ... line.** He is 'giving them enough rope to hang themselves'.

186. 'Inch-thick' and 'knee-deep' refer to the supposed love of Hermione and Polixenes. So does 'o'er head and ears' at first, but the words suggest the growth of horns and so change their meaning as Leontes speaks, referring now to his being a cuckold.

187–90. This is the first of a series of theatrical metaphors. 'Issue' means *outcome* but also the actor's exit; 'hiss', 'contempt and clamour', refer to the reaction of the people to Leontes' disgrace, but within the metaphor apply to a dissatisfied audience.

190–207. **There have ... not.** Leontes seeks comfort in thinking how many others are in the same position as himself. The speech is a 'direct address' to the audience (see l. 193: 'Now, while I speak this') and suggests the frequency of adultery *in the real world*. Coarse language is used to convey a sense of revulsion. 'Sir Smile' looks back to the 'practis'd smiles' of l. 117. 'Gates' are the floodgates opened for 'sluicing', in the fishing metaphor used for the sexual act. Leontes goes on to find a cause in astrology for the prevalence of adultery. The second metaphor is taken from siege operations, a frequent figure for sexual love.

200. [**there's.** Pope and some subsequent editors read 'there is', to give a regular number of syllables to the line. But see l. 70, note.]

211. **honest man**: *a good boy*, but also with a secondary meaning, *a legitimate child*.

217. They're . . . already. The people are already mocking me (with a gesture (V) signifying cuckoldry, which Leontes possibly makes).

224–8. The metaphor in 'soaking', 'draw in', 'blocks', is from the process of dyeing hats on hat-blocks. Camillo's head 'absorbs' more than the others. 'Lower messes' are so called because those of inferior rank sat at table below the salt; it is assumed that they would be lower in intelligence also. Leontes in his perversity describes as 'finer natures' those who can detect adulteries.

230. Ha! Leontes had expected a different end to Camillo's sentence.

233. Satisfy. Leontes seizes on this word and thinks that by it the courtier Camillo intends to convey delicately that he knows of Hermione's (supposed) adultery.

237. [chamber-councils. Some editors have suggested that these chamber-councils—or, according to Wilson, *chamber-counsels*—refer to Leontes' secret sins. They believe Shakespeare intended to hint that Leontes had himself been guilty of adulteries; hence his present jealousy. This would destroy the pattern of the play, which goes from happiness to misery and back to happiness again. The general suggestion of the dialogue has surely been that Leontes and Hermione have *up to this time* been happily married. And if the chamber-counsels or -councils referred to secret sins, would they not be among 'the nearest things to his heart'? If so, why does he speak of 'the nearest things to my heart, *as well (as)* my chamber-councils'? 'Nearest things to my heart' must be private matters; 'chamber-councils', matters of State. It is perhaps with reference to these latter that Camillo has been like a confessor to him: the stock Renaissance figure of the Good Counsellor, directing his prince away from private caprice to public duty. But more probably 'wherein . . . reform'd' refers back to 'the nearest things': Camillo has helped him, like a confessor, to cope with his sins—but these need not have been sexual. Had Shakespeare intended to make Leontes guilty of sexual sins, he would have left no room for doubt in a matter so important for our understanding of the play.]

238–9. Note the change from the personal 'I' to the royal 'we', as Leontes stands upon his dignity.

241. seems so : for it is not real integrity, Leontes thinks. Here and in the following speech he accuses Camillo of knowing the adultery of Hermione and concealing it.

244. hoxes : metaphor taken from cutting the hamstrings, the sinews behind the knee, in horses or cattle, so as to lame them. Leontes says that, if Camillo inclines towards honesty, i.e. prefers to be honest, yet his cowardice maims his honesty, so that he does not do what he ought to do ('restraining . . . requir'd').

248–9. i.e. who sees a game played to the end and the money that has been pledged taken up by the winner, and thinks it is all a joke and not in earnest. Camillo may be foolish enough to regard what Leontes believes to be adultery as a harmless flirtation.

254–64. In your . . . free of. 'If in your affairs, my lord, I was ever wantonly neglectful, it was my foolishness; if I deliberately took things lightly, it was because I neglected to see how important the matter was; if I ever feared to do something of which the outcome was doubtful, and which, when once it *was* done, clearly appeared as something that *had* to be done, it was a fear that the wisest often have : these, my lord, are the sort of allowable weaknesses that every honest man has to some degree.'

267–73. Ha' not . . . slippery? Take 'my wife is slippery' as a noun clause, object of three verbs, 'seen', 'heard', 'thought'. Leontes begins with 'Have you not seen?' but breaks off, for Camillo *must* have seen, unless he is blind, that Hermione is fickle ('slippery'). Metaphorical blindness is expressed by reference to cataract ('the pin and web' of l. 291), a thickening of the lens of the eye, which Leontes characteristically compares to a cuckold's horn. 'Have you not heard?' he goes on; 'for there must be plenty of gossip about something that can be so clearly seen ('a vision so apparent'). Then, 'Have you not thought?' &c. The passage 'for cogitation . . . think' cannot mean flatly 'for there is no thought in the man who does not think'; therefore take 'my wife is slippery' after both 'thought' and 'think'. 'Have you not thought my wife is fickle?— for the man who does not think so is incapable of thinking.'

273–8. If thou . . . justify 't. 'If you will admit the fact—for boldly to deny it would be the same as denying that you can see, hear, and think—then put it crudely and say that my wife's a "hobby-horse" (wanton), deserves as coarse a name as any linen-maker who has sexual intercourse before her betrothal : say it and show it to be true.' In Elizabethan times betrothal was more solemn than a modern engagement and constituted an indissoluble union : it was therefore not sinful for the couple to have sexual intercourse *after* betrothal but before the church wedding (see IV. iv. 415, note).

284–92. Is whispering . . . nothing? This description of the supposed lovers' behaviour arises wholly from Leontes' imagination.

295. nor . . . nothings. Negatives do not normally cancel one another in Shakespeare's English. The piling up of negatives in this speech stresses the intensity of Leontes' assertion.

297. Camillo introduces the metaphor of disease, which is appropriate to Leontes' corrupted mind. Sin is a spiritual disease. Note how the image is bandied about later. To Leontes, who is diseased in 'opinion', it appears that every one else is diseased and he alone well.

304–6. were . . . glass continues the disease metaphor. The play on words— 'liver . . . life . . . live'—survives in the old joke: 'Is life worth living ?' 'It depends on the liver.' Puns in Shakespeare, however, are not always meant to be funny : their chief function is to express a point neatly and memorably by suggesting in verbal *form* the relationship that exists between two *meanings*.

312. undo more doing : either 'make further action unnecessary' (on the part of Leontes and his supporters) or 'make further action impossible' (on the part of Polixenes and Hermione). Note the word-play: 'do', 'undo', 'doing'.

316. [**gall'd,** the reading of F, should not be changed to 'galled': the *time* of an unstressed syllable is taken up at the pause.]

324. Camillo, who has been as intimate as a confessor with Leontes, begins an appeal based on his affection for him and so uses the familiar 'thee'. Leontes interrupts, not having attended to Camillo's last few words and referring, not to them, but back to Hermione's honour: 'If you are going to argue about *that*, you may go and rot.' Leontes' mind is made up and he wants the company only of those who will agree with him.

[There may, however, be some error in the text : the courtly Camillo is not likely to have used the familiar second person singular to his King.]

325. so muddy, so unsettled : cf. *Troilus and Cressida*, III. iii. 314:

> My mind is troubled, like a fountain stirr'd;
> And I myself see not the bottom of it.

329. This list of stinging things shows the sensitive state of Leontes' nerves.

355–61. The spiritual heavens, the created universe, the individual, the state: Shakespeare and his contemporaries treat these four concepts as analogous and often draw parallels between any two of them. In the present instance individual psychology is expressed by analogy with the state, a parallel so familiar to his audience that Shakespeare's simple reference was in effect a sort of shorthand. If Leontes is in rebellion with himself, it could mean only that the lower elements, the passions, have risen against their natural sovereign, the reason. In this state, says Camillo, he will have his followers to be rebels too—but 'rebels' is meant literally this time, for they are to strike an anointed king. Camillo takes the orthodox Tudor and Stuart view of 'divine right'. 'Anointed' is an important word, reminding us of the almost sacramental power of the unction at coronation. He asserts that (*a*) if there had been any number of successful assassinations of kings, he would not do such a deed, and (*b*) that, as no single one is recorded, even a villain should, for his own sake, avoid the crime. These words would carry their meaning over from the play world to the real world, especially at the royal performance on 5 November 1611, the anniversary of the Gunpowder Plot.

377–80. Polixenes utters disconnected phrases in his bewilderment. Some words must be supplied to bring out his probable meaning. 'What! dare not? surely you mean " do not"? (He pauses and reflects; then, perceiving Camillo's meaning,) Do you know and dare not admit that you know? Give *me* the information; it must be that you know and dare not admit the fact to *me* ("'tis thereabouts"); for, as far as *you* are concerned, you *must* know what you know, and it would be absurd to say that you dare not admit it to yourself.'

381–4. Commentators are surely wrong in making 'complexions' refer to a literal pallor. Polixenes means rather Leontes' 'lip of much contempt' (l. 373) and Camillo's uncommunicativeness— changes in *countenance* or *regard*, for which 'complexions' is metaphorical. The whole passage is difficult to understand, yet 'for I must . . . with 't' has never been commented upon. Perhaps we might paraphrase: 'The change in Leontes' face and yours shows how my own must appear changed too; for I must be concerned in this alteration, when I find myself altered at the same time.' This is not quite sense. If we could read 'and' instead of 'for', it would yield the satisfactory, if illogical meaning: 'and I must be concerned in the matter, when I find myself disturbed by it.' But there is insufficient reason for altering the text. The whole speech reflects Polixenes' confusion of mind, and in this play from time to time Shakespeare expresses the disturbed minds of his characters by giving them the muddled logic and false syntax that they would use in real life (cf. ll. 400–402 below, note).

384–7. The riddling answer has a long tradition in fiction and reality (going back to the Greek oracles, &c.), and the Elizabethans and Jacobeans especially loved 'dark meanings'. Camillo continues the imagery of disease.

388. The **basilisk** or cockatrice is one of the strange creatures in whose existence Shakespeare's contemporaries believed, largely

through the influence of Pliny's *Natural History*. It was said to be
so poisonous that even its look could kill. In origin it was even
more remarkable, being hatched by a toad or snake from a soft
egg laid by an aged cock. The name basilisk (Greek, βασιλεύς =
king) has special significance in the context. Polixenes has not
been a monarch whose looks killed (i.e. a tyrant) but one who
behaved graciously.

392–4. which ... gentle. It was a favourite and enlightened belief
of Shakespeare's time that a gentleman should be as much re-
spected for his learning as for his high descent.

400–2. 'I enjoin you by all the duties that an honourable man
recognizes—and not the least of them is this petition of mine. . . .'
As frequently in this play, where Shakespeare catches so much of
the human mind in disorder, the sense is clearer than the grammar.
The special 'duty' is not strictly Polixenes' petition ('suit'), but
the duty of yielding to it, of telling a man of any danger known to
be threatening him.

414–17. vice — *screw up*, as in a vice, but with a pun on *vice* =
wickedness. Leontes swears to Polixenes' guilt as if he had himself
urged him to it.

419. his ... Best : Judas Iscariot, who betrayed Our Lord. The
religious reference at this point shows that Hermione stands for a
very high degree of virtue. It also emphasizes the innocence of
Polixenes, leaving no doubt at all in the mind of the audience.
'Infected' (l. 418) and 'infection' (l. 423) carry on the disease
metaphor.

426. influences : the effects that stars were thought to have in
governing the temperaments of people and the course of events on
earth.

426–31. you may ... body. Leontes is as fixed in his belief as the
laws of nature, by which the moon governs the sea (cf. ll. 293–4,
above). His 'folly' is conceived as a building founded on his
faith and which will last as long as his body (i.e. as long as he lives).
There is terrible irony here : Leontes' 'faith' is belief in Hermione's
unfaithfulness.

442–6. I ... sworn : 'I have told you the truth, but if you want to
prove it, I dare not remain with you; nor will you be any safer
than one whom the king himself has condemned and immediately
sworn to have executed.'

445. [Many editors regularize the line by ending it with 'thereon' from the
line following. We retain the F reading and suggest that the *time* is

taken up by emphasis—which the sense requires—on the last two words:

> Than óne/condémn'd/by the kíng's/ówn/moúth.

The resultant extra foot in l. 446 does not jar, since the line is divided between two speakers.]

458–60. The grammar is again loose. Most editors take 'good expedition' as subject to 'comfort' as well as 'be', explaining that the queen will be comforted to know of his safe departure. But surely the subject of 'comfort' is left unexpressed: 'May speed be my friend and may (God) comfort the gracious queen.'

459–60. [nothing ... suspicion. Furness, followed by Moorman, takes this phrase to mean that Hermione 'is not yet the fatal object of his (Leontes') ill-founded suspicion'. This would make Polixenes' running away less like a desertion of the queen at a time when she needed him to help clear her name. But Camillo has already told him that Leontes believes him to have 'touch'd his queen forbiddenly' (ll. 416–17). Shakespeare, especially in this play, is free enough in his use of language for 'suspicion' to signify *what he suspects*, and, if this be allowed, all difficulty disappears from the *meaning*, though we are left with an unchivalrous and panicky Polixenes. Such, however, would seem to be Shakespeare's intention.]

ACT II, SCENE I

The pleasant opening, with Hermione and the ladies of the court at leisure with the young prince, is changed by the entry of Leontes. Having just heard of the escape of Polixenes and Camillo, he is enraged, accuses Hermione of adultery and, although she is soon to bear a child, has her imprisoned to prevent her having opportunity to murder him. The courtiers all protest against this action, making it quite plain that they believe in Hermione, not Leontes, and the latter informs them that he has sent for advice to the oracle at Delphos. Except for some speeches of Leontes, the verse is simpler and less intense than in Act I. Hermione is the central figure, maintaining her position not by outbursts of passion but by quiet self-control.

24. For this winter's tale within *The Winter's Tale* see Introduction, p. 15.

38–44. There may ... spider. The image is drawn from a common belief that spiders were poisonous, but only if the victim *saw* what he swallowed. Leontes has already said without imagery what he repeats in this form. He had been 'blest' with a correct opinion about his wife and Polixenes, but that blessing was a curse too.

How much better if he had known nothing about it; then his happiness would not have been destroyed.

49–51. The first thought is that Leontes is comparatively helpless now that his enemy has escaped; he is 'pinch'd' or narrowed in his operations (cf. 'cabin'd, cribb'd, confin'd': *Macbeth*, III. iv. 24). But dolls were made by 'pinching' cloth, and so the word gives rise to the further notion that he is a 'trick' or puppet to be moved at his enemies' will. This progression from image to image by word suggestion is common in Shakespeare.

61–63. **But . . . nayward.** Hermione has not yet fully realized how serious Leontes is; she remains relatively calm. 'Even if you inclined to deny my faithfulness, I know you would believe my word if I only told you that I am innocent.'

[**nayward**: the only instance of this word in O.E.D. Might it be an error of printer or copyist for *nayword* = *refusal*?]

68–77. Leontes still believes that all in the court must have noticed Hermione's supposed ill behaviour. Their praise of her appearance will be followed by a significant gesture or sound instead of praise of her 'honesty'. Such tokens of disapproval he describes as 'brands' made by 'calumny'. Then he pauses. He is 'out' in his speech, like an actor who has forgotten his lines. For calumny (backbiting) will attack—'sear' the flesh of, brand, attach a bad name to—even the virtuous. When the person spoken about is infamous, it is merciful to use a shrug or a broken exclamation rather than to speak out her fault.

77–80. Furness quotes Lady Martin, *On Some of Shakespeare's Female Characters* (Edinburgh, 1891), p. 351: 'In a kind of stupor Hermione listens to these vituperations, until Leontes brands her, to the wonder-stricken circle of his lords, as an "adultress". Upon this the indignant denial leaps to her lips. (But at the word "villain") she checks herself. The name "villain" must not be coupled with his,—her husband, and a king,—and with a voice softened, but resolute she adds, "You, my lord, do but mistake."'

81–86. **O thou . . . beggar.** In saying 'thou thing which', &c., Leontes tries to avoid using such a word as *whore* or *harlot*: 'You are a thing which I will not call anyone in your high position, lest those who are opposed to civilized order should follow my example and use the same terms for people of all classes and so make no polite differentiation between the highest and the lowest in the social scale.'

89. [federary: known only in this passage. Elsewhere Shakespeare uses *fedary* but in neither form is the word used by any other writer. It may be a variant of *feudary = feudal tenant, retainer,* but used by Shakespeare in a sense derived from erroneous association with Latin *foedus* = treaty. The lengthening or shortening of words by adding or omitting a syllable was a recognized poetic liberty, derived ultimately from Aristotle's *Poetics*: see Puttenham: *The Arte of English Poesie,* Bk. III, ch. xi.]

95–97. How . . . me! Take 'that/You . . . me!' in apposition to 'this'. 'How sorry you will be about this, when you understand things better—that you have publicly used such terms of me.'

99–102. No . . . top. In the Ptolemaic system the earth was believed to be the centre of the universe. The association of 'centre' and 'school-boy's top' is a witty bringing together of remote terms, and the whole reference continues Leontes' large, cosmic imagery for his assurance, begun in Act I, Scene ii (e.g. ll. 293–4).

104–14. There's . . . perform'd! Hermione puts down the whole matter to the influence of the stars, for in her great charity she will not blame her husband. She will use the virtue of patience until the 'aspect' of the stars, their relation to one another and to the earth, is more propitious. Her appeal for charitable judgement is dignified, dismissing tears as 'vain' and stressing the fact that her grief is 'honourable'. The repeated imagery of wet and dry, water and fire, emphasizes her spiritual power, since she repudiates the element of water, associating herself with its opposite, fire, which was believed to lie highest in the universe and nearest heaven. 'Judge me with your minds directed by charity' is her characteristic request.

114. Shall . . . heard? Hermione has spoken unhurriedly and the court have listened to her instead of obeying Leontes. In spite of his interruption she goes on quietly making arrangements for her attendance in prison, where it now seems her child must be born.

120–1. this . . . grace. Some editors follow Dr. Johnson in taking 'action' in the legal sense of 'indictment, charge or accusation'. Others take it as meaning merely 'what I am going to do'; but Wilson suggests that it is a military metaphor: Hermione is going on a campaign for her honour (taking 'grace' as *honour, reputation*). This last is probably the best interpretation, but there is surely also a strong theological implication in 'grace' (cf. I. ii. 105, note). Moreover, the sufferings of the saints are traditionally spoken of in military terms—the metaphor of the Christian as soldier, derived from St. Paul—so that the whole phrase carries

two layers of meaning, the deeper one interpreting the behaviour
of Hermione in terms of Christian saintliness.

133–4. I'll keep . . . her. If Hermione is unchaste, says Antigonus,
all other women, including his own wife, must be unchaste also.
They must, in fact, be mere animals. So much is clear from the
speech taken as a whole. Probably 'I'll keep my stables', &c.
means 'I'll keep my horses and my wife in the same building'—
since she will be no better than they. The animal reference is then
continued, with a change from horses to dogs, in the next phrase:
'I'll go in couples with her', meaning 'I'll go everywhere with her,
like dogs that are leashed together.'

142. land-damn has defied two centuries of comment. Its meaning
is unknown but it must be an energetic expression.

151–3. but I . . . feel. Presumably Leontes tweaks Antigonus' nose
or pulls his beard at the words 'doing thus'—probably the former
as he refers in the previous line to 'a dead man's nose'. Leontes
sees and feels 'this business', i.e. is sensitive to what he believes
has happened between Hermione and Polixenes, as Antigonus
literally feels and sees the fingers at his nose (or beard). 'The
instruments that feel' are Leontes' fingers. The subject of 'see'
in l. 152 is 'you' understood, not 'I'. 'Feel' in l. 151 is emotion;
in l. 152 sensation on the part of the sufferer; in l. 153 sensation
on the part of the aggressor.

164. [which : used as in Dickensian and later Cockney ('which I wouldn't
go if I was you'). It has no grammatical place in the sentence but merely
indicates a general connexion with what has gone before.]

176–8. That lack'd . . . deed : a parenthesis. **all other . . . deed.**
All other known circumstances added up to 'the deed' of adultery,
indicated that it had taken place—only 'sight', i.e. a direct witness,
was lacking to make the case complete (see ll. 176–7).

181–6. I have . . . spur me. In locating the oracle of Apollo on an
island called Delphos (it is called an island later: see III. i. 2)
Shakespeare is following Greene. The famous oracle was at
Delphi on the mainland of Greece, but Apollo was born at *Delos*
and had a shrine there. In *Pandosto* it is Bellaria (corresponding
to Hermione) who appeals to the oracle, but Shakespeare makes
Leontes show this act of faith, and publicly declare that he will
accept the oracle's guidance, so that his repudiation of the oracle
later will have the full force of a defiance of the gods.

190. to th' minds of others. Though acting with outward piety and in real faith, Leontes lacks humility: he is sure beforehand that the oracle will confirm his own opinion of Hermione.

197. **raise us all**: usually explained as 'rouse us all'. Leontes believes that Hermione is not only an adulteress but that with Polixenes and Camillo she is plotting against his life and the state. This would certainly 'rouse' the nation. But Leontes is complacent about his 'smartness' in detecting the supposed adultery and plot, and seems pleased at the prospect of a public speech, so that there may be the added sense of *raise = elevate, dignify*, which would give more point to the acid comment of Antigonus. King James I was proud of his own detective work and professed to have discovered the Gunpowder Treason himself just in the nick of time. Shakespeare would certainly not intend any sneer at his royal patron, before whom this play was performed, but the example of a king who took pride in secret service activities might well have suggested a Leontes who hoped to be raised in his people's esteem by a similar display of cleverness.

197. *s.d.* Antigonus' comment is perhaps addressed more to the audience than to his fellow lords.

ACT II, SCENE II

Paulina visits the prison and triumphantly carries off Hermione's newly-born baby, with which she is determined to face Leontes. Her forthrightness is akin to that of Antigonus but without his crudity of metaphor.

2–4. **Good lady . . . prison?** Addressed to the absent Hermione.

6. [**who.** The use of nominative for accusative and vice versa is frequent with the relative pronoun in Shakespeare.]

8. Leontes had particularly (expressly) forbidden the high-spirited and dangerous Paulina to be admitted to the queen.

19–20. This is complicated, the wit depending on a play of metaphorical and literal meanings in 'stain' and 'colouring'. 'There is more fuss here to make what is no stain into a stain (i.e. to make the innocent appear guilty) than the dyer makes'—in dyeing ('colouring') a garment. *To colour* also means *to make plausible* and *to palliate, excuse*: thus 'as passes colouring' means, in addition to the literal sense given above, 'as passes all plausibility' (Leontes' 'ado' lacks the colour of truth) and 'as passes all excuse' (it is beyond excusing).

33. **blister.** Falsehood was said to blister the tongue; cf. *Pandosto*: 'report hath a blister on her tongue', i.e. is often false. The passage occurs in the account of Bellaria's thoughts in prison. Presumably Shakespeare had remembered it, consciously or unconsciously, since he here uses the figure in *his* prison scene.

34–35. Wilson explains: 'Heralds were loud-voiced persons dressed in red and often bore candid, or insulting, messages; their "trumpet" was a man who preceded them.'

43. **[is.** The singular verb is common in Shakespeare with a composite subject: 'attraction' takes place between the verb and that singular noun, forming part of the subject, which lies nearest to it.]

55. **come something nearer :** in order 'to visit the next room' (l. 47).

61. **enfranchis'd :** given the rights of a free man (after slavery or serfdom); also, freed from prison. There is a play on both meanings: the child (i) attains personality, and (ii) is no longer 'prisoner to the womb'.

ACT II, Scene III

Leontes, in a state of irritation from worry and sleeplessness, is confronted by Paulina carrying the infant princess. Paulina rebukes him sharply; with her boldness of speech she symbolizes Conscience. Driven almost mad by her persistence in protesting Hermione's innocence, and faced with an unsympathetic court, Leontes condemns the child to be abandoned in a desert place. The opening of the scene is highly serious but the tone changes to what is almost music-hall farce, with the slanging match between Leontes and Paulina and jokes about hen-pecked husbands, then modulates to a quiet but tense conclusion.

3. **The cause** of his insomnia—Hermione. She is, he goes on to say, only part of the cause, but she is the only part that he can touch, Polixenes being too far away (ll. 4–6) and too powerful (ll. 19–21). The association of insomnia which sin is usual: it is a recurrent theme in *Macbeth*.

8. **Given . . . fire.** Death by burning was the punishment for women found guilty of high treason or petty treason. (Petty treason is the murder or conniving at the murder of husband or master.) Leontes thinks Hermione guilty of both.

20. **[Recoil :** attracted into the plural by proximity to 'revenges'.]

38. Honest as either. 'Paulina here refers to herself. She is as honest in intention as either healing or truth.' (Furness.)

38–39. to purge . . . sleep. Paulina carries on the disease metaphor of previous scenes: she will drive out the jealous 'humour' that keeps Leontes from sleeping. Her plain speech and her medicinal purpose support her function as symbol of Leontes' conscience.

44. I knew she would : the first note of comedy. Leontes has clearly been scared of Paulina all along and, while forbidding her the court, has been gloomily conscious that she would disobey him. Allegorically this applies to the way in which conscience breaks through the mental barriers we erect to keep out the thought of our sin. Shakespeare makes a *serious* point comically, as elsewhere in this play, especially in Act III, Scene iii.

49. Commit . . . honour. There is a double play of wit : (*a*) 'commit me' to prison for 'committing honour' (doing an honourable deed)—a pun ; (*b*) we should expect 'committing' to be followed by the name of a crime or sin but Paulina substitutes a virtue, 'honour'. By this witty use of the unexpected it is implied that, to Leontes, 'honour' is a crime.

51–52. Antigonus uses 'horsy' language as in II. i. 133, though it has here no unpleasant significance.

53–55. [professes, dares : third person for first; perhaps misprints, perhaps Shakespeare's irregular grammar. 'Professes' is less likely than 'dares', because nearer to 'I'.]

53–57. 'I *am* your loyal servant, &c., but I dare to appear less so, when it comes to countenancing your evils, than those who seem to be most attached to you (i.e. hers is a deeper loyalty than theirs, for she shows him his faults while they pander to them).' *Comforting* is used in the legal sense of *aiding and abetting*.

60. combat : the trial by single combat, in which a champion fought to vindicate a lady's honour.

71. To tell a king to his face that he is mad would be, especially in Shakespeare's time, a remarkable feat of plain speaking which would require great courage.

74–75. unroosted . . . Partlet. From the reference to falconry in 'woman-tir'd', Shakespeare moves to the poultry-yard and the old tale of Reynard the Fox, well known in Chaucer's version, *The Nonne Preestes Tale*, where the hen's name is Pertelote (=Partlet).

85–86. slander . . . sword's. The phrase has lingered in Shakespeare's mind from the play which he almost certainly wrote immediately before this: cf. *Cymbeline*, III, iv. 35: 'slander / Whose edge is sharper than the sword'.

88. He cannot be compelled because he is the king.

91–92. **beat . . . bait(s)** were pronounced almost alike: a pun.

96. **old proverb.** It can be found in Overbury's character of a sergeant: 'The devill cals him his *white sonne*; he is so like him, that hee is the worse for it, and hee takes after his father.'

98–99. **print, matter** (i.e. subject-matter), **copy,** are terms used by printers.

106–7. **lest . . . husband's.** To suspect this she would have to have been unfaithful to her husband, which is certainly not what Paulina means. In her angry sarcasm she has confused the sexes. The eighteenth-century editor Malone thought it was *Shakespeare* who had 'forgotten the difference of sexes'. In that century it was hard to believe that serious and comic strands should be so closely interwoven. The passage is, of course, a joke on Shakespeare's part, though not on Paulina's.

109–11. **Hang . . . subject:** the perennial joke. The tone is now so completely of the music-hall that normal courtly politeness is forgotten.

114–15. Leontes is the heretic, not Paulina, for it is he who holds wrong views about Hermione. Burning by the secular authority was the most extreme punishment of religious heresy. The witty parallel between faith in God and faith in a lover or spouse is usual in this period.

115. **tyrant.** The sixteenth and early seventeenth centuries produced many books on the 'conduct of princes': their common teaching is that the ruler who allows his passions to govern his reason (and who is therefore in a state of internal rebellion—see I. ii. 355–61, note) must necessarily become a tyrant, and that his people will suffer under him. 'Tyrant' was the worst name that could be applied to a king, and even Paulina is reluctant to use it without qualification.

118. **weak-hing'd fancy.** His mind is in a precarious state, since his 'fancy'—we should call it 'imagination'—is like a creaky door whose hinges are insecurely fixed.

121–3. **Were . . . one.** The much-harassed Leontes makes a good point here. We are bound to believe that he *is* a tyrant, (*a*) because of his unjust actions and (*b*) because the oracle so declares him (III. ii. 132), and the whole plot hinges on the truth of its pronouncements. But he is much too civilized and sensitive to be a really effective tyrant, and his cruelty proceeds more from a desire to settle his own tortured mind than from a thirst for power. His *actions* are sufficiently tyrannical to remind us at times of Richard III, but, whereas Richard acted in deliberate defiance of justice, Leontes, in his jealous dream, constantly believes that he has justice on his side. This, together with his earnest desire not to be accounted tyrannous (shown here and in III. ii. 4–5), indicates that he is not hardened beyond the possibility of repentance.

126. **What needs . . . hands?** They are pushing her from the room. [**needs** is an impersonal use. Later folios unnecessarily alter to 'need'.]

143–52. The courtiers, through First Lord, speak out too freely for this to be the court of an habitual tyrant.

159. **Lady Margery.** Wilson explains that *margery-prater* was the cant term (used among thieves and beggars) for a hen, so that 'Lady Margery' is the same as 'dame Partlet'.

161. **this beard** must be Antigonus'. Leontes is still young, but Antigonus has only a little blood left (l. 165) and is called 'old' by the Shepherd (III. iii. 104), who had not seen him—it is Shakespeare's knowledge of his age that has allowed the word to slip out at that point. The king probably pulls Antigonus' beard as he had either his nose or his beard on a previous occasion (II. i. 152). It is unnecessary, with some editors, to alter 'this' to 'thy'.

167. **Swear . . . sword.** 'It was anciently the custom to swear by the cross on the handle of a sword, or by the sacred name of Jesus, which was sometimes engraven on the top of the blade or on the pommel of the sword' (Halliwell Phillips). This Christian custom is introduced at an important point in the play : the Cross figures in the disposal of Perdita as it does in her finding (see III. iii. 109, note).

177. [**it own.** 'It' is the old possessive case. Both 'it' and 'its' are found in Shakespeare. Variation between the forms may be due to Shakespeare himself or to either the copyist or the printer.]

179. **in justice :** Leontes' perversion of a cardinal virtue. According to him the bastard, being through its father foreign, deserves banishment.

181. **strangely** has a possible further meaning, *as a foreigner* (to Sicilia), since Leontes thought it the child of Polixenes.

185–8. The ravens fed Elijah (1 Kings xvii. 6) ; Romulus and Remus,

legendary founders of Rome, were suckled by a wolf. There are many
stories similar to the latter in legendary history.

188–91. **Sir . . . loss !** (*To Leontes*) 'I trust you will be more prosperous than this cruel deed would allow you to deserve. (*To the
baby*) And may (God's) blessing be on your side, opposed to this
cruel deed, poor thing, condemned to be abandoned.'

ACT III, Scene I

This scene, though short, is the turning-point of the play. We have
so far followed the uninterrupted course of an evil passion. We now
note the beginning of a divine action which will encounter and conquer it. A pagan religious service is described in the language of
Christian devotion, so as to express the power and mystery and bene-
ficence of God, who providentially orders the lives of men and brings
good out of evil. The messengers are shown on their journey to the
court, not yet knowing the contents of the oracle.

1–3. Shakespeare uses images of natural goodness and fertility to
express the supernatural goodness of the Creator, just as he uses
images of decay and barrenness to express the *uncreating* or
destructive power of evil. For this, and for the language of this
scene generally, cf. the speeches of Duncan and Banquo before
Macbeth's castle (*Macbeth*, I. vi), where the purpose is to express
the holiness of the king—and, more generally, to remind us of the
power of God, before embarking on the concentrated evil of the
scenes within the castle.

3–8. Cleomenes has described the effects of divine goodness in the
natural order (ll. 1–3); now Dion gives a condensed description of
the *supernatural* quality of religious worship. The passage is
crowded with words which evoke the atmosphere of devotion
through their constant use in relation to the worship of the
Church.

8–11. The association of the oracular voice with thunder recalls the
giving of the Law on Mt. Sinai, especially as Jove, the Thunder-
bearer, stands for God in this period, when classical myth was being
put to Christian uses.

11. **That . . . nothing.** In mystical devotion the worshipper often

experiences a feeling described as the annihilation of the self, although, of course, the self does not really cease to exist.

21. **fresh horses!** They are at an inland stage in their journey and require a change of post horses. They cannot be, as some editors head this scene, at *A Sea-port in Sicilia*, or the cry would be for 'horses', not 'fresh horses'.

Act III, Scene II

Throughout her trial Hermione maintains the dignity and forbearance of a saint. Her appeal to the oracle brings the religious theme directly into the personal conflict, since she and Leontes have both recognized the same divine arbiter. When, however, the oracular message is read, Leontes blasphemously refuses to give it credit. He is immediately punished with the death of Mamillius and as immediately repents. The supposed death of Hermione, which follows, will be maintained so that the king may live heirless, in penitent obedience to the oracle, until Perdita is found again.

4–5 **clear'd ... tyrannous** : referring to Paulina's accusation in the previous act; see II. iii. 121–3, note.

s.d. Silence. Many editors give this to the Officer, others to a 'Cryer' invented for the purpose. We revert to the F reading, which there is no adequate reason for altering. A hush of awe and expectancy spreads over the crowd and upon this Hermione enters.

21–53. In this and the following speeches of Hermione, she is making a public defence of her conduct, in a court of law. Shakespeare uses to the full the rhetorical devices which in his time were diligently taught in school and university. The actress playing Hermione should deliver these speeches with a more formal manner of diction and gesture than in her usual dialogue.

21–27. 'Since all I can say in my defence will be a denial of the charge, and since there is no one to give evidence for me except myself, it will not be any use to say "Not guilty": my innocence is already taken as guilt, and when I plead my innocence it will be taken in the same way.'

28. **as they do.** The three monosyllabic words occurring together call for emphasis. They powerfully assert Hermione's religious

faith and the theme upon which the whole play is built: that
human actions are known to God and overruled by Him. There is
a similar phrase at the same point in *Pandosto* but its implications
are not brought out by Greene, as they are by Shakespeare, in the
work as a whole.

29–31. Personifications somewhat soften what is in effect a counter-
accusation directed at Leontes: Hermione is identified with innocence and patience, Leontes with false accusation and tyranny.

32. [who. F has 'whom': cf. II. ii. 6, note.]

34–36. which ... spectators : i.e. which unhappiness is greater than
any stage play can imitate, though it is composed and performed
to impress an audience.

We have here one of the occasions when Shakespeare reminds
the audience that his play is only a play and causes them to have
play world and real world in mind at the same time. Hermione's
words (a) emphasize her grief (in the play world) and (b) apologize
to the audience for the inadequacy of the dramatic medium. The
actress should treat the real audience as part of the stage audience
and include them in a sweeping gesture at the word 'spectators'.
The audience itself is thus given a double status: (a) as real-world
audience, receiving the playwright's apology; (b) as stage audience,
caught up into the story.

40–41. Hermione's distaste for the vulgar publicity, which is not
the least of the cruelties Leontes has inflicted upon her refined
sensibility, comes out in these lines, especially in 'prate and talk'.
('Prate' (=*chatter idly*) contemptuously reduces the court pro-
ceedings to a sort of idle gossip.)

41–44. For life ... stand for. Now that she no longer has Leontes'
love, life is only grief to her: she therefore values her life as she
does grief—she would be glad to have done with it. But her
honour (or dishonour) is 'derived', or inherited, by her children
and it is on that account that she defends herself.

48–49. With what ... thus : noun clause after 'I appeal / To your
own conscience' (to declare) ... Paraphrase: 'in what way my
behaviour has stretched beyond the conventional that I should
have to appear in court.'

The argument is *a fortiori*: 'I have not even broken the conventions, let alone committed adultery.'

53–56. I ... first. Leontes means that those who are guilty of such
sins as adultery are not likely to hesitate about a mere lie in
denying their guilt.

[There is some confusion as a result of the succession of negative ideas. As the words stand, we should now require to substitute 'more' for 'less': '. . . lacked more impudence to deny . . . than to perform . . .' or, perhaps, 'lacked impudence to deny . . . any more than to perform . . .' Shakespeare writes as if 'wanted' had a positive sense (= *had*, *possessed*), with which 'less' would be correct. In his time the grammar of negatives was hesitating between the Chaucerian practice, by which one negative intensifies another, and the modern, by which they cancel one another. Or perhaps 'less' = *the lesser* and 'Than . . . first' follows from a confusion of this idea with the sense already suggested.]

58–60. More . . . acknowledge. 'I will not confess myself to be possessor of (i.e. accountable for) more than what is charged against me as a fault'—which is, as she goes on to say, her (really innocent) friendship with Polixenes.

70–72. Now . . . how. 'As for conspiracy, I do not know what it feels like to be a conspirator, though you are doing your best to make me feel like one.' (Conspiracy is being 'dished up' in the indictment for her to taste.)

80–83. Hermione, who sees the case clearly, says that her life is within range of (i.e. about to be forfeit to) Leontes' 'dreams' or delusions. Leontes, who takes good for evil, and dream for reality, retorts that what she calls *his dreams* are in fact *her actions*. 'You had . . . dream'd it' is bitterly ironical.

97. infectious reminds us of the sin-disease parallel used frequently in earlier scenes.

100. post. Public notices in Shakespeare's day were fixed on to posts.

104. i' th' open air. Fresh air was thought to be dangerous to invalids.

107–13. Therefore . . . law. 'Go on with the trial', Hermione says, but then she decides to add something more—not to plead for her life but for her honour. So she asks their attention and proceeds: 'Do not misunderstand me. It isn't life I ask for—I value it not at all. But as for my honour, which I wish to vindicate, if I shall be condemned on mere conjecture, with no proof but what is invented by your jealousy, it is cruelty not justice.' Shakespeare got the last phrase from *Pandosto*: 'therefore if she were condemned without any further proofe, it was rigour, and not Law.'

118. In *Pandosto* the Emperor of Russia is father-in-law of Egistus (= Polixenes). On the so-called anachronism here, see Introduction, p. 28. This speech of Hermione is not intended for the *stage* audience: Hermione would not voluntarily or involuntarily burst out with such an intimate revelation of her feelings. It is a purely conventional aside, intended to convey to the *real* audience what she is feeling but would not in fact speak aloud.

122. **pity, not revenge !** Hermione feels the need of pity but does not have any desire for the vengeance that her father might have been moved to take. Her attitude is again that of the Christian saint.

123. Cf. II. iii. 167 and note.

138–52. Leontes' blasphemy is immediately followed by divine punishment and he at once repents : he is not hardened in his sin.

161–3. **though ... done** : though I did threaten him with death not doing it (i.e. if he did not do it) and encourage him with reward (it) being done (i.e. after it should be done).

> [In this figure various parts of a compound sentence having the same grammatical functions are grouped together. It has been termed the 'respective construction'. In rhetoric it is treated as a species of *isocolon*, a figure concerned with rhythm, since it produces equality among different parts of the sentence (see Aristotle's *Rhetoric*, Bk. III, ch. 9—1410*a*).]

166. [The line is metrically short. The later folios read 'certain hazard', which is quite a Shakespearian use of oxymoron and may be correct : Camillo is certain to run the risk of every kind of uncertainty in his hasty flight. But perhaps Shakespeare wanted a short line here.]

169. **Through** : pronounced as a dissyllable, 'thorough', to which Malone and subsequent editors alter it.

171. **cut my lace** : i.e. the lace of her stays, to prevent fainting. Stage costume was 'modern' with minor modifications to suggest period or place. Cleopatra also asks for her lace to be cut (*Antony and Cleopatra*, I. iii. 71).

173. **tyrant.** Paulina has now overcome any previous reluctance she may have had (see II. iii. 115, note) to call a spade a spade : she baldly asserts that Leontes is a tyrant. In the long speech following—strongly sarcastic—she virtually speaks as his own conscience. Although she has this symbolic function she is at the same time kept sufficiently human. No doubt she is meant, as a human character, to believe at this point that the queen is really dead, so that her grief is the psychological occasion of her outburst.

174. The line is metrically short but there is no need to suspect any omission : the list of tortures demands slow and emphatic enunciation and takes up the time of a full line.

177. **most worst.** The double superlative is doubly emphatic.

187. **kill a king.** How did Paulina know ? She was not present for Leontes' confession at ll. 157–9 above. Had Camillo told her

before he left ? Such questions arise only in the study, not in the theatre. Shakespeare was surely thinking of Leontes, not Paulina, as he wrote this speech, which is a summary of Leontes' sins and their consequences. He would most likely endow Paulina with knowledge of Leontes' projected murder without asking how in reality she could have acquired it.

191. **water . . . fire :** tears in hell-fire, implying pity in the least likely place, (*a*) because devils have no pity and (*b*) because water is the element opposed to fire (cf. ii. i. 104–14, note).

192. **[is't.** The 'it' is redundant, or else the construction alters as the sentence proceeds—beginning as if it were to be 'nor is it . . . that you killed . . .']

205–12. **But . . . wert.** For a brief time Paulina counsels despair. Her attitude is that of the Old Testament : Leontes has sinned too deeply for recovery. When the conscience speaks thus in a would-be penitent it must be ignored. Paulina, and by implication Leontes, will soon recover from this unhealthy state. For it is not *acts* of penance that in themselves atone for sin : God's grace produces penitence, and out of this the acts flow which God in His mercy accepts as if they were sufficient, though it is through his faith in Christ that the penitent is in fact saved.

   The vividly pictorial expression of penance in lines 208–12 is extremely powerful. We have (i) the multitude of people involved, (ii) the length of time, (iii) a series of deprivations : of clothing, of food, of fertility ('barren mountain'), of sun, of fair weather. Leontes and Hermione are to pass through a period of self-denial which might be pictured thus. The opposite images (of fertility, warmth, &c.) are soon to be associated with Perdita and the new life that is preparing for Leontes and his queen.

217–18. These words apply as much to Leontes as to Paulina and continue the theme of repentance. Paulina's *volte-face* suggests the quick recovery of a fundamentally healthy conscience after a moment of despair.

220–1. **What's gone . . . grief :** cf. *Richard II*, ii. iii. 171, 'Things past redress are now with me past care', and *Macbeth*, iii. ii. 11, 'Things without all remedy / Should be without regard.' This is proverbial. As used by Paulina, it is also sound doctrine, for whereas *remorse* looks to the past, true *penitence* is concerned with the good that can be done in the future.

221–4. **do not . . . forget :** 'do not give yourself up to affliction because I have urged you to (i.e. at lines 207–8 especially, when she told him to yield to despair); rather than that, punish me for recalling to you what you should forget (the list of his sins).'

238. **recreation** has normally in Shakespeare the sense of *diversion*, *pastime*, and this sense is borne out by 'exercise', in l. 239. But there is a further sense fundamental for a full understanding of the play: *recreation* = *re-creation*, *making anew*, *restoration*, which can apply to physical, but is here used of Leontes' spiritual, health. In keeping with this sense, 'exercise' has its common technical meaning of *spiritual exercise, devotion, prayer*. It is interesting to note that the more obvious meaning of both words in their context is metaphorical, taken from sport, and their deeper meaning literal. It is by means of wit in the form of a double pun that the leading idea of the play is revealed at the close of this important scene.

ACT III, Scene III

Act III, Scene i was the true turning point of the play, since it expressed the omnipotence of divine Providence and turned our contemplation from the destructive activity of sinful man to the constructive activity of God. In Scene ii we saw God's grace at work in the penitence of Leontes. The transition from Scene ii to Scene iii expresses the same movement from negative to positive after its process has begun in Leontes' soul. It is conceived as a movement from one 'world' to another. As Leontes turns from sin to repentance, we move from the stifling, suspicious atmosphere generated by Leontes at the Sicilian court to the pure air of Bohemia and the theme of 'life renewed'. The scene is remarkable for its wealth of symbolic reference, for the way in which it turns tragedy into comedy, and for the alternation and intermingling of comic and serious, reminding us how much depends on 'point of view'.

1–2. [Shakespeare followed Greene in giving Bohemia a sea-coast. The bargee-poet Taylor visited Prague in 1620 and, when he came back, wrote an account of his travels, in which he jibes at the ignorance of London aldermen by making one of them—a fictitious Sir Gregory Gandergoose—ask him about the arrival of 'the last fleet of ships' in Bohemia. In the *Autobiography* of Lord Herbert of Cherbury it is said that a French statesman, de Luynes, whom the author first met in 1619, had once asked whether Bohemia 'lay upon the sea'. It would appear that most people knew well enough that it did not, and that there was a joke of the 'Swiss navy' type current about 1620 both in England and abroad, of which the subject was Bohemia's well-known non-existent coastline. Perhaps it originated from *Pandosto*, which was widely known and had been translated into French in 1615. It could scarcely have arisen from the unpublished *Winter's Tale*. It is, however, unlikely that a joke so widespread would arise from a piece of bad geography in a novel at a time when such mistakes were not uncommon. If it were an old joke of unknown origin, then Shakespeare, and even Greene, might have been aware of it, and used the sea-coast of Bohemia to imply that the Bohemia of this 'old tale' is to be found not on the contemporary map of Europe but in the realms of the imagination, and that the story is not to be taken too literally (cf. Introduction, pp. 12 ff.). Although Shakespeare changes around the countries of Bohemia and Sicilia he (very carefully ?) preserves this old 'error'. The unfanciful Ben Jonson in a conversation with William Drummond of Hawthornden in 1619 criticized his fellow dramatist for having 'in a play, brought in a number of men saying they had suffered ship-wrack in Bohemia, wher ther is no sea neer by some 100 miles'.]

15–16. The verse of this speech at times seems to burlesque an outmoded type of melodramatic 'vision' poetry—such as *The Mirror for Magistrates*, with its series of informative ghosts—and this prevents the audience from taking it too seriously and leaves them emotionally free to speculate about the nature of the vision. (Many editions of *The Mirror*, with varying contents, appeared between 1554 and 1587, and a further enlarged edition in 1610.)

[The question of apparitions was much debated in Shakespeare's time. The extreme Protestant view (as of the Puritans) was that either the appearance of the dead was assumed by angel or devil or that it was illusory. The traditional Catholic belief (to which High Anglicans would incline) was that for some purposes, good and ill, the dead were themselves permitted to return. Antigonus, it seems, had previously taken the Protestant line but was converted by the vision he goes on to describe. The matter is complicated for the audience by the fact that *in this instance* he was wrong: Hermione was not dead. Was the vision angelic (to assure the proper disposal of Perdita) or diabolic (attempting to induce despair in Antigonus and the destruction of Perdita), or was it meant to be an appearance of Hermione's separated soul during the period of her unconsciousness after the trial ? The audience does not yet know that Hermione is alive: they would be divided into the well-known Protestant and Catholic camps, since the evidence appeared compatible with either theory. Later, at the end of the play, if their minds recurred to the vision, both parties would be forced to a reconsideration and possible revision.]

18–36. To me . . . air. This description of the vision presents a surprising mixture of stylized burlesque and serious significance. Shakespeare in his last period frequently conveyed his serious matter by means of *wit*, and even in the course of comic dialogue and 'business'. The positions of the head (formalized movement), 'vessel . . . sorrow', the three bows, the gasp, the eyes as 'two spouts', the 'fury spent', the 'shrieks' with which 'She melted into air', are all, in matter and expression, old-fashioned, the effect being to burlesque an earlier style. The white robes 'like very sanctity' more seriously suggest the 'gracious' Hermione.

20–21. a vessel . . . becoming makes free with grammar and employs

wit. 'Vessel' means *creature*, especially thought of as made by
the Creator (cf. the Biblical 'vessels of wrath', &c.). But here, to
express the vision's grief, 'vessel' is given in addition its primary
meaning of jar, crock, container, used metaphorically: 'vessel of
sorrow' is at the same time *sorrowful creature* and *jar of tears*
'So fill'd' goes with the second meaning. 'So becoming' does not
fit with either meaning in strict grammar; expand: 'I never saw a
vessel of like sorrow, so filled and to which the being filled was so
becoming.'

42–43. this . . . Polixenes. Not only is Antigonus wrong about the
nature of the vision (see note on ll. 15–16, above) but he is also
viciously wrong about its *meaning*. At last he comes to believe—
after all his vigorous protestations to the contrary—that Hermione
has been an adultress. Visions can mislead or they can be wrongly
interpreted. In Shakespeare's time the Puritans claimed the
freedom of the individual to act on what he regarded as divine
inspiration, whereas Hooker and the High Church divines advocated a 'testing of the spirits' by their consonancy with Church
teaching and by reason. When he thinks himself most Catholic
(which is probably the secondary significance of 'superstitiously'
in l. 39), Antigonus is, in fact, most Protestant: he hastily attaches
to his vision an interpretation which his moral sense should have
repudiated; the doubtful—for it may be a diabolic—vision weighs
more with him than what he knows of Hermione's purity. It is
significant that he is converted to the unbelief now no longer shared
even by Leontes, immediately before being eaten by the bear.

50. Weep I cannot. He cannot obey the injunction of the vision
(l. 31).

55–56. A savage . . . chase. 'Clamour', according to Dr. Johnson,
refers to the noise of hunters and dogs, pursuing the bear, which
then appears. Antigonus' 'This is the chase' refers, he thinks, to
the *animal pursued*. We hear in the Shepherd's first speech that
there are hunters about, and this would help to confirm Johnson's
reading. But there need not be any connexion between the hunters
who scared the Shepherd's flock and the appearance of the bear:
perhaps the clamour is made by the bear alone, or the bear and the
rising storm, and 'This is the chase' may mean 'I'll have to run
for it'.

s.d. Exit . . . bear. This *s.d.* is in F. Wilson produces evidence of the
use of a real bear, a polar bear, in dramatic performances about
1610–11, and in one instance by Shakespeare's company: in the
play *Mucedorus* a special scene was inserted, in which a clown,

pursued by a bear, falls over it on the stage. There is little doubt that the same performing bear would be used to pursue Antigonus and that the incident would be designed as farce.

58. **ten.** Some editors have altered this to 'thirteen' or 'sixteen', but it is surely part of the joke that the old Shepherd makes these juvenile delinquencies start so early. His is a comically extreme expression of the attitude of age to youth.

62. **Hark you now !** Spoken directly to the audience, as all this speech is, and probably to draw their attention to what he is going to say rather than to 'hunting noises off'.

66–67. **browsing of ivy.** Shakespeare is following *Pandosto* closely here: 'browsing on the sea Ivy, whereon they greatly doe feede.'

67. **[what... here?** Many editors insert *s.d.* '*Taking up the Child*', but this he does not do until later.]

68–69. 'Barne' is a dialect form, still found in Cumberland; it is akin to the Scottish 'bairn'. In Shakespeare's time its use was not restricted to the north. 'Child' was used in west country dialect for *baby girl*. Wilson observes that 'west country dialect was the conventional speech of yokels on the Elizabethan stage. The expression ('A boy or a child') probably sounded as ridiculous to Londoners then as it does now.'

74–75. **yet . . . come.** Changing his mind and leaving the baby on the ground.

78–79. **to talk . . . rotten.** Shakespeare's 'clowns' (i.e. rustics and members of the populace, not the professional jesters who 'corrupt words' and chop logic deliberately) are frequently comic through their unintentional breaches of logical and rhetorical propriety. The Shepherd here produces a good specimen of an 'Irish bull'.

81–99. In Shakespeare a storm at sea usually symbolizes human passion, since in the analogy of microcosm (man) and macrocosm (the physical universe) *blood* corresponds to *sea*, and blood is the physical basis of the passions. The ship and its crew thus perish in the storm as we move from the tragic episodes in Sicilia to the new life of Bohemia: tragedy takes its victims and itself dies before our eyes. Antigonus, the last to disbelieve in Hermione's innocence, perishes at the same time, to the audience's laughter. These deaths are made comic because good is to come out of ill and, this being the law of the universe, death is not a final or irremediable evil.

[The Clown labours to be expressive but makes what a contemporary audience would recognize as a series of elementary errors in rhetoric. To describe the storm properly he should use figures which 'augment' it: i.e. by comparison with other great and terrifying things, by hyperbole and so forth, he should make his audience feel its power, as Lear does on the heath (see *King Lear*, III. ii. 1). Instead he persistently uses figures of diminution: (*a*) the bodkin; (*b*) 'boring the moon', as with an auger; (*c*) the cork in the hogshead; (*d*) the flap-dragon—all refer to small and familiar domestic objects. This is (i) an amusing exercise in bad rhetoric, for which the audience will laugh at the Clown, but (ii) it also shows us the storm from the eternal point of view, as a mere 'storm in a teacup', reminding us that all is under divine guidance and control (as the storm in *The Tempest* is controlled by Prospero, who in part symbolizes divine Providence).

There is more bad rhetoric in the way the Clown uneasily moves between one part of his tale and another, from the ship to Antigonus and back again, with his comments on the process: 'but that's not to the point'; 'And then for the land-service'; 'But to make an end of the ship'. Observe also (*a*) 'land-service', which could only be jocular and so is out of place; (*b*) balance of phraseology with comic effect (not intended by the Clown) owing to the forcing of the later phrase into conformity with the earlier; so that the 'poor gentleman' is said to 'roar' (a term more appropriate to a clown receiving a beating) and the bear to 'mock' him.]

96. **A flap-dragon** was a small object, usually a raisin, floating in a glass of lighted spirits, the game being to extinguish it in the mouth and swallow it. Cf. the Christmas game of *snap-dragon*.

104–5. **old man :** see II. iii. 161, note.

107. **your charity . . . footing.** i.e. your assistance would have been useless. The phrase is taken from the *footing* or proper legal foundation of an institution (such as a charitable foundation), and there is the obvious pun on the lack of footing in the sea. There is no need to think that the Clown wished his father had been drowned, or that he, as an heir, disapproved of charitable institutions. In such comic dialogue as this there are no psychological implications: ill wishing between comedians is an ancient and perennial source of fun.

109–10. **Now bless . . . born.** The tone changes suddenly to extreme seriousness. The actors can convey this by a solemn pause while the Clown looks at the infant as if awe-stricken and then makes the sign of the Cross. For a moment there is almost a tableau, which would surely suggest a Nativity scene, especially to an audience that remembered the Miracle plays. This symbolic moment is interpreted by the dialogue: 'things dying . . . things new born'. By the Cross, and, in anticipation, by the Infant Christ, things dying ('the old man') became 'new born'. Baptism is new birth, according to the Scriptures, and baptism is indirectly referred to below: 'a bearing-cloth for a squire's child!' Now, in this scene,

Leontes' 'old man' and the world of sin are drowned and consumed, that his new life, symbolized in Perdita, may grow. There is a triple reference: (a) on the story level, to the renewed fortunes of Leontes; (b) to spiritual regeneration by baptism into the Church; (c) to the historical events of the Incarnation and Crucifixion, by which new life was won for the world.

[The name Antigonus occurs in Plutarch but also in Josephus' *Antiquities of the Jews* (which would be familiar in Shakespeare's day), where it is borne by a highly significant figure—the last truly Jewish king of Judaea, who was executed by the Romans and succeeded by the non-Jewish Herod, in whose reign Our Lord was born. This would seem to have been common knowledge in the seventeenth century, for it is used with no flourish at all in an Italian work on sermon conceits (by Emanuele Tesauro and incorporated into his *Il Cannocchiale Aristotelico*) as one of the proofs that Our Lord came when human malice had reached its extremity. This transition scene is thus surely intended to represent the movement from Old Testament to New, as well as, correspondingly, from the spiritual death of sin to the new life of grace, as we move from tragedy to comedy.]

111. **squire's :** the highest rank he is accustomed to.

114. **changeling.** It was thought that the fairies occasionally stole away human babies and left their own in exchange. Here is meant a human child stolen by the fairies—to the Shepherd the most reasonable way of accounting for the presence of a child in such a place.

116. [**made.** F reads 'mad' but the phrase 'made for ever' occurs in the corresponding place in *Pandosto*. 'Made' and 'mad' were pronounced similarly in Shakespeare's time and a pun may be intended.]

119. **close.** 'To divulge the possession of fairies' gifts was supposed to entail misfortune' (Staunton).

126. **a good deed** may refer to the apocryphal book of *Tobit*; see especially xii. 13: 'And when thou didst not delay to rise up, and leave thy dinner, that thou mightest go and cover the dead, thy good deed was not hid from me: but I was with thee.'

ACT IV, SCENE I

'Time' enters as a 'chorus' to bridge the sixteen years gap needed for the penitence of Leontes and the growth of Perdita. This device has been criticized as clumsy, but we should remember that Shakespeare showed in *The Tempest* that he could keep the 'unity of time' (i.e. restrict the action to one day) when he wanted to; also, that, when he did so, he gave an air of parody to the long dialogue summing up the previous history of his chief characters, and that in *The Winter's Tale* his cheerful defiance of the neo-classical 'laws' is equally deliberate. 'Time' is an amused gesture of disregard for those who wanted to put the drama into a critical strait jacket.

Some commentators maintain that Shakespeare did not write this speech, which they consider to be very different from and inferior to the rest of the play. But it would have been wrong to write a chorus, an external commentary, in precisely the same style as the rest of the dialogue. The rhythm is 'flatter', less dramatic, but appropriate for the familiarity of 'direct address' to the audience, and the rhyme distinguishes Time's speech from that of the story characters. In spite of assertions to the contrary, there is nothing wrong with the rhymes (a half-rhyme can be a pleasant variation), the obscurity is packed with meaning, and some lines are very fine.

This scene bridges the time-lapse, but, as we have already implied, it is not the turning-point of the play. In addition, however, to its purely technical function of indicating the passage of time, it serves to bring to the forefront of our minds two interlocking themes which the play presents : first, the relation of time and eternity, men's deeds and God's providence ; secondly, the various 'planes of reality' (see Introduction, p. 25). Time tells us that even 'this present'—the *now* of the audience—will itself become an old tale : our own lives are given the same degree of reality or unreality as the tale of Leontes, and only Time is timeless.

1–2. 'I who bring pleasure to some and trial (*or* testing) to all men, who am joy to good men and terror to bad, through whom mistakes are made and afterwards brought to light . . .'

both joy . . . bad. Cf. III. ii. 161–3, note.

[**makes and unfolds.** Strict grammar would require the first person, but Shakespeare, as elsewhere, employs a colloquial looseness.]

6. [**leave . . . untried.** Dr. Johnson thought that '"untried" is not, perhaps, the word he (the poet) would have chosen, but (that) which his rhyme required'. There is no need to take this view : 'untried' means either that the sixteen years growth is *unattempted* by the dramatist or *not tested, not sampled*, by the audience—or it may mean both.]

7. **wide gap.** Cf. *Antony and Cleopatra*, I. v. 5, 'this great gap of time / My Antony is away'—a passage which has never been denied to Shakespeare.

7–9. **since . . . custom.** This is a witty apology of the dramatist for his 'licence' in respect of time. He makes Time himself explain that he overthrows law and in the same hour may start a new custom and destroy an old one. Thus the dramatist in ignoring the critics' laws about time is only doing what Time himself does with laws and customs in general.

9–15. Let me . . . it. 'Let me pass' = *consider me to be*. Times
change but 'Time' is always the same. Indeed, Time considered
abstractly, without beginning or end, is not really Time but
Eternity. This meaning is borne out by the use of 'I am' (l. 10),
both because it is the Old Testament name for God (Exodus iii. 14)
and because its present tense stretches from before the 'ancient'st
order' (i.e. before order was first brought out of chaos at the creation) to the moment of speaking. 'Time' is *now* the present witness
to the past times that brought in the first order (regulating human
society) and that which is now maintained. In the same way,
Time *shall be* in future the surviving witness to the things which
are today 'fresh' or new, when they shall in turn, through the
power of time, become old and 'stale', as the tale of Leontes now
seems to this present age. Time considered apart from our day-
to-day experience is an eternal present, so what harm is there in
leaping a gap of sixteen years?—or sixteen and more centuries
between Leontes and James I? Shakespeare's wit at the same time
apologizes for his dramatic practice and presents a philosophy of
literature and history which denies the view so popular in the
twentieth century, that things are no longer important when they
are past. Past, present, and future are all on the same level before
the judgement of eternity.

19. [imagine me : 'me' is ethic dative—'imagine for my sake . . '.]

22. I mention'd. Editors have been puzzled because Time, the
Chorus has *not* mentioned the king's son. But Time is imagined as
narrator of the whole story presented in dramatic form: he mentioned him when he was spoken of by Polixenes (I. ii. 165 ff.).

27–28. [The rhyming of 'daughter' and 'after' indicates that they were
pronounced similarly. Both '*dafter*' and '*auter*' are known pronuncia-
tions, so that it is impossible to tell which sound was intended by
Shakespeare.]

31–32. The meaning of 'that Time' has been disputed. We suggest:
'If you have never spent time worse before now, yet that time
(which you are spending so badly) does himself say that he wishes
you never may (spend time worse in future).'

ACT IV, SCENE II

Polixenes and Camillo show us the present situation: that Florizel
probably is in love with Perdita, that Polixenes would disapprove,
and that Camillo is anxious to see Leontes and Sicilia again. The
conversation is in prose, being chiefly concerned with matters of
fact.

4. **fifteen years.** We have just heard that it is sixteen, but this is the sort of inaccuracy, frequent in Shakespeare, which makes him seem so 'natural'.

13–17. **Thou . . . done.** Camillo, an expert administrator, has started enterprises of State that only he can carry through. If he leaves Polixenes without completing these tasks, he does in effect take away with him the good that he has done.

24. [**are**: attracted into the plural by proximity to 'queen and children'.]

44–45. i.e. that (about the shepherd's daughter) is also part of my information; but, I am afraid, she is the cause of my son's being attracted there.

'But' has puzzled commentators. It has its usual sense by implication: 'She is a wonderful girl, I hear, *but* she is the cause of my son's absence'—the point against her.

ACT IV, Scene III

This scene introduces Autolycus and shows him at work. Autolycus is the invention of Shakespeare: he has no place in the source. Critics have a good deal sentimentalized him. He is not a lovable rogue with a heart of gold, but a mean and wholly selfish sneak-thief who was once a courtier. Shakespeare's point is not that roguery is endearing and superior to 'conventional' morality, but that even the least satisfactory people have their share of God's sunlight and can play a part—often unwittingly, as Autolycus does later—in the operation of God's grace.

1–12. This song is *not* an Elizabethan 'nature' lyric but a product of Jacobean wit which incidentally parodies the Elizabethan simplicities (as Donne parodied Marlowe's 'Come live with me and be my love'). Shakespeare takes the usual poetic ingredients—spring, flowers, birds—and sets them in contrast with the petty thief and his immoral companions. The humour lies in the unexpectedness of some of the words, e.g. 'doxy' after, and in alliteration with, 'daffodils'—we might have expected 'With heigh! the blackbird . . .' or some such thing. From Harman's *Caveat or Warning for Common Cursetors* (1567) we may learn about the organized gangs of beggars who roamed the English countryside: they had their own class distinctions, their own laws, and their own 'canting' speech, which Shakespeare employs in this song and elsewhere in the dialogue of Autolycus.

4. **pale.** Grammatically a noun = *bounds, domain*; but there is probably a pun on the adjective *pale* (in colour). 'The red blood reigns within what were once the boundaries of winter' *and* '. . . instead of the pallor of winter'.

7. **pugging.** *Puggard* was a cant word for a thief. 'Pugging tooth' is coined on analogy with *sweet tooth*, and there is also a play on words, since (according to Wise) 'pugging tooth', in Shakespeare's native Warwickshire, was a dialect phrase for *dog tooth, canine*. 'Set . . . on edge' here implies eagerness to taste, not the more usual meaning of *reluctance* to taste or disapproval on tasting.

8. He would buy the ale with money paid him for the stolen sheets (cf. l. 23).

15–22. 'Shall I mourn because I am out of work? No, I have the moonlight to steal by, and I do best when I am wandering about. So long as tinkers are allowed to go around, carrying their tools in their pouch, I shall be able to give an account of myself (saying that I am a tinker) and affirm it when I am put in the stocks.'

23–24. It has been debated whether Autolycus meant to compare or contrast himself with the kite. This bird was notorious for stealing small pieces of linen for nest-building; but Autolycus steals sheets. Surely he *compares* himself to the kite and so wittily *diminishes* the size of the sheets and, by implication, the heinousness of his crime!

24. **Autolycus** was in classical mythology the son of Mercury by Chione; he was noted in Homer for thievery and swearing. In Golding's translation of Ovid's *Metamorphoses* he is described as 'such a fellow as in theft and filching had no peere'. Shakespeare may have used Golding here and for the Proserpine story (IV. iv. 116–18), but he could equally have gone to the Latin original. Mercury was patron of thieves; it was therefore appropriate that Autolycus and his father should be born under the influence of the planet Mercury, to which the characteristics of the god had been transferred.

28–30. **Gallows . . . of it.** 'Gallows and knock' = 'beating and hanging' in reverse order. It has been suggested that, since he is afraid of beating and hanging, Autolycus avoids highway robbery, limits himself to the 'silly cheat', and so has no worries about the future ('the life to come' taken as his future days here on earth). But even petty theft was punishable by hanging, and vagabonds were liable to be beaten, so that he could scarcely escape such worries. The point lies in '*too* powerful': the authorities are more vigorous in detecting and punishing highwaymen, so that Autolycus limits himself to petty theft, for he is afraid of beating and hanging even as a sneak-thief—the terror would be greater if he went in for armed robbery. He has fears, then, so far as *this* life is concerned; but *as for the life to come*—i.e. the world to come—he gives it no thought. That Autolycus does fear hanging, though limiting himself to petty theft, is made clear by IV. iv. 623–4 (and see note on that passage).

43–44. **psalms to hornpipes.** He sings psalms to the rapid and rollicking hornpipe tunes. The setting of sacred words to lively popular airs has been the practice of heretical or 'nonconformist' movements from the Arians to the Salvationists. The Clown perhaps wishes to say that even this one Puritan is of the more cheerful sort.

49. **I' th' name of me !** 'Me' is surely not the beginning of the word 'mercy', interrupted by Autolycus. The whole exclamation, though not found elsewhere, seems best taken as a very mild oath, similar to 'Before me' in *Twelfth Night*, II. iii. 197.

54. [**offend** : attracted into the plural.]

65–66. [**if this ... service.** There is probably a play on *horseman = man on horseback* and *horse-soldier*, and *service = use* and *military service*. The Clown's query (l. 62), however, surely means 'By a man on horseback or on foot ?'—without any suggestion of military desperadoes. The military significances, if any, are limited to ll. 65–66 and are not literal but merely provide a secondary, metaphorical reinforcement of the surface meaning.]

85–89. A Shakespearian 'clown', like a modern comedian in the lighter sort of entertainment, may step out of his usual character of dullard in order to make a witty remark. Here, Autolycus begins the satire by suggesting that virtue is driven from the court. The Clown seems to disagree but, by a surprising twist of thought, comes to say almost the same thing : they do not drive virtue from the court; they lavish care upon it to try to make it stay, but even so it will *just stay and no more*—i.e. it is always on the point of taking its departure, like a discontented guest. This satire on the court is taken up by Autolycus later (IV. iv. 713 ff.) and recalls the unhealthy atmosphere of the court of Sicilia during Leontes' jealousy.

ACT IV, SCENE IV

This unusually long scene (of nearly 900 lines) presents the love
story of Florizel and Perdita, their interrupted troth-plight and their
escape. With its mixture of lovely poetry and earthy humour, it
reveals the best side of country life, while not ignoring its less
attractive qualities—the crudity of the Clown and the general
credulity which allows Autolycus an easy success. Through the
poetry, especially in relation to Perdita, is built up a symbolic
suggestion of 'new life', redemption, and restoration. The love of
Florizel and Perdita, frankly sexual yet completely chaste, contrasts
strongly with the morbid sophistication of Leontes in his jealousy.
It is their attitude of faith which will conquer all obstacles and
restore the drooping life of Sicilia.

1. **unusual weeds.** This is 'not the ordinary costume for the queen
   of the sheep-shearing, "no shepherdess, but Flora" (cf. l. 10 : "Most
   goddess-like prank'd up"). Florizel is not paying a compliment
   merely, he is telling the audience what the costume signifies; and it
   appears from ll. 9–10 that he had designed it, with no doubt for
   himself a becoming swain's attire to match, which though Perdita
   complains of it (ll. 7–9, 12–13) was rich enough to suggest the
   court to Autolycus and the two shepherds (ll. 671–3, 725–32). This
   last is an important point since it has puzzled many why
   Autolycus is mistaken for a courtier after donning the prince's
   "swain's wearing". I owe the elucidation of it to Mr. Granville-
   Barker who tells me that when he produced the play in 1912 the
   lovers both wore "fancy-dress"' (Wilson).

   It may be added that an audience of the time of James I would
   not be surprised to find a prince designing what are in effect
   masque costumes. It is not explained why, if the two shepherds
   later took the swain's costume for a courtier's, they should have
   accepted it without question at the feast; but this element of
   illogical convention is to be found in Shakespeare as in modern
   musical comedy. It is a matter of dramatic convenience : (i) Florizel
   and Perdita *must* have rich costumes to please the eye, but (ii)
   Florizel must not be suspected before the plot requires it, and (iii)
   Autolycus *must* be taken for a courtier. In the swing of a performance audiences do not niggle about completely naturalistic true-
   ness-to-life.

2. **[Does** : singular by attraction to 'part'.]

2. **Flora.** In *Pandosto* 'shee seemed to bee the Godesse Flora her
   selfe for beauty'. Acting on this hint, Shakespeare associates

Perdita throughout with the spring, flowers, sunlight, the fruitful earth—there will be no need to point out the instances individually —so that she represents, as it were, the sum of *natural* goodness which is produced by *supernatural* grace.

6. This distorted word-order and the compressed and metaphorical language that follows, sufficiently prove that energetic rhythm, obscurity, &c. are not specially characteristic of the jealous Leontes but extend even to the healthy simplicity of Perdita. In fact, the verse of this play does not normally reflect character but complexity of meaning (see Introduction, p. 22).

10–12. **But ... custom** : i.e. there is always foolishness at feasts and the feasters 'swallow' it because it is traditional.

13–14. **sworn ... glass.** It is as if Florizel in his peasant's clothes had sworn to show Perdita as in a mirror what she herself really is.

[The eighteenth-century emendation of 'sworn' to 'swoon', with its suggestion that Perdita would faint at the sight of her fine array, is out of character and out of period, part of a general, and to some extent unconscious, rewriting of Shakespeare to suit later 'climates of opinion'. Perdita is neither a 'shrinking violet' nor the sort of coquette who would talk about swooning in order to interest a lover.]

14–16. **I bless ... ground.** In *Pandosto* also the first meeting of the lovers took place when the prince was hawking.

22. **Vilely bound up.** This metaphor from bookbinding has been declared inappropriate to the rustic Perdita, but the only propriety that Shakespeare usually seeks in a metaphor is propriety in relation to meaning, not character (though some have noted the feminine activity of pattern-cutting in l. 380 below).

23. **borrowed** is the reading of F and need not be elided to 'borrow'd' : if the third syllable is fully pronounced it naturally reduces the second almost to an elision (*borr'wed*).

25–31. **The gods ... now.** Cf. *Pandosto* : 'Neptune became a ram, Jupiter a Bul, Apollo a shepheard : they Gods, and yet in love.' Shakespeare seems to ridicule the passage—perhaps also the pastoral mode, and perhaps the pagan gods—by adding the comically realistic phrases 'and bellow'd', 'and bleated'.

33–35. i.e. nor with so chaste an intention, &c. Unlike the gods mentioned, Florizel, as he goes on to explain, purposes honourable matrimony.

37. This line could be made numerically regular by a double elision

such as is quite normal in this text, making 'of the king' into 'o'
th' king'. But F does not elide and the line, though irregular, is
easily scanned:

Oppós'd/as it múst/bé/by th' pówer/of the kíng.

38–40. 'One of these two things must necessarily happen, as will
then be quite clear: either you must change your purpose (of
marrying me) or I must change my way of life (and, refusing to have
anything more to do with you, become a mere shepherdess again)'
—cf. ll. 445–8. It has been suggested that 'Or I my life' implies
that she fears execution as a traitor, but to '*change* my life' (for
this is the verb understood) can scarcely mean to die.

43–45. **for I . . . thine.** He is truly himself—*in* himself and in his
relations with others—only when he is hers. This is the true and
highest doctrine of love between the sexes, as it had been worked
out through the Middle Ages and the Renaissance. Love of the
chosen woman and love of God had been thought of as analogous,
so that each helped in the understanding of the other: cf. 'whose
service is perfect freedom' (Book of Common Prayer).

s.d. **Mopsa, Dorcas.** Dorcas is a Biblical name (Acts ix. 36, 39).
It has been observed that Mopsa, as well as other names in this
play, is to be found in Sidney's *Arcadia*; but the Shepherd's wife
in *Pandosto* is called Mopsa, and Shakespeare must have had this in
mind.

55. From the speech beginning here it can be seen that the Shepherd,
unlike other characters, is given verse expressive of his nature.
It is simple and slow-moving. (See Introduction, p. 21.)

61. [This is the punctuation of F. Some editors omit the comma after
'labour' and insert one at the line end, thus suggesting that the fire
in the dame's face was increased by what she drank!]

73. **those flowers.** In Shakespeare's time flowers, like animals,
had their proper 'meanings'. Perdita's distribution of flowers
would be much fuller of significance for the Globe audience than
for an audience today.

74–76. [Rosemary and rue, preserving their good qualities through the
winter, are appropriate gifts for the aged (ll. 78–79). *Rosemary* was
much loved and used in the past: preserving colour and scent for a
long time, it was a symbol of remembrance and therefore of enduring
friendship. Although properly derived from *ros marinus* or *maris*
(= sea-dew) it was quibblingly explained as 'Rose of Mary'. Such
fictitious derivations were not necessarily due to ignorance; their
invention was a recognized form of wit, explained in and based on
Aristotle's *Rhetoric*, Bk. II, Ch. 24 (1400*b*). *Rue*, from *ruta*, was wrongly
connected with *ruth* (perhaps a genuine error; perhaps wit), and this,

together with its bitter taste, rendered it a fitting symbol for repentance; whence it was also called Herb of Grace.

Perdita uses these plants symbolically, referring to 'Grace and remembrance'. It is fitting that she who symbolizes the new life of Leontes, won by repentance arising from grace and by the grace-inspired self-denial of Hermione, should begin her flower-distribution with the symbols of remembrance and Our Lady, penitence and grace.]

79–103. [Sir . . . me. Perdita tactfully explains why she has not given Polixenes and Camillo the most beautiful flowers of late summer, appropriate to late middle-age. This leads to a long discussion of the advisability of planting carnations, in which we have a good example of the way Shakespeare and the 'Metaphysical' poets of the seventeenth century can manipulate an apparently superficial thought so as to express several layers of deeper meaning, an ability largely depending on an agreed association of specific objects (flowers, for example) with certain moral meanings obtained by the process of 'witty' analogy. Several points should be noticed:

(a) The terms *carnation* and *gillyvor* seem both to have been applied to the same range of flowers, pinks and carnations, though *gillyvor* or *gillyflower* has been at times extended to cover sweet-williams, wall-flowers, and stocks. The streaked *gillyvor* was probably the clove carnation or pink.

(b) Although she does not directly say so, Perdita seems to have a *moral* objection to growing what 'some call nature's bastards' (l. 83). These flowers were, in fact, associated with the idea of sexual immorality: *gillyflower* could mean *a light woman*; and cf. Spenser's *Shepheardes Calender, Aprill* (l. 136):

Bring hether the Pincke and purple Cullambine,
    With Gelliflowres:
Bring Coronations, and Sops in wine, worne of Paramoures.

(*Coronations*: carnations. *Sops in wine*: yet another name for the same kind of flower, because they were used to flavour wine and beer.) Probably the 'streaks' suggested 'painting' and so, as always with the Elizabethans, prostitution; Perdita has this in mind at l. 101. She will not grow the flowers that symbolize unchastity.

(c) Her direct argument is (ll. 86–88) that these 'streaked' or 'pied' flowers are produced by the gardener's art and not by 'great creating nature' alone, and that this is wrong. It appears that in Shakespeare's day, when gardens were much loved and the art of horticulture widely studied and practised, there was discussion, in relation to experiments with gillyflowers, as to whether interference with nature, to alter colour &c., was justified. Shakespeare thus introduces a topical question into his pastoral scene. Perdita takes the negative side, but, in traditional feminine fashion, advances no argument. Polixenes is given a subtle piece of reasoning on the positive side (ll. 88–97). He argues that nature makes the means by which nature is improved, so that above (and therefore controlling) the art that 'adds to nature' is a further art devised by nature. That is to say, the gardener can 'improve' nature only by observing nature's laws. Polixenes takes grafting as his example: a 'gentler scion' (nobler offspring) is married to a wild root (as domestic apples are grafted on to the stronger root of the crab) and the result of the union is an improvement, indeed a change, in nature; but the art of grafting is itself governed by nature or, as he

has put it before, by 'nature's art'—i.e. it is nature, not the gardener,
that says when the operation must be performed, where is the best
place for the graft, &c., and it is nature which runs the sap from the
wild root into the cultivated branch that has been grafted. At a time
when Bacon and others were beginning to assert that man can 'conquer' nature—a theory which has produced the man-made deserts
of today—Shakespeare, through Polixenes, presents the view that man,
in applying his 'art' to nature, must work in subordination to the laws
of nature itself, i.e. the laws of God for natural operations. Perdita's
attitude is, of course, even more anti-Baconian.

(d) Behind the argument about gardening lies the wider question of
the relation of art to nature. Polixenes states the opinion of classical
critics, from Aristotle to Longinus, and the Renaissance theorists
dependent upon them: that nature is itself art (the art of God) and
that art is natural, being subject to the same laws as operate in nature.
Perdita's view of the superiority of nature to art was advocated in the
seventeenth century at least by one Italian writer of impeccable
theological orthodoxy—Emanuele Tesauro, in *Il Cannocchiale Aristotelico*—to whom it appeared that nature, the art of God, must be
truer than the art of fallen man. As usual Shakespeare has given us
both sides of the argument, and in this instance it is impossible to discover to which side he inclines, though we may perhaps on general
grounds suppose him to favour Perdita.]

97. **So it is.** In addition to its various meanings already discussed,
Polixenes' speech contains (ll. 92–97) strong dramatic irony. For it
can apply to the union of his own 'gentler scion' to Perdita's
supposedly 'wildest stock'—a union to which he is soon violently
to object. Perdita's apparent agreement—'So it is'—applies to
this point only: she has at once thought of Florizel and herself.
There is no other explanation of her words, since she shows
immediately (ll. 99–100) that she is not convinced on the question
of gillivors.

104. [Herbs were much cultivated in sixteenth and seventeenth-century
England. Lavender signified true love.]

105. [**The marigold,** associated with Our Lady by witty derivation (Mary-
gold; cf. ll. 74–76, note), has been said by some to be the sunflower but
is probably the same as the modern marigold, *calendula officinalis*.
It was particularly dear to the age of wit, since it always turns towards
the sun (being therefore called *turnesol*), opening as it rises and closing
as it sets. Called *Sponsus Solis* (spouse of the sun), it symbolized
marriage and the virtue of obedience. Significantly, the only flowers
Perdita has are marigolds. She has herbs in addition, notably rosemary
and rue, but the other flowers are merely spoken of.]

107. **given:** in the heraldic sense, *used to represent*. Certain commentators think that Perdita presents these flowers not to Polixenes and Camillo but to other members of the company. But
Camillo's words at ll. 109–10 look like a complimentary reply to
the welcome of l. 108. Perhaps Perdita, penitent for her first

gift of the flowers of old age and having no flowers of *late* middle-age, now errs on the other side and gives Polixenes and Camillo tokens which she believes to apply to men somewhat younger than they are. The tone would be mildly comic.

113–16. The feast is in the late summer so that middle and late summer flowers are available but not those of spring. In most pastoral poetry flowers of all seasons bloom together, as they were said to do in the golden age: Shakespeare is more realistic. The analogy between seasons of the year and the ages of life (spring = youth, &c.) is implied throughout. The further analogy between sexual development and the relation of earth to sun (often figured as sexual) is strongly felt. The marigold is married to the sun and has the wife's portion of joy and tears, but the spring flowers do not experience Phoebus (the sun) as a bridegroom (ll. 122–5).

115–16. The young people are figured as plants or trees.

116–18. O Proserpina! . . . waggon! According to the myth, Proserpine was gathering flowers when Dis (Pluto) seized her and carried her off to his underworld kingdom. In her fright she let fall her flowers. (See IV. iii. 24, note).

118. A short line. Coleridge wanted to insert 'golden' before 'daffodils'; but there need be no error. A longish pause before beginning the list of flowers would be appropriate, and this would make up the 'time' of a full line.

120–2. violets . . . breath: 'dim', perhaps because dimly seen in woodland and hedgerow; perhaps *less bright* than the daffodil; perhaps both. 'Sweeter' does double duty: *more lovely* than Juno's eyelids; *sweeter-scented* than Cytherea's breath. Cytherea = Aphrodite (Venus), from the island of Cythera, in whose waters she was born of the foam.

122–5. pale . . . maids. In contrast with the marigold, the bride of the sun, the primrose figures as a young girl with no experience of Phoebus' love: Perdita, who has recently had misgivings about the future course of her own love, thinks of herself as she adds 'a malady . . . maids'.

125. oxlips are larger and sturdier than cowslips. As they stand tall and straight in face of the sun, they are said to be 'bold' in wooing him.

126. The crown imperial, a tall yellow fritillary, was introduced into England from Constantinople late in the sixteenth century and soon became popular.

127. The flower-de-luce or *fleur-de-lis,* although classified by Shakespeare among the lilies, was probably the iris.

131. or if. Perdita in the frank enthusiasm of young love wants flowers to 'strew' over Florizel. He playfully suggests that that sounds like a funeral. She begins by rejecting the idea, and for 'corpse' substitutes 'bank' as the image implied in her 'strewing'; then she has a second thought:—'or if' (i.e. if like a corpse, a 'body'), then not for burial but alive and in her embrace.

> [Critics have compared Beaumont and Fletcher's *Philaster*:
>
> > I could wish
> > I rather were a corse strew'd o'er with you
> > Than quick above you
> >
> > > (IV. iv. 4).
>
> (It is the flowers that are being addressed.) If Shakespeare had the passage in mind, he has completely reversed the original thought, turning a melancholic desire for death into a triumphant assertion of love and life. Playwrights and other poets at that time sometimes indulged in deliberate references to one another, and it may be that Shakespeare wished to counter the unhealthy sentiment of Beaumont and Fletcher in this way. (See Introduction, pp. 21-2.)]

134. Whitsun pastorals. The Whitsuntide 'games' were probably May games with a king and queen, usually identified with Robin Hood and Maid Marian, who was also called 'white-pot queen' (see IV. iv. 161, note). The May queen was descended from the Flora of the pagan Roman festival, so that Shakespeare links a late-summer sheep-shearing with spring festivities, suggesting the whole range of nature's development from first growth to fruition, and further links the natural order in its pagan expression (references to pagan deities) with the Christian supernatural (Whitsun)—as, indeed, they were historically related in the evolution of the Church's liturgy (see Introduction, p. 30). The complication of planes of reality (see Introduction, p. 15) is remarkable in this passage, where a boy actor plays a princess, thought to be a shepherdess, playing a queen's part at a festival and comparing herself to one who plays another queen's part at another festival!

135-46. What ... queens. The whole speech is one conceit, of which the *Arcadia* perhaps provides the immediate source. Of the lover and his beloved it is there said that 'what soeuer she doth is euer in his eyes best. And that best, being by the continuall motion of our changing life, turned by her to any other thing, that thing againe becommeth best ... If she sit still, that is best, ... If she walke, no doubt that is best, ... ' &c. Sidney refers to sitting, walking, silence, and speech. Shakespeare makes the activities more various and significant. Speaking, singing, dancing, are what Florizel praises, but, whether by intention or not, we are also made to imagine Perdita as buying and selling, 'ordering her affairs', and praying and giving alms—the duties of social life and of religion. The lover's dream is brought down to earth and raised up to heaven, made practical, as it should be. For a further treatment of this speech as poetry, see Introduction, pp. 21–22.

142. The short line allows for lingering stress on the last four words, which produce a wave effect, with the two 'stills' at the crest.

145–6. The metaphor in 'crowns' and 'queens' is taken from Perdita's present function as queen of the feast and reminds the audience of her royal lineage.

[An illogicality is wittily resolved: 'crowns' surely means *elevates above the rest*: everything she does in turn seems best. But they cannot all *be* best, although that is what Florizel says. The proper conclusion *without metaphor* would be nonsense: 'so that all your acts are best' or 'bests'. The whole statement, however, is figurative and 'queens' *seems* to follow from 'crowns', but there can be more than one queen as there cannot be more than one best. Thus the figure has subtly shifted its meaning (see footnote) and the logic is apparently, though not really, saved. Truth is, of course, stated by this disguised illogicality: the excellence of whatever Perdita does.

Furness takes 'the present deeds' to 'refer to the distribution of flowers then taking place, and his paraphrase is adopted by Moorman and Wilson. But the passage beginning 'each your doing' forms a concluding statement after a point-by-point 'praise' of Perdita's behaviour, and we should expect it to summarize what has gone before and to echo the opening proposition. If it had been intended to refer to the distribution of flowers, it would surely have been more specific. 'Each your doing' most naturally means *each of the activities just named*, i.e. speaking, singing, dancing. Each thing she has done *in the past*, however, cannot be said to crown what she is doing *at present*. That would be a 'dispraise'. 'The present deeds' must mean 'at present', not in the sense of *now* but of *the time when the activity in question is taking place*: 'everything you do is such that when it is being done it seems best.' The plural 'deeds' adds a further difficulty: presumably each activity or 'doing' is thought of as involving many contributory 'deeds'—the 'particulars' of l. 144.]

148. **the true … 't.** He is blushing. 'It' is his 'youth': it is through his youth, i.e. his youthful complexion, that the blood peeps—'fairly', because he is handsome. (Perdita is honest in her praise.) The blood is 'true' because practised deceivers in love have passed the stage of blushing. In ll. 147–55 both lovers make it clear that their aim is honest marriage.

155. **I'll … 'em** has a frank and pleasant heartiness.

159. **Too noble.** It was held that noble blood must necessarily show itself in the behaviour of its possessor. Polixenes' speech is thus dramatic irony: the audience know, though he does not, that Perdita's behaviour proceeds from her royal blood.

161. **The queen . . . cream** refers to the 'white-pot queen' of west-of-England May games (see note to l. 134, above). 'White-pot in old cookery was a kind of custard, made in a crust or dish with cream, eggs, pulse of apples, sugar, spices, and sippets of white or manchet bread.' (Douce, quoted Wilson.) The relation of royalty to rural simplicity in Perdita, symbolizing the proper relation of court and country, is summed up in this phrase.

162–3. **garlic . . . with.** Even coarse rustic humour has a witty form in this play. The smell of garlic is not normally attractive; but, according to Dorcas, it would improve ('mend') Mopsa's breath. The implied argument may be termed literally an example of *a fortiori*.

168–71. The first line and a half are the general rumour. 'He is called Doricles and (they say) he declares he has a good farm; but *I* have it from himself and I believe it—he looks honest.'

181. **the pedlar** in Shakespeare's day brought the news and the wares of the city to his country clientele. It is the younger generation who pursue him most avidly: town ways are slowly coming to the country, though the process will take three more centuries to complete.

182–3. **tabor and pipe.** The piper had a little drum (tabor) and played both instruments to accompany a morris dance, in which he was himself a performer. See the well-known illustration of the pre-Shakespearian clown, Tarlton, who was famous for his jigs, which were performances of this type with comic verse dialogue. The **bagpipe** was used in rural England as well as in Scotland: its form varied with the locality.

185. These **ballads** are not the fine traditional poetry, chiefly of border exploits, which we so much value today. They are doggerel verses describing some startling contemporary event, a murder, a hanging, or the birth of a two-headed calf, as parodied in the dialogue of Autolycus later.

grew to = were attracted by. The metaphor is perhaps from a plant that grows towards another which will support it (cf. eyes 'glued on' an object). This growth of ears may by Shakespeare—though not by the servant—be meant to imply that their possessors became asses.

188–90. doleful . . . lamentably. A similar nonsensical oxymoron has been used before (*Midsummer Night's Dream*, v. i. 57, 'very tragical mirth'), and there may be a lingering joke at the title-page of Preston's *Cambises* (a play ridiculed by Falstaff in *1 Henry IV*, ii. iv. 427 ff.): 'A lamentable tragedy mixed full of pleasant mirth.'

191. of all sizes. He means 'kinds', but 'sizes' slips out because he is thinking of the gloves to which he is about to compare them.

194. which is strange. The servant's surprise at the absence of bawdry (jokes about sex) is a reflection on the usual wares of the pedlar. The comic effect is extended when it appears from what follows that Autolycus' ballads do not deserve this commendation. The 'delicate' refrains 'of dildos and fadings' (ll. 194–5) are, in fact, sexual in significance and found in indecent songs.

215. [of these pedlars : a partitive genitive.]

246. clamour : from an English root *clam* = *to clog*, *glue together*; used in bell-ringing of ringing all the bells together before a silence. The spelling may arise from confusion with *clamour* = *noise*. Perhaps *clammer* would be better.

248–9. tawdry lace. Such laces were sold at the annual fair of St. Audrey (hence the name) or, more properly, St. Etheldreda, at Ely. The saint died of a swelling in her throat, which she ascribed to her having been too fond of necklaces in her youth. The present meaning of *tawdry* clearly derives from the quality of these memen-toes and other trinkets sold at the fair.

259. for then . . . true. This pathetic belief in the veracity of the printed word is usual among simple people. ('It must be true. Oi seed it in the papers.')

273. of a fish. Malone quotes a title of 1604: 'The most true and strange report of A monstruous fishe that appeared in the forme of A woman from the wast vpward Seene in the Sea.' There were many such ballads. The ballad-writer, however, strains credulity only in requiring us to believe in mermaids, of which there have been reports in every age. Shakespeare's title is not an imitation but a fantastic burlesque, with its impossible date, the enormous height of the 'fish', the ballad it sang, and the comic-indelicate explanation. Lines 260–3, above, contain a similar burlesque.

290–4. In view of the nonsense still often talked about illiterate Elizabethans, it is worth noting that the milkmaids Mopsa and Dorcas are going to read the words at sight, and the tune, which they 'had a month ago', they have presumably learned from the music. Yet Shakespeare presents them as typically dull and credulous rustics. In the sixteenth and seventeenth centuries education was widespread, and the nation was musically accomplished to an extent which is hard to believe today. An educated man or woman read a madrigal at sight; lutes were kept in barbers' shops for the customers to play; and the country folk had skill in singing and instrumental music. Autolycus in the role of pedlar claims music as his occupation.

325–6. men of hair . . . Saltiers. They are dressed as satyrs. 'Saltiers' (probably pronounced *sautiers*) provides a pun on *satyrs* and the French *saulteurs* (*leapers*, as in *somersault*). Perhaps the pun is not designed to be deliberate on the performers' part but is to be taken as a happy mistake of the servant, due to a mishearing of 'satyrs'.

336. before the king : see Introduction, p. 8.

341. As the chief characters step forward at the end of the dance, this is said as if in reply to the Shepherd, suggesting that a conversation has taken place.

342–3. Polixenes' question is rhetorical: he has already made up his mind that the love of Florizel and Perdita has gone too far and must be stopped. This he has decided from his talk with the Shepherd, who is referred to in l. 343.

357–8. which . . . deliver'd : 'which' refers to 'heart', thought of as a package of gifts; 'given . . . But not deliver'd' means that he loves her but has not made a formal declaration—they are not yet espoused. There is a pun on *deliver'd* as goods and *deliver'd* = *spoken*.

358–60. O ! hear . . . lov'd. Furness thinks 'this ancient sir' is Camillo, but the words that follow surely refer to Polixenes' speech above, about the time when he 'handed love'. Therefore, from 'O ! hear' Florizel addresses not Polixenes but Perdita and refers to Polixenes as witness.

362. The 'Or' is glided over and 'Ethiopian's' is a trisyllable, so that the line has the usual time-value.

364–5. Florizel's similes make whiter what was white already. Polixenes has a note of irony here.

375–6. The so-called 'respective construction' (see III. ii. 161–3, note). 'Commend them (his various good qualities) to her service or condemn them to their own perdition'—i.e. to be lost or destroyed. There may be a play on words: Perdita or perdition are the alternatives before him.

380–1. She means that his intentions must be like hers.

415. **contract.** Wilson observes that this was to have been a 'pre-contract' or betrothal of the sort that Shakespeare himself probably went through with Anne Hathaway (see I. ii. 273–8, note).

418. [**affects** : Shakespearian second person singular; perhaps for euphony.]

421. **who** : F 1 'whom', perhaps for euphony.

424. **More . . . state** : 'homely' has a punning double meaning, (i) plain-looking (the modern American sense), and (ii) humble, low in the social scale. The phrase thus means 'more unattractive than your social position is humble'.

429. **Farre . . . off.** Polixenes says that he will not recognize Florizel as related to him, not even when their ancestry is traced farther back than Deucalion. As Deucalion is the classical equivalent of Noah and therefore the common ancestor of all, the statement is strictly nonsense. It is, of course, hyperbole intended to express his indignation.

432. [**dead.** 'Dread' is a possible but unnecessary emendation.]

433–5. i.e. worthy enough (bride for) a herdsman; yes, and for him too who, except for his royal blood ('our honour therein') makes himself unworthy of you (—by acting as he has done, without consulting his father and without thinking of his duty of marrying within his station).

439. **Even here undone!** Perdita's love affair is 'here'—i.e. at this time and place—fallen to pieces, finished. 'I was not much afeard' follows after a pause, in a reminiscent wonder at herself: she had thought she would be unable to face Polixenes' anger (ll. 17–24).

442–4. Cf. St. Matthew v. 45 : 'for he maketh his sun to rise on the evil and on the good, and sendeth rain on the just and on the unjust.' Although this Scriptural passage lies behind Perdita's remark, we must not assume that court and cottage stand for evil and good: the point is that God's gifts are equally available to all and that that gives all men a certain equality before Him. Perhaps a word 'both' or 'all' has been omitted after 'Looks on'; but F 1 may be correct—an intransitive use.

450. He dare not admit his knowledge to himself—dare not think about it.

454–6. Hanged men were buried at the gallows' foot with 'shards, flints, and pebbles' (*Hamlet*, v. i. 253) thrown upon them. Presumably the Shepherd was too agitated to realize that Polixenes had pardoned him (ll. 431–2).

[In the first Prayer Book of Edward VI, the rubric at the burial reads 'Then the priest castyng earth upon the Corps, shall saye.' This was the medieval practice. The second Prayer Book of Edward VI reads 'Then whyle the earth shalbe cast upon the body, by some standing by, the priest shal say.' It is likely that country clergymen kept up the custom of casting the earth themselves, and even more likely that octogenarians would think of burial in terms of the ancient ceremonies. The old Shepherd attains here the dignity of sorrow: his rural piety is expressed in his desire to be constantly associated with familiar things, to die in the family bed and be buried in the family grave.]

469. **his highness.** F 1 prints 'Highnesse' with a capital and it *may* be merely a title.

471. **I think, Camillo?**—recognizing him through his disguise. Camillo probably removes it as he replies.

475–7. **and then . . . within !** These seeds are the 'germens' of *Lear*, III. ii. 8 and *Macbeth*, IV. i. 59 : the sources of life and growth in the created world. Their destruction would be the end of all things.

480–3. 'I am "advised" and by love: if my reason will follow the dictates of love, I am content to be rational; if not, my senses (by which love is mediated) prefer madness and welcome it.'

There is a play upon *fancy = imagination* (in our modern sense) and *fancy = love*; but there is a real relationship between the meanings, since love arises in the fancy, whence it *ought* to be submitted to the judgement of reason, which is the faculty that properly exercises authority over the rest. Shakespeare seems at times, especially in his later work, to question this orthodox Elizabethan view of things: *reason* comes to have rather the sense of *worldly wisdom*, and there is a hint that something akin to 'intuition' (which the Elizabethans would have included under 'reason', as its highest operation) is alone to be trusted.

485–90. **Camillo . . . belov'd.** Florizel uses large cosmic references as did Leontes (see II. i. 99–102, note), but to swear to his faith, not his unfaith. In his love he is the exact opposite of Leontes in his jealousy and so helps to symbolize the 'new life'.

504–5. **Hark, . . . by.** This crude device of a talk aside to permit another character to come forward and make a 'direct address' to the audience is repeated at l. 592 and l. 658. Shakespeare is concerned in this part of the scene principally with managing his plot, and so, now the tension is lowered, he has an opportunity of detaching the audience (who will have been concerned over Florizel and Perdita) and renewing for them the atmosphere of 'an old tale' by telling it in the 'old' way. (Even more obvious examples of old-fashioned technique are the use of Gower as Chorus in *Pericles* and Posthumus' dream in *Cymbeline*; in *The Tempest*, I. ii. the near-parody of the narrative method entailed by the unities has a similar effect of 'detachment'.)

522-3. This is the language of the courtier: Camillo knows well enough that Florizel has no plan.

529-31. [In the eighteenth century editors inserted 'I'll' or 'I will' before 'strive'; but in 1790 Malone omitted it, returning to F—to which our present text adheres—and explained the passage by taking 'strive' after 'you may' (l. 525) and treating 'with my ... absence' as a parenthesis: 'And where you may, by letters, entreaties, &c., endeavour to soften your incensed father, and reconcile him to the match; to effect which, my best services shall not be wanting during your absence.' This paraphrase, however, depends too much on the insertion of phrases of which there is no clear equivalent in the original. Moreover, the whole insistence of the speech is on what *Camillo* will do, and it is more natural that he should claim chief place in a future reconciliation. But Shakespeare is never very strict about antecedents, and by understanding 'I'll' from l. 524 we can retain the F reading and paraphrase intelligibly and closely, as in the footnote.]

549. **divides him**: a rhetorical term. He keeps referring to both subjects, his former unkindness and his present kindness, putting them in separate categories—condemning the one and wishing the other to grow more quickly than a thought comes to mind or time passes.

557. **deliver** does not imply forged *written* messages. Camillo is only to write (l. 558) notes to remind Florizel what to say.

568-70. 'Nothing about you will be as safe as your anchors, and the best they can do will be to keep you in some place that you will detest'—which, it is assumed, is better than being on the high seas, for sea travel was not comfortable in Shakespeare's day.

568. [**anchors, who.** 'Who' with a neuter antecedent is frequent in Shakespeare.]

570-7. **Besides, ... such.** Camillo utters the worldly wisdom of his years and profession: affliction, he says, alters both the appearance and the heart. Perdita, however, will admit only the former, and the old courtier is himself pleased with her sturdy faith.

576-7. [Wilson thinks this remark was addressed to Florizel but (*a*) Perdita was not born at his father's house, so why 'another'?—and (*b*) would Camillo call the king's palace 'your father's house'? Surely the point is simply that there will not be any more pretty—and wise—maidens at home like Perdita—with dramatic irony, because the audience know that (a) she was not born where Camillo thinks, and there cannot be any more like her born in a shepherd's cottage, and (b) Leontes will live without an heir until Perdita is found.]

578–9. 'She is (in wisdom, &c.) as much ahead of (what you would expect from) the way she has been brought up, as she is below me in birth.' That 'breeding' means *upbringing*, not *accomplishments*, is confirmed by v. ii. 37, and this makes emendation unnecessary.

579. [The first two syllables of this line are metrically redundant and should be pronounced rapidly and unemphatically.]

585. [Some commentators suggest medicine = doctor, from the French *médecin*; but this, if it exist at all, is rare, and is quite unnecessary here.]

590–1. **as if . . . mine** : one of the metaphors from the playhouse (see Introduction, p. 15)—'as if I myself were in your place'. This is rather patronizing on Camillo's part, but either his courtliness or Shakespeare's nods a little here.

606–7. **stuck in ears** : cf. '. . . all their sences climbd into their eares'—Chapman in *Hero and Leander*, 5th sestiad, l. 88.

615. **alive . . . army :** a comic metaphor, by which Autolycus' theft becomes a military enterprise against an army of purses. It is the more apt in that he is not strictly a pickpocket but a *cutpurse* and uses cold steel.

616. This continues the conversation they are supposed to have been holding aside.

620. [**Who :** for 'whom'. Cf. ii. ii. 6, note.]

624. **hanging :** the punishment for theft of over twelve pence. Clearly Autolycus *did* fear for his earthly future (cf. iv. iii. 28–30, note).

649. Perdita is to remove her 'fancy dress', under which she would presumably have her peasant's blouse and skirt.

651. **eyes over.** There may be an error or omission in the text: as it stands the phrase is strange though not impossible.

652–8. **the play** continues the stage metaphor, which is persistent while this rather theatrical escape is carried out and old-fashioned stage-technique employed. Cf. note on ll. 504–5, above.

659–64. This is not meant as a betrayal. Camillo expects that the young couple will be married before Polixenes and he can reach Sicilia, but, as we learn later, they have a rough passage and their marriage is delayed.

669. a good nose : i.e. to 'smell out' or discover the most likely
purses for cutting.

670–1. I see . . . thrive : cf. Psalm xxxvii. 36 (Book of Common
Prayer), 'I myself have seen the ungodly in great power : and
flourishing like a green bay-tree'.

676–9. If I . . . profession. This is grammatically awkward : the
hypothetical construction *implies*, 'But I do *not* think it honest to
tell the king, and so I *will* tell him'. Some critics have seen the
difficulty and suggested emending by transferring the 'not' to a
position after 'were' or after 'thought' : 'If I did not think it
honest, I should do it.' Perhaps they are right.

> [Furness sees no difficulty and gives a paraphrase containing the same
> difficulty as the text; Moorman and Wilson ignore it. Retaining the
> reading of F, the best way to take it is to consider Autolycus as hesitat-
> ing, and so teasing the audience, who are on the side of Florizel and
> Perdita. 'If I thought it was honest, I shouldn't do it', he says, imply-
> ing that, as it would be knavery, he will do it. Then a pause and, to
> the audience's relief, he changes his mind : it is greater knavery to
> keep silent. The speech is, of course, a witty self-justification : he will
> be constant to his profession of knave. If we are to interpret in terms
> of character we must call it ironic wit on Autolycus' part : no knave
> would talk like this in pure seriousness. Perhaps it is better taken con-
> ventionally : Autolycus speaks the literal truth of himself as he would
> not do in real life, and the wit is Shakespeare's, not the character's.]

695–8. There is a good deal of alteration of character for local purposes in the treatment of the Shepherd. When he is with the
serious characters he is himself of some dignity, but with the
Clown he becomes predominantly comic, though still retaining
the integrity and feudal feeling of his generation. He is as much
outraged as Polixenes at the way in which Florizel and Perdita
would flout 'degree' in their marriage.

701. I know how much. Hanmer inserted 'not', but there is no
need to alter F, if the Clown's assertion were accompanied, as
Furness suggests, with a knowing wink. This would not only be
the more comic assertion, but would fit better with Autolycus'
'Very wisely' of l. 702.

708–9. An apology to the audience, continuing the wit of ll. 676–9
(see note, above) and to be similarly interpreted. In what
is he going to be honest ? Not in misleading the Shepherd and
Clown to help Florizel : he regards it as knavery to keep the flight
of Florizel and Perdita from the king. Presumably he refers to the
removal of his false beard : he is to present his true and therefore
'honest' countenance.

710. excrement : 'I am not ignorant that hayre is noted by many as an excrement' (Chapman, 'A Justification of a Strange Action of Nero', in *Poems*, ed. Bartlett, p. 347).

718–22. To give the lie means to accuse some one to his face of lying, an insult which a soldier would instantly requite with 'stabbing steel'. But tradesmen 'give the lie' to a soldier in another sense, by telling lies about their goods, and these lies the simple fellow pays for in coin of the realm; so that, in fact, they do not *give* the lie, but *sell* it.

723–4. A comment on Autolycus' self-correction: 'they . . . give us . . . the lie'; 'they do not give us the lie'. 'Your worship nearly gave us one, if you had not taken yourself in the act' (metaphor from catching a thief with the goods upon him).

726–7. Florizel's 'swain's wearing' (l. 9) has transformed Autolycus into a courtier (see l. 1, note). This whole speech is ironic. Autolycus becomes an instrument for satire directed against the court, a reminder to us that the rural virtues are badly needed there.

738–9. The Clown confuses the royal court with a court of justice. It was a common practice to bribe a justice of the peace with gifts in kind; hence his natural error about 'advocate'. Some commentators would amend 'pheasant' to 'present' and so make the Shepherd mishear; but, as Wilson argues, the Clown would not then urge the Shepherd to say he has none: they are prepared to offer a bribe, as we see later.

741–3. Autolycus goes into verse, and rhymes 'men' with the preceding 'hen' in the Shepherd's line, which is verse also, but standing alone would not have been noticed as such. This comic 'elevation' in a prose context produces the Clown's admiring comment.

744–9. The Shepherd has more sense of true gentility than the Clown: the younger generation of rustic was more easily impressed by vulgar display.

748–9. the picking on's teeth. There are many contemporary jokes about 'toothpickers', which were introduced from Italy about 1600 and were an affectation of the would-be-fashionable.

752. [lies such secrets : singular verb *before* plural subject is frequent in Shakespeare.]

758. Man was said to be compounded of the four elements, fire, air, water, earth. In the ideal man they were equally mixed, but in most people one element or another predominated, giving rise to four 'humours' or temperaments, the choleric, the sanguine, the phlegmatic, the melancholic.

780–1. **and a dram :** i.e. and rather more. Comic, since it implies that 'three quarters' refers to weight or bulk in the phrase 'three quarters dead'.

817. **look . . . hedge :** i.e. to relieve himself—the most obviously comic of the excuses used, in this revival of old stage-technique, to allow of a direct address.

ACT V, Scene I

In Sicilia his courtiers urge Leontes to re-marry, but Paulina, symbolizing his conscience even more clearly than in earlier scenes, reminds him of Hermione and of his former sins and their consequences. Florizel and Perdita arrive at Leontes' court, closely pursued by Polixenes. Leontes promises to be their advocate with his old friend. In this scene we note especially the great change in Leontes, who appears grave, quiet, humble, almost saintly, the result of his sixteen years penance. The verse given to him is rhythmically smoother and more musical, suggesting his religious composure and leading towards the poetic climax of the last scene. Perdita appears among the courtiers as a symbol of natural goodness, creativity and the rural virtues : the poetry in which she is described combines the qualities of that used in the description of Delphos (Act III, Scene i) and that which first presents her to us as rural 'queen' and 'goddess' in Act IV, Scene iv.

16–20. **I think . . . seldom.** If we contrast Leontes' treatment of Paulina before his repentance, we can see the extent of his reformation.

30. **well :** i.e. spiritually. Cf. *Antony and Cleopatra*, II. v. 32, 'we use/To say the dead are well'.

56–60. Leontes says that, as there can be no more wives like Hermione, he will have no wife at all; if he were to take a worse wife and treat her better, it would be enough to make the sainted Hermione's soul reanimate her body and upon this earth, where we sinners dwell, begin a reproachful speech : 'And why to me ?' (i.e. 'And why to me this insult ?')

Here again we have the metaphor of *stage* for *world*.

[Lines 59–60 in F read:

        (Where we Offendors now appeare) Soule-vext,
        And begin, why to me ?

There must be an error here, and many emendations have been suggested. We have adopted that of Capell, Malone, and Steevens, because, with a minimum of alteration, it gives what seems both the best sense and the aptest and easiest rhythm.]

84–85. *s.d.* **[Gentleman.** Theobald substituted this for the *Seruant* of F, and it is today less liable to be misunderstood, although the servants of royalty were in Shakespeare's time well known to be gentlemen.]

94–95. Perdita, symbol of natural goodness, is described as a 'piece of earth' and associated with the fructifying sun (see her flower speech (IV. iv. 110–29) for the bridal relationship of earth to sun (Phoebus)). This carries on the imagery of fertility, &c., used in Act III, Scene i for the divine creativeness and so links up Perdita with the good Providence signified by the oracle.

98–103. **Sir, . . . better.** The 'so' of l. 99 refers forward to '"She had not been . . ."' This serving-gentleman is a court poet. Paulina addresses him : 'Sir, you yourself have spoken and written so (i.e. in the way I am going to quote).' She then interpolates : 'but your poetry now is colder (has less life in it) than Hermione who was its theme.' (Note the irony, for Hermione is alive, as Paulina knows.) After this harsh criticism of his recent verse, she goes on to give his old theme more precisely, the passage placed, as most editors have it, in inverted commas, although it is 'reported speech', not a direct quotation : 'She had never been and never would be equalled.' His verse, she says, had once 'flowed' thus with her beauty. The metaphor is usual and is taken from a flowing stream ; but in what follows it is sharpened into wit, for now, says Paulina, changing the image from stream to sea, it is ebbed—the tide of his verse is gone out—when he can say he has seen one superior to Hermione.

Paulina, as usual, speaks vehemently and inaccurately. ' 'Tis' (l. 102) refers to 'verse' (l. 101) but the gentleman has written no verse about Perdita : the reference changes 'written poetry' (l. 101) to 'poetic ability' (l. 102).

106–9. **This . . . follow.** 'This is such a creature that, if she started a new religion, she would 'put out' (extinguish) the devotion of all who believed differently, and make converts of all that she merely told to follow her.' The court poet's linking of Perdita so decisively with the theme of religion assists the development of Shakespeare's 'inner meaning'.

131. **princess,—goddess !** She is royal and, more than that, seems to have something divine about her. This combines the suggestions of Act IV, Scene iv, the 'queen' references and 'Flora'.

132–4. 'Twixt heaven and earth' has no clear meaning after

'wonder' or 'begetting'; it must be taken with 'stood'. Leontes, who has just proclaimed Perdita a goddess, says that he lost a couple who might have stood between heaven and earth—being something more than human—causing all men to wonder, as this gracious couple do. This continues the treatment of them as divinities, which is also implied in 'gracious' (with again the theological connotation behind the social), and helps the 'inner meaning'.

136–8. **my life** is by some explained as an adverbial phrase, 'while I live', 'before I die'. Clearly, however, the meaning is that Leontes, though life is misery to him, yet desires to live in order to see Polixenes again (cf. I. i. 38: 'desire yet their life to see him a man'). 'Him' (l. 138) after 'whom' (l. 136) is redundant.

147–56. **O, ... person.** The opening remarks, full of penitent good-ness, are addressed to the absent Polixenes. Leontes in his new humility is overwhelmed by what he supposes to be the other's kindness. Then he welcomes Florizel and Perdita. 'As is the spring to th' earth' reminds us of Perdita's resembling the goddess Flora at the sheep-shearing feast. Thinking of her crossing the sea, his mind reverts to the baby whom he had exposed to its dangers. He is 'a man not worth her pains', a new Leontes indeed.

168–78. **The blessed ... you!** The opening sentence is reminiscent of the island of Delphos—'The climate's delicate, the air most sweet', &c. (III. i. 1)—and, although the word 'climate' bears a different meaning here (= visit), the general effect is again to stress the relationship of Perdita to the oracle and both to the divine Good-ness. The rest of this speech continues the religious references, so as to emphasize the holiness of Leontes—his is the holiness which he humbly but not very accurately ascribes to Polixenes. Note the succession of words of religious import: 'holy', 'graceful', 'sacred', 'sin', 'heavens', 'bless'd', 'heaven', 'merits', 'goodness', 'goodly'.

193. **Camillo ... me:** not intentionally; see IV. iv. 659–64, note.

206–7. The thought is concerned with rank: the stars will kiss the valleys before the high-born (and therefore star-like) Florizel will marry the low-born Perdita (who resembles the valleys because they are farthest from the stars). Then follows the conviction that in such affairs Fortune makes no distinction between high-born and low-born: it is no easier for them because Florizel is a prince than if he had been a beggar.

[Some editors believe there is also a play on 'high' and 'low' as terms for false dice. Wilson explains: 'Fortune is a cheater who beguiles princes and shepherds alike with his false dice.' But this is surely wrong. If 'high' and 'low' signify (a) the dice and (b) princes and shepherds, the passage cannot mean that princes and shepherds (meaning (b)) are cheated by false dice (meaning (a)). It must mean simply, 'The chances for "high" and "low" are equal', 'high' and 'low' signifying *at the same time* dice and social classes. Moreover, the reference cannot be to *false* dice: it is only with *true* dice that the chances would be equal.]

223. **I'd beg . . . mistress :** no doubt suggested by the source, where Pandosto falls in love with his daughter (see Introduction, p. 17). Shakespeare, however, makes of this, first, a harmless sally of wit, and then (ll. 227–8) a deeply pathetic touch of dramatic irony, as Leontes shows himself to be drawn to Perdita because she reminds him of Hermione—whom we know, though he does not, to be her mother.

230. Leontes will not be influenced by rank: he will help Florizel and Perdita, provided they remain chaste until marriage.

ACT V, Scene II

We hear at second hand, through the conversation of the courtiers, whose language parodies fashionable court jargon, how the kings met and Perdita's identity was discovered. This crucial event is not directly presented, but reported, so that we are left with one undoubted climax in the restoration of Hermione. The use of 'rumour', 'report', adds yet another to the many 'planes of reality' in the play: heaven, earth, theatrical performance, dream, and now reality as seen through the refracting glass of other men's minds. Further, the restoration of Hermione is the more emphasized in that it is wholly serious, whereas, in contrast, this report of Perdita's discovery is comic—another instance of Shakespeare's capacity for making the serious comic by altering the 'angle' or point of view. Yet, as in the previous discovery of Perdita, as an infant (Act III, Scene iii), the comic dialogue is shot through with phrases of deep significance for the 'inner meaning'.

11. **very notes of admiration :** i.e. absolute exclamation marks. Throughout the dialogue of the courtiers we have the wit of the period made ridiculous by excess or inappropriateness: the purpose is parody. The changes of countenance in the king and Camillo expressed extreme 'admiration' (=*wonder*). This allows of a witty hyperbole: they were 'notes of admiration', which means 'signs, marks of wonder' and also, punningly, *exclamation marks*.

12–13. tear . . . eyes : another hyperbole, inappropriate as express-ing extreme discomfort. 'Cases' are eyelids.

14–15. they look'd . . . destroyed : an instance of the intrusion of the serious in a comic context (cf. III. iii. 109–10, note). The simile is taken from the ransoming of the world by Our Lord on the Cross, and its destruction at the Last Day as a preliminary to the 'new heaven and new earth'. It thus relates to the theme of redemption and restoration which the whole story symbolizes, particularly in the characters of Perdita and Hermione.

15–16. a notable passion of wonder : the common note of Shake-speare's romances.

24. ballad-makers composed verses on new and marvellous events (cf. IV. iv. 185, note).

28. like an old tale : see also l. 60, below, and Introduction, p. 12.

43–45. so . . . tears. They were weeping because their sorrow had been turned to joy, so the ingenious Third Gent. personifies sorrow and makes her weep at parting from them. It is not a helpful figure ; the legal 'so and in such manner' is inappropriate ; and the hyperbole of 'waded', later, is comically excessive.

54–55. which . . . reigns : 'conduit', because he is weeping. There is a pun on *reigns—rains*. While not departing from the elaborate wit characteristic of this gentleman, Shakespeare strikes a deeper note in comparing the old Shepherd with a worn statue that has conveyed rain-water throughout the reigns of many kings. What the Shepherd stands for—the rural values of loyalty and use-fulness and the whole pattern of rustic life—will survive the vicis-situdes of kings and the changing fashions of courts.

[**which :** either for *who* or proleptically, referring to 'conduit'.]

73–74. one eye . . . elevated : i.e. she was torn between joy and sor-row. The remarkable behaviour of Paulina's eyes should be enough to warn us that Third Gent. is not a wholly serious character. The 'one auspicious and one dropping eye' of *Hamlet*, I. ii. 11, cited by Furness, is no true parallel, being an emblematic, not a physically descriptive statement. Third Gent. has, as usual, been injudicious in his choice of figure : he speaks as if describing Paulina physically and uses terms—'declin'd', 'elevated'—*both of which* can signify directions as well as states of mind.

81–82. angled . . . fish. Third Gent. is in bad trouble with this image. 'Angled for mine eyes' = *demanded my attention*. 'Water' = *tears*. But what are 'the fish' ? They cannot mean his eyes (i.e.

his attention), as they should, for that was caught or he would not have wept. The image *looks* clever but fails to 'work out'.

84–87. how attentiveness . . . tears. Wounded by Attention (personified) she bleeds tears—another instance of a simple fact made to sound difficult by a superficial exercise of wit.

88–89. Who . . . colour. This has the appearance of paradox, for marble cannot change colour: but 'marble' is used metaphorically (petrified with wonder, rigid with attentiveness—or, perhaps, hard-hearted), while 'changed colour' is literal. Again the wit adds confusion, not clarity, and the point could have been better made without it.

95. Here is an 'anachronism' which Shakespeare cannot have committed ignorantly: he must have known that Romano was a 'modern'. Julio Romano, an Italian painter, died in 1546. According to an epitaph, quoted by the sixteenth-century art-historian, Vasari, he was also a sculptor and an architect. We cannot tell whether Shakespeare knew that, from the epitaph or in some other way, or whether he intended to name Romano only as the *painter* of the statue. It has also been debated whether Shakespeare had seen Romano's works, and, if so, whether in England—there were sixteen in Charles I's collection, but we do not know how long they had been in this country—or in Italy.

[It has been argued by Elze that Shakespeare knew the special quality of Romano's painting—its vivid lifelikeness—and that he had seen his works in Mantua and the original Latin epitaph there, to which his own words approximate. *Videbat Jupiter corpora sculpta . . . spirare* may have suggested 'and could put breath into his work'. There is, however, no reason to doubt, as Elze seems to, the ability of Shakespeare to read Italian, so that he might have read Vasari's book which quotes the epitaph. But all this is mere conjecture, and based on very dubious premisses. For the description in Shakespeare's text is *not* a criticism especially appropriate to Romano but a commonplace eulogy such as was applied to any painter or sculptor—and, as such, it is to be expected from Third Gent. The similarity between Shakespeare's phrase and that in the epitaph is therefore unremarkable. Shakespeare need not, in fact, have known more than the painter's name; though his associating Romano with sculpture, and the fact that the text needs some wresting to make him merely the colourist of the statue, would render it likely that he was in some way acquainted with the statement of the epitaph, which is the only known authority for Romano as *sculptor*.]

95–98. who, . . . ape: i.e. if he had two properties of Nature that he has not, her immortality and her ability to make her works live, he would steal her trade from her (like a rival shop-keeper), he imitates her so closely.

[Nature is eternal according to Greek philosophy but not in Christian doctrine. Either Shakespeare makes Third Gent. an unthinking devotee of classical commonplaces, or by 'eternity' he means here *that length of existence which Nature has in contrast with the earthly lifetime of a human individual.* The latter is the more probable. In contrast with Nature, the artist can neither make his work live nor himself live more than a short span.]

103–5. **she hath … house.** Shakespeare dodges the awkwardnesses of Hermione's survival: what was buried in her coffin, how she was fed, took exercise, and was attended, during sixteen years. Here is just a hint of Paulina's activity in the matter, enough to satisfy an audience that is not too concerned about the factual details of this 'old tale'.

125. **gentlemen born.** It has been pointed out that, according to *The Booke of Honour and Armes* (1590) a gentleman born is one who is 'descended from three degrees of gentry on the mother's and father's side'. But the Shepherd's claim for his grandchildren is probably no more than many an Elizabethan merchant might have made on acquiring a country estate. It is the Clown who makes nonsense of the phrase, in the speech following.

126–31. The comedy here includes satire against the new gentry of Elizabeth and James I. According to the Clown, the two notes of a gentleman are his clothes and his quarrelsomeness. He urges Autolycus to 'give him the lie' as a means of provoking a duel (cf. iv. iv. 718–22, note).

149–50. The old countryman has some notion of the obligations entailed by gentility. He is a type of the old feudal retainer.

156–70. The Clown presents more marks of the 'modern' gentleman : to use oaths, to lie for a friend, to admire 'toughness', to patronize the undeserving.

ACT V, Scene III

The 'coming to life' of Hermione is a far-fetched and 'theatrical' incident, but the hushed and awesome poetry in which it is presented —simple in diction ; melodious ; profoundly religious in significance— transforms the 'transformation scene' into a hint of what Shakespeare felt about the life of Christian devotion, here and hereafter. The quality of life which he expresses is that which comes of redemption, restoration, renewal, through Christ by means of divine grace, in this life, but which cannot be fully known until the life to come.

It is a measure of the humility of our greatest poet that he conveys this very indirectly, through what is on the surface a mere theatrical trick. The theme throughout is 'life', 'warm life', rising from cold death (the marble; the sixteen years separation): the life of heaven is thus symbolically expressed in terms of the full richness of human and earthly life and love.

18. [**Lovely.** F read thus but in the old lettering, 'louely'. Hanmer emended to 'lonely' and almost all editors have followed him: 'u' for 'n' was a very easy error in printing, especially from manuscript. The emendation is noted because it is plausible: it is not adopted, because (*a*) it is unnecessary; F makes good sense; (*b*) 'lonely' produces a tautology: there is no need to follow it with 'apart'; (*c*) 'lovely, apart', expressing the cloistered beauty of Hermione, is so much more meaningful that it is surely what Shakespeare wrote. Because an error *could* have been made is not sufficient reason to think that it *has*, especially when the 'correction' damages the poetry.]

39–42. The image here extends to a brief allegory: the *magic conjures* his past sins up again (like evil spirits) and takes away the *spirits*, or *life*, of Perdita, making her like a marble statue.

The theme of 'black' and 'white' magic runs through the scene (see ll. 96–97, 104–5, below). The good supernatural brings life out of death, but there is still a reminder of the bad, the diabolic, which serves sin and destruction—a reminder of the evil from which we are redeemed.

52. Commentators have tried to add a syllable to this line, on the assumption that the compositor dropped one, but the heavy stresses, 'só lóng líve', and the pause following, make up the time of a blank verse line.

54–56. Polixenes was not the *efficient cause*, though he was the *material cause* or *occasion*, of Leontes' jealousy. He asks that, as he was concerned in Leontes' trouble, he may share his sorrow and so diminish the load of it.

62. **Would . . . dead.** Staunton is surely right in taking this as an imprecation. Leontes begins to say, 'May I die, if I do not think that already it is moving', but he breaks off to ask about the sculptor.

67–68. The contrast of 'fixure' and 'motion' suggests a subordinate meaning: 'Although the eye is fixed, it appears to move.'

94–95. **It . . . faith.** Faith is necessary for the 'resurrected' life of the Christian in this world.

96. [**On.** Presumably regarding this as absurd after the injunction in the preceding line to 'stand still', many editors emend to 'or' with no

punctuation following. 'On' for 'or' is a possible error, but 'on' makes
quite good sense: 'let us go on, proceed, with what has to be done.'
This being so, a change is unwarranted.]

99. **be stone no more.** 'Paulina had, it seemed to me, besought
Hermione to play the part of her own statue, in order that she
might hear herself apostrophized, and be a silent witness of the
remorse and unabated love of Leontes before her existence became
known to him, and so be moved to that forgiveness which, without such proof, she might possibly be slow to yield' (Lady Martin).
This, by an actress who had played Hermione to the Leontes of
Macready, is as good a way as any of accounting for Hermione's
submitting to the theatricality of the statue pose, except that she
would doubtless have forgiven Leontes from the beginning: her
withdrawal was not in anger but to fufil the oracle. It is more
likely that she would need proof of his love in order to gain courage
to return to him who had once rejected her. It is unlikely, however,
that Shakespeare troubled to give himself a psychologically consistent account of the matter: the symbolic significance of this
'resurrection', the new life that comes from divine grace and
human penitence, has swallowed up all naturalistic questionings.
But whatever we think about the situation itself, Hermione's conduct of it is consistent with her previous character: gracious, re-
strained, yet warm and forgiving. She speaks no word to Leontes—
her only speech is a blessing on her daughter—but the wordless
reconciliation, something rare in the Elizabethan theatre, where
what would be silent in real life is usually translated into poetry,
provides a welcome natural touch in a highly symbolic scene. It
is also a further mark of Shakespeare's humility: he will not express
the inexpressible. The greatest master of words is also a master of
silence.

101. **I'll fill . . . up.** No one has commented on this somewhat
obscure remark. Presumably Paulina means that, by summoning
Hermione to move, she is making it impossible for her to return
to the 'grave' of her retirement.

102–3. Such phrases in this scene are all capable of a secondary
meaning expressing Christian doctrine. The Christian at baptism
abandons the 'old man' to death and is redeemed by Christ, who
is the 'dear life' of all.

109. [**suitor?** Some editors put '!' instead of '?'; which need not imply
any error, since in F '?' does duty for '!' also. But the remark seems
more natural as a question, Paulina urging Leontes out of his amazed
stupor and conscience-stricken shyness.]

116–17. **hooted . . . tale.** Shakespeare allows that the tale is thin, and yet coolly closes the scene without answering the questions which begin to trouble the characters and no doubt occur to the audience. Paulina in her forthright way points out (ll. 128–30) that such explanations are inappropriate to the occasion—a point which could be taken to apply to audience as well as characters. Factual completeness would merely distract the audience's attention from symbolic significance.

121–3. In her first words Hermione prays for 'graces'. Grace and its theological significance have been associated with her throughout (see I. ii. 105, note).

132. **turtle.** The turtle-dove, as symbol of true love (cf. IV. iv. 154–5), when left alone mourns for her mate. Moorman compares Lodge's *Rosalynde* (source of *As You Like It*):

> A turtle sate upon a leaveless tree,
> Mourning her absent pheare,
> With sad and sorrie cheare . . .

148. **holy looks:** contrast the 'practis'd smiles' of I. ii. 117. Hermione perhaps hesitates, wondering how to treat Polixenes; Leontes then addresses her with a direct and penitent reference to his old sin against them both. Their looks, he now knows, were holy: his warped vision has been adjusted and he sees good and evil as they truly are.

150–1. **[whom ... daughter.** Two grammatical constructions are confused: 'whom' serves as accusative after 'directing' and also instead of 'who' as subject of 'Is'. This is a further example of Shakespeare's colloquial usage in matters of grammar. Or perhaps the 'm' is supplied for euphony, and 'whom' should be taken as a nominative, subject to 'Is', with 'heavens directing' as a nominative absolute.]

150. **heavens directing.** This states a doctrine which governs the whole action of the play. The interrupted betrothal of Florizel and Perdita, the consequent return of the latter and the 'restoration' of Leontes, Hermione, and the country of Sicilia dependent upon them, have been under the direction of heaven. God's good providence has cared for, and is caring for, all.

153–4. **part/Perform'd.** The analogy between theatre and world (*theatrum mundi*), as we have seen, supplies Shakespeare with many images; it is, moreover, characteristic of the whole period of 'wit'. The actors on the stage and the actors on the stage of life have a certain freedom of will to 'interpret' their parts, but there is a script they must adhere to; and behind the mere spectacle of stage and world is a deeper and more real life from which they derive their energies and their significance and to which all must ultimately retire.

SELECT LITERARY CRITICISM

The Shakespearian Romances

... Strangely remote is the world of Shakespeare's latest period ; and it is peopled, this universe of his invention, with beings equally unreal, with creatures either more or less than human, with fortunate princes and wicked step-mothers, with goblins and spirits, with lost princesses and insufferable kings. And of course, in this sort of fairyland, it is an essential condition that everything shall end well ; the prince and princess are bound to marry and live happily ever afterwards, or the whole story is unnecessary and absurd ; and the villains and the goblins must naturally repent and be forgiven. But it is clear that such happy endings, such conventional closes to fantastic tales, cannot be taken as evidences of serene tranquillity on the part of their maker ; they merely show that he knew, as well as anyone else, how such stories ought to end.

Yet there can be no doubt that it is this combination of charming heroines and happy endings which has blinded the eyes of modern critics to everything else. Iachimo, and Leontes, and even Caliban, are to be left out of account, as if, because in the end they repent or are forgiven, words need not be wasted on such reconciled and harmonious friends. It is true they are grotesque ; it is true that such personages never could have lived ; but who, one would like to know, has ever met Miranda, or become acquainted with Prince Florizel of Bohemia ? In this land of faery, is it right to neglect the goblins ? In this world of dreams, are we justified in ignoring the nightmares ? Is it fair to say that Shakespeare was in 'a gentle, lofty spirit, a peaceful, tranquil mood', when he was creating the Queen in *Cymbeline*, or writing the first two acts of *The Winter's Tale* ?

Attention has never been sufficiently drawn to one other characteristic of these plays . . . the singular carelessness with which great parts of them were obviously written. Could anything drag more wretchedly than the *dénouement* of *Cymbeline* ? And with what perversity is the great pastoral scene in *The Winter's Tale* interspersed with long-winded intrigues, and disguises, and homilies! For these blemishes are unlike the blemishes which enrich rather than lessen the beauty of the earlier plays; they are not, like them, interesting or delightful in themselves; they are usually merely necessary to explain the action, and they are sometimes purely irrelevant. One is, it cannot be denied, often bored, and occasionally irritated, by Polixenes and Camillo and Sebastian and Gonzalo and Belarius; these personages have not even the life of ghosts; they are hardly more than speaking names, that give patient utterance to involution upon involution. What a contrast to the minor characters of Shakespeare's earlier works!

It is difficult to resist the conclusion that he was getting bored himself. Bored with people, bored with real life, bored with drama, bored, in fact, with everything except poetry and poetical dreams. He is no longer interested, one often feels, in what happens, or who says what, so long as he can find place for a faultless lyric, or a new, unimagined rhythmical effect, or a grand and mystic speech. . . .

Is it not thus, then, that we should imagine him in the last years of his life? Half enchanted by visions of beauty and loveliness, and half bored to death; on the one side inspired by a soaring fancy to the singing of ethereal songs, and on the other urged by a general disgust to burst occasionally through his torpor into bitter and violent speech? If we are to learn any-thing of his mind from his last works, it is surely this.

LYTTON STRACHEY, Books and Characters (1922)

THE remaining three plays of the traditional Shakespearean canon exhibit an altered mood, a kindlier and happier view of man's life and character. It is true, as Mr. Lytton Strachey has pointed out, that there are no worse characters anywhere than Iachimo and others, and that these plays are full of hideous crimes. But when he makes this a ground for questioning the 'serenity' of Shakespeare's final outlook, the answer is simple. These last plays end on a new note. The crimes do not triumph as they do in the tragedies. They fail. And the criminals are forgiven. The final word is no longer mere acquiescence in fate;

it is forgiveness, reconciliation, recovery, peace. And the curtain falls now on life, not on death. In the tragedies those for whom we have most cared—Othello, Desdemona, Brutus, Hamlet and Ophelia, Lear and Cordelia—all die at or before the end of the play. Now they all live. If they have died or seemed to die, they are miraculously restored to life. The sins of the stupid—a Cymbeline, a Leontes—are not now irretrievable or repented in vain. The end is atonement: the lost are found, the estranged are reconciled, the quarrelling fathers and daughters, husbands and wives, whose quarrels have made the play, end it by becoming one family again.

JOHN BAILEY, *Shakespeare* (1929)

SHAKESPEARE still thought of the graver trials and tests which life applies to human character, of the wrongs which man inflicts on man; but his present temper demanded not a tragic issue,—it rather demanded an issue into joy or peace. The dissonance must be resolved into a harmony, clear and rapturous, or solemn and profound. And, accordingly, in each of these plays, *The Winter's Tale, Cymbeline, The Tempest*, while grievous errors of the heart are shown to us, and wrongs of man to man as cruel as those of the great tragedies, at the end there is a resolution of the dissonance, a reconciliation. This is the word which interprets Shakespeare's latest plays—reconciliation, 'word over all, beautiful as the sky'.

EDWARD DOWDEN, *Shakspere: a Critical
Study of His Mind and Art* (1874)

WE may pass at this point to the theme of finding that which is lost. The circumstances in which the characters in each of the four plays are lost differ in each case. In *Pericles*, Marina is lost through the action of the murderous Dionyza, and of the robbers who sell her to the brothel; Guiderius and Arviragus are lost through the revenge of Belarius on the injustice of Cymbeline; Perdita is lost through the 'jealous sickness' of Leontes; and Ferdinand is lost to Alonso through the action of Prospero which arises in the last resort out of the action of Alonso and Antonio years before. In each case therefore the loss occurs as a direct result of the evil doings of other characters; these other characters are in three cases parents of the lost child, and in the other case Dionyza has been foster-parent to Marina. What actuates Dionyza in occasioning the loss of Marina is a jealousy in the interests of her own child; in *Cymbeline* the sin is of injustice and of revenge; in *The Winter's Tale* it is a wild un-reasoning sexual jealousy; in *The Tempest* it is the love of power and possession. It is, it need hardly be said, dangerous to seek a precise symbolism in all that is to be found in these plays. Yet here again, where a situation is repeated, in essence, four times, it is difficult to avoid the conclusion that in it is a clue to an important element in what Shakespeare was, in his last work, labouring to convey. We may believe therefore that in this part of his mythology, he is seeking to body forth his sense of the loss by man, through his own evil, of his most treasured possession, 'the jewel of his soul'. It is impossible to avoid the parallel with the constant use of the theme in the Gospels, the theme of the finding of that which is lost.

But let us in the first place concentrate on the loss. The loss is due to man's evil, which in each case is a sudden, in-explicable evil arising out of a former state of happiness, love, and loyalty. In *The Winter's Tale*, which unlike the other plays has not such figures of extreme evil as Cloten and Caliban, what of evil is shown is concentrated, but for Autolycus, in Leontes. Here Shakespeare elaborately portrays the state of perfect love which precedes Leontes' fatal jealousy. It is emphasized repeatedly in the most beautiful language; it is described by Camillo in the opening scene. And again by Polixenes, when he says

> We were as twinn'd lambs that did frisk i' th' sun,
> And bleat the one at th' other: what we chang'd
> Was innocence for innocence; we knew not
> The doctrine of ill-doing, nor dream'd
> That any did.

And equally is the previous love of Leontes and Hermione stressed, only to be followed at once by the first signs of the jealousy of Leontes. From that time on his jealousy burns like a disease. Indeed it is repeatedly described as a 'sickness'. 'Good my lord', says Camillo,

> be cur'd
> Of this diseas'd opinion, and betimes.

And again

> There is a sickness
> Which puts some of us in distemper; but
> I cannot name the disease.

Again it is a 'madness'; Leontes has a 'weak-hinged fancy'. There can be little doubt that Shakespeare is setting out the evil of Leontes as a sudden eruption into disease of what originally was healthy. And although this theme has an emphasis which it has not in the other plays, it is present in them also. It is from outbursts of sheer evil, on the part of the characters who in their former nature were otherwise, Dionyza and Cleon, Cymbeline, Leontes, Antonio, that the loss occurs. And where, as in *Pericles* and *Cymbeline* the loss of Marina and the exile of Posthumus are not due directly to Pericles and Cymbeline, it is yet due to evil in someone closely related to themselves; Pericles entirely trusted his friends Cleon and Dionyza; Cymbeline thought it 'vicious to have distrusted' his Queen. Similarly with Prospero and Antonio. The originating evil in these cases issued from persons who, by their intimacy with them, were identified with Pericles, Cymbeline, and Prospero.

In each case what is lost through the agency of this evil is a person of the greatest beauty and incomparable worth. And that person is in each case restored; and with that restoration comes the recovery, to those who have lost them, of their true nature. Pericles has no active evil to be purged from his nature; but he is brought out of desolation, and also sees the characters of Cleon and Dionyza in their true light. Cymbeline similarly has not the record of a Leontes or an Antonio; yet he is dis-intoxicated from his love for the Queen and sees her for what she was. And all four, Cleon and Dionyza, and the Queen and Cloten, are destroyed by death. Leontes, though the gods have destroyed his jealousy, knows fulfilment only with the return of Perdita; and Antonio and Alonso are changed by the finding

of Miranda and Ferdinand. Clearly, the most satisfactory
interpretation we can place upon this striking repetition, in
four plays, of a single theme, is Shakespeare's imagination of
human life as a descent into a necessary tragedy and evil which
is seen as a sudden irruption into what is originally perfect, and
as a sudden loss of innocence; and as the recovery of a lost perfection, the achievement of a condition which is not merely an
innocence but which, in its achievement, is an 'affliction'
having

> a taste as sweet
> As any cordial comfort.

D. G. JAMES, Scepticism and Poetry (1937)

SHAKESPEARE fell in love with Stratford, with its memories, its
quiet pastures and wide skies, with all the wild life of bird
and beast and flower, with the pleasant friendships and domes-
ticities of the little town, with his house and garden, with his
own family, and especially perhaps with his younger daughter.
Can any explanation of his retirement be more natural and more
complete than this, if we remember that when poets love they
love with a passion which cannot be gainsaid? One can feel it
growing in the plays, from the contrast drawn by Belarius
between the slippery life of the court and the honest freedom
of the countryside, through the sheep-shearing scene of *The
Winter's Tale*, up to the inaccessible island cut off from civilisa-
tion, full of

> Sounds and sweet airs that give delight and hurt not.

But most of all is it felt in the innocent figures, especially of
young girls, that now take the centre of his stage: Marina,
playing with her flowers by the water's brink, Imogen and
the 'flower-like boys, Guiderius and Arviragus', Perdita as
Flora at the country-feast with her Florizel, and to crown all,
the peerless couple Miranda and Ferdinand.

J. DOVER WILSON, The Essential Shakespeare (1932)

The Winter's Tale and the Stage

The Winter's Tale and *Cymbeline* show us the accomplished
artist amusing himself, playing with his art, with the ease that

comes of perfect mastery, the carelessness that is so sure-footed and so certain of its power, and in the last resort, of its control. Nowhere is Shakespeare's adroitness more triumphant than in the way in which in both plays, after letting itself go, it might almost seem at random, the mechanism is reassembled for the tableau of the final scene. Yet it may be said of both of them, I think, that they are more delightful to read than to see acted. The stage is an exacting mistress; and as a servant, has her limitations. Shakespeare is loosening his grasp of the theatre: or alternatively, the theatre is loosening its grasp of Shakespeare.

J. W. MACKAIL, The Approach to Shakespeare (1930)

The Winter's Tale is one of the best-acting of our author's plays. We remember seeing it with great pleasure many years ago. It was on the night that King took leave of the stage, when he and Mrs. Jordan played together in the after-piece of the Wedding-day. Nothing could go off with more *éclat*, with more spirit, and grandeur of effect. Mrs. Siddons played Hermione, and in the last scene acted the painted statue to the life—with true monumental dignity and noble passion; Mr. Kemble, in Leontes, worked himself up into a very fine classical frenzy; and Bannister, as Autolycus, roared as loud for pity as a sturdy beggar could do who felt none of the pain he counterfeited, and was sound of wind and limb. We shall never see these parts so acted again; or if we did, it would be in vain. Actors grow old, or no longer surprise us by their novelty. But true poetry, like nature, is always young; and we still read the courtship of Florizel and Perdita, as we welcome the return of spring, with the same feelings as ever.

W. HAZLITT, Characters of Shakespear's Plays (1817)

Anachronisms

So much has been said about the anachronisms of this play, that it seems needful to add a word concerning them. We have already seen that the making of seaports and landing of ships in Bohemia were taken from Greene. Mr. Verplanck conjectures that by Bohemia Shakespeare meant simply the land of the

Boii, an ancient people several tribes of whom settled in the maritime parts of France: but I hardly think he would have used the name with so much license at a time when the boundaries of that country were so well fixed and so widely known. For the events of the Reformation had made Bohemia an object of special interest to the people of England, and there was much intercourse between the English and Bohemian Courts. I have no notion indeed that this breach of geography was a blunder: it was meant, no doubt, for the convenience of thought; and such is its effect, until one goes to viewing the parts of the work with reference to ends not contemplated in the use here made of them. And the same is to be said touching several points of chronological confusion; such as the making Whitsun pastorals, Christian burial, Julio Romano, the Emperor of Russia, and Puritans singing psalms to hornpipes, all contemporary with the Oracle of Delphi; wherein actual things are but marshalled into an ideal order, so as to render Memory subservient to Imagination. In these and such points, it is enough that the materials be apt to combine among themselves, and that they agree in working out the issue proposed, the end thus regulating the use of the means. For a work of art, as such, should be itself an object for the mind to rest upon, not a directory to guide it to something else. So that here we may justly say 'the mind is its own place'; and, provided the work be true to this intellectual whereabout, breaches of geography and history are of little consequence. And Shakespeare knew full well, that in poetical workmanship Memory stands absolved from the laws of time, and that the living order of art has a perfect right to overrule and supersede the chronological order of facts. In a word, history and chronology have no rights which a poet, as such, is bound to respect. In his sphere, things draw together and unite in virtue of other affinities than those of succession and coexistence.

H. N. HUDSON, *Shakespeare: his Life, Art, and Characters*
(1872)

The Structure of the Play

CRITICS have accused *Pericles* and *The Winter's Tale* of this common fault: that each has a double plot which is also a separated plot—separated by the break between Acts III and IV. In *The Winter's Tale*, it is urged, the first three Acts make a complete independent tragedy. By the end of them the boy Mamillius is dead; Antigonus is dead; and—far worse—for aught we know Hermione is dead, of a broken heart. The words of the Oracle are fulfilled; and Leontes, childless as well as wifeless, is very righteously left to a lifelong remorse. So far Shakespeare has worked strictly in terms of tragedy; and the action, tragically conceived, has been tragically rounded off. Then (say the critics) in the last two acts, after a supposed interval, Shakespeare tacks on a complete independent comedy, which, picking up the thread of the story at its most tragic point, conducts us out into a garden of pleasant romantic devices where old wrongs meet to be reconciled as in this world they never do and never are.

I lay little store by this fault-finding. To start with, I think it unfair to drag *Pericles* into the comparison, since . . . the first two acts of *Pericles* are not Shakespeare's work. . . .

Next, ruling out *Pericles* for this reason and taking *The Winter's Tale* by itself, I find the fault-finders pedantic. They seem to me to be enslaved by stock definitions. 'Here,' they say, 'in Acts I, II, III, we have Tragedy; there, in Acts IV and V, we have Comedy. *Therefore* Shakespeare is guilty of the attempt to work into one drama two different stories in two separate categories of Art. Q.E.D.'

Quite so. *That is precisely what Shakespeare was attempting to do.*

In a world where Nature mixes comedy with tragedy and often shades one into the other indistinguishably, Art, if she be Nature's mirror (as Shakespeare held), must always be impatient of hard definitions. They have their disciplinary uses: again and again while he is learning his trade they may restrain the artist from 'mixing up things that differ'—which Horace rightly put in the forefront of his *Ars Poetica* as the prime offence against Art. But in the end they must be for him a matter of tact rather than strict law, which *de minimis non curat*. They are, after all, conventions: they are, at the best, inductions from the practice of great artists who have gone before; as Aeschylus, Sophocles, Euripides preceded Aristotle, and but for them he would have had not only no theory but nothing to theorise about. . . .

Be this granted or not, no one can begin to understand Shakespeare's later plays who does not perceive that they have one common and constant aim—to repair the passionate errors of men and women in the happiness their children discover, and so to renew the hopes of the world; to reconcile the tragedy of one generation with the fresh hope of another in a third form of drama which we may call 'romantic' if we will.

Moreover—and for a minor point—it is not true of this particular play, *The Winter's Tale*, that Acts I–III make a rounded play in themselves. A number of threads are deliberately left hanging. For example, while the doom of the Oracle has been exacted, its promise of hope yet waits to be fulfilled— *The King shall live without an heir if that which is lost be not found*. The pith of an oracular response lies always in the riddle, and this is the sole riddle in the answer brought by Cleomenes and Dion from Delphi. 'That which is lost' is, of course, Perdita, as her name tells us: and the story of her putting away has already been introduced, and very carefully, into Act III. We do not know, to be sure, that Hermione lives: yet if, as members of the Globe audience, we know our Shakespeare of old, we ought to have guessed, in Paulina's protestations, a something held up her sleeve. I grant that it takes a guess, and that Leontes must by no means be allowed to surmise the truth.

But—to return to my main argument—if the critics be unintelligent who condemn the general structure of *The Winter's Tale*, they multiply stupidity when they proceed to convert and use it in condonation of certain flagrant faults: as, for example, when they argue that *because* Shakespeare, by compressing two plots into one play, overcrowded the time at his disposal, *therefore* we must overlook the monstrously sudden growth of Leontes' jealousy; that he left himself no room to develop it rationally: or, for another example, as when Gervinus, to excuse the unworkmanlike trick by which Shakespeare scamps the recognition scene between Perdita and her father, sagely pleads that 'The poet has wisely placed the event behind the scenes; otherwise the play would be too full of powerful scenes.'

ARTHUR QUILLER-COUCH, *Shakespeare's Workmanship*
(1918)

IN no play is the passage from complication to resolution so clearly marked as here. In the course of the Middle Act, Antigonus deposits the infant, and exit, pursued by a bear— the complication which is connected with Sicilia is played out. Then the Shepherd and Clown enter and discover the child— the resolution of the plot and the Bohemian side of the story begin. This change from complication to resolution is marked by a change from verse to prose.

RICHARD G. MOULTON, *Shakespeare as a Dramatic Artist*
(1885)

BUT why introduce that bear? The ship that brought Antigonus is riding off the coast of Bohemia and is presently engulfed with all her crew. The clown sees it all happen. Then why, in the name of economy, not engulf Antigonus with the rest— or, better still, as he tries to row aboard? I can discover no answer to that. If anyone ask my private opinion why the bear came on, it is that the Bear-Pit in Southwark, hard by the Globe Theatre, had a tame animal to let out, and the Globe management took the opportunity to make a popular hit.

ARTHUR QUILLER-COUCH, *Shakespeare's Workmanship*
(1918)

The Pastoral Element

AND here I must plead as earnestly as I can for allowing more than the usual virtue and weight to the fourth act of *The Winter's Tale*. There are several reasons why it has been taken too lightly. It has been far too much the property of vague young women doing eurhythmics at Speech Days or on vicarage lawns; and, when it is acted professionally, the part of Perdita is usually taken by some pretty little fool or pert suburban charmer. Also, it is usually thought that joy and virtue are inferior as poetic themes to suffering and vice; or that the earthly paradise taxed the resources of Dante less than Ugolino's tower. It would seem that the truth is the other way round, because convincing pictures of joy and virtue are extremely rare, while those of suffering and vice are comparatively common. Shelley succeeds in describing the sufferings of Prometheus; the earthly bliss brought on by them is, except in patches, a shoddy affair in comparison. Shakespeare never did anything finer, more serious, more evocative of his full powers, than his picture of an earthly paradise painted in the form of the English countryside. The old problem of adjusting realism and symbol is so well solved that we are quite unconscious of it. The country life is given the fullest force of actuality, as when the old shepherd describes his wife's hospitality at the shearing feast [Tillyard quotes IV. iv. 55 ff.]. Yet the whole country setting stands out as the cleanest and most elegant symbol of the new life into which the old horrors are to be transmuted.

E. M. W. TILLYARD, *Shakespeare's Last Plays* (1938)

PASTORAL is never to be mistaken for a transcript of rustic life. The significance resides, not in any fidelity to the fact of the peasant, but in its relation to the state of mind of the world-wearied courtier or scholar who writes it. And the contrast is generally brought into the foreground of the picture. Consciously or unconsciously, the shepherds, or some at least among them, are masquerading. So it is in *The Winter's Tale*, where the rude manners and the open-mouthed simplicity of the real farm-folk only serve as a foil to the natural nobility of the king's son Florizel and the king's daughter Perdita.

E. K. CHAMBERS, *Shakespeare: A Survey* (1925)

Implications of the Imagery

THE thought constantly in Shakespeare's mind in this play, or perhaps more correctly the idea in his imagination, seems to me to be the common flow of life through all things, in nature and man alike, seen in the sap rising in the tree, the habits and character of flowers, the result of the marriage of base and noble stock, whether it be of roses or of human beings, the emotions of birds, animals and men, the working of the poison of disease

alike in mind and in body, the curative power, the tonic
'medicine' of gay or honest presence, and, above all, the oneness of rhythm, of law of movement, in the human body and
human emotions with the great fundamental rhythmical movements of nature herself.

Much of this analogy between things human and natural is
of course to be found all through Shakespeare's imagery;
indeed without it imagery itself would have no meaning or
existence.

The likeness in the life of a tree and of a human being,
brought out here in the roots of affection in youth which branch
in age (I. i. 22), the 'sap' or life essence in human counsel (IV.
iv. 563), the source of poison in a rotten root (II. iii. 89), is, as
we have seen, worked on continually in the historical plays;
the likeness of the sickness of body and mind, emphasised here
(Leontes' 'diseased opinion' (I. ii. 297), Paulina's 'medicinal'
words (II. iii. 37) and so on), is constantly found elsewhere, as in
Macbeth or *Hamlet*, as is also the similarity in human and animal life and emotion, here illustrated by the children like
lambs frisking and bleating in the sun (I. ii. 67), or the constant
love of turtle doves (IV. iv. 154); but I have never noticed elsewhere so much insistence—and this in the most imaginative
similes—on the likeness between human and natural processes
and characteristics, and on the oneness of rhythmical movement
and law.

The art of grafting and what it achieves is touched upon
elsewhere, but it is discussed here at length by Polixenes and
Perdita in language which today we might apply to eugenics:

> we marry
> A gentler scion to the wildest stock,
> And make conceive a bark of baser kind
> By bud of nobler race;
>
> (IV. iv. 92)

and flowers—the marigold, primrose and oxlip—are here more
markedly than anywhere else endowed with human characteristics and emotions.

The great natural movements seem the normal mode of
expression and comparison; so the old shepherd, seeking to

convey to Polixenes the force of Florizel's love of Perdita and her attraction for him, does so most successfully when he says:

> for never gaz'd the moon
> Upon the water as he'll stand and read
> As 'twere my daughter's eyes.
>
> (IV. iv. 172)

In the same vein is the ardour of Leontes' greeting to Florizel, 'Welcome hither, as is the spring to the earth' (v. i. 151); so also is Florizel's answer to the query as to whether he is married, when in his despair at achieving his wish, he cites in old ballad fashion the most unlikely event in nature:

> We are not, sir, nor are we like to be;
> The stars, I see, will kiss the valleys first.
>
> (v. i. 205)

More in this play than anywhere else is the ebb and flow of emotion exquisitely mirrored in the ebb and flow of blood in the face, obeying, as it does, the same laws, and responding to the same inner stimulus. 'I'll blush you thanks' (IV. iv. 582), cries Perdita to Camillo. . . .

So also the immutability of the laws of nature, working alike in the human and in the natural world, is in the poet's mind when he makes Camillo cry,

> you may as well
> Forbid the sea for to obey the moon
>
> (I. ii. 426)

as hope by threat or counsel to move the stubborn human will, based upon what is a genuine even though it be a false belief.

And as the human will can be immovable and unchangeable as is the moon's influence on the tides, so also the influx and withdrawal of energy in these same tides of the sea come and go as do the tides of fluctuation of human emotion itself. This then is naturally the metaphor Paulina uses when, moved to anger on hearing the unknown Perdita praised as

> the most peerless piece of earth . . .
> That e'er the sun shone bright on,
>
> (v. i. 94)

she turns on the unwitting courtier, reminding him curtly that in time past, when his emotions ran high about her beloved queen, Hermione, just so did he speak and write about her:

> 'she had not been,
> Nor was not to be equall'd'; thus your verse
> Flow'd with her beauty once; 'tis shrewdly ebb'd
> To say you have seen a better.
>
> (v. i. 100)

And, above all, it is perfectly and exquisitely in keeping with this central imaginative idea, that Florizel, in the height of his emotion and adoration of the beauty and wild natural grace of Perdita, should see the poetry of the motion of her young body as a part of the ordered and rhythmic flow of nature herself in the movement of the tides, and would have her stay for ever part of that larger movement, so that he cries in ecstasy,

> when you do dance, I wish you
> A wave o' th' sea, that you might ever do
> Nothing but that.
>
> (IV. iv. 140)

CAROLINE F. E. SPURGEON, Shakespeare's Imagery (1935)

Style

THE style of these last plays is a further development of the style of the Tragedies. The thought is often more packed and hurried, the expression more various and fluent, at the expense of full logical ordering. The change which came over Shakespeare's later work is that which Dryden, at an advanced age, perceived in himself. 'What judgment I had,' he says, in the Preface to the *Fables*, 'increases rather than diminishes; and thoughts, such as they are, come crowding in so fast upon me, that my only difficulty is to choose or reject, to run them into verse, or to give them the other harmony of prose.' The bombasted magniloquence of the early rhetorical style has now disappeared. The very syntax is the syntax of thought rather than of language; constructions are mixed, grammatical links are dropped, the meaning of many sentences is compressed into one, hints and impressions count for as much as full-blown propositions.

WALTER RALEIGH, Shakespeare (1907)

The Characters

THE jealousy of Leontes is the aberration of a weak mind and owes nothing to external pressure. The husband's feeble wrath is finely contrasted with his wife's gentle composure and patient fortitude in the presence of unwarrantable suffering which moves pathos of an infinite poignancy. The boy Mamillius is of near kin to the boys in *Cymbeline*. Nowhere has the dramatist conveyed more convincingly boyhood's charm, quickness of perception, or innocence. Perdita develops the ethereal model of Marina in *Pericles* and shows tender ingenuous girlhood moulded by Nature's hand and free of the contamination of social artifice. The courtship of Florizel and Perdita is the perfection of gentle romance.

SIR SIDNEY LEE, *A Life of William Shakespeare* (1898)

Leontes

THE idea of this delightful drama is a genuine jealousy of disposition, and it should be immediately followed by the perusal of *Othello*, which is the direct contrast of it in every particular. For jealousy is a vice of the mind, a culpable tendency of the temper, having certain well known and well defined effects and concomitants, all of which are visible in Leontes, and, I boldly say, not one of which marks its presence in *Othello*;—such as, first, an excitability by the most inadequate causes, and an eagerness to snatch at proofs; secondly, a grossness of conception and a disposition to degrade the object of the passion by sensual fancies and images; thirdly, a sense of shame of his own feelings exhibited in a solitary moodiness of humour, and yet from the violence of the passion forced to utter itself, and therefore catching occasions to ease the mind by ambiguities, equivoques, by talking to those who cannot, and who are known not to be able to, understand what is said to them,—in short, by soliloquy in the form of dialogue, and hence a confused, broken, and fragmentary manner; fourthly, a dread of vulgar ridicule, as distinct from a high sense of honour, or a mistaken sense of duty; and lastly, and immediately, consequent on this, a spirit of selfish vindictiveness.

S. T. COLERIDGE, *Literary Remains* (1836–9)

In the delineation of Leontes there is an abruptness of change which strikes us, at first view, as not a little a-clash with nature: we cannot well see how one state of mind grows out of another: his jealousy shoots in comet-like, as something unprovided for in the general ordering of his character. Which causes this feature to appear as if it were suggested rather by the exigencies of the stage than by the natural workings of human passion. And herein the Poet seems at variance with himself; his usual method being to unfold a passion in its rise and progress, so that we go along with it freely from its origin to its consummation. And, certainly, there is no accounting for Leontes' conduct, but by supposing a predisposition to jealousy in him, which, however, has been hitherto kept latent by his wife's clear, firm, serene discreetness, but which breaks out into sudden and frightful activity as soon as she, under a special pressure of motives, slightly overacts the confidence of friendship. There needed but a spark of occasion to set this secret magazine of passion all a-blaze.

. . . It is true, Shakespeare had a course of action marked out for him in the tale [i.e. of Pandosto]. But then he was bound by his own principles of art to make the character such as would rationally support the action, and cohere with it. For such is the necessary law of moral development and transpiration. Nor is it by any means safe to affirm that he has not done this. For it is to be noted that Polixenes has made a pretty long visit, having passed, it seems, no less than nine changes of the Moon at the home of his royal friend. And he might well have found it not always easy to avoid preferring the Queen's society to the King's; for she is a most irresistible creature, and her calm, ingenuous modesty, itself the most dignified of all womanly graces, is what, more than anything else, makes her so. What secret thoughts may have gathered to a head in the mind of Leontes during that period, is left for us to divine from the after-results. And I believe there is a jealousy of friendship, as well as of love. Accordingly, though Leontes invokes the Queen's influence to induce a lengthening of the visit, yet he seems a little disturbed on seeing that her influence has proved stronger than his own [Hudson quotes I. ii. 86 ff.].

There is, I think, a relish of suppressed bitterness in this last speech [i.e. 'Why, that was when Three crabbed months' &c.], as if her long reluctance had planted in him a germ of doubt whether, after all, her heart was really in her words of consent. For the Queen is a much deeper character than her husband. It is true, these notices, and various others, drop along so quiet and unpronounced, as hardly to arrest the reader's attention. Shakespeare, above all other men, delights in just such subtle insinuations of purpose; they belong indeed to his usual method of preparing for a given issue, yet doing it so slyly as not to preclude surprise when the issue comes.

So that in his seeming abruptness Leontes, after all, does but exemplify the strange transformations which sometimes occur in men upon sudden and unforeseen emergencies. And it is observable that the very slightness of the Queen's indiscretion, the fact that she goes but a little, a very little too far, only works against her, causing the King to suspect her of great effort and care to avoid suspicion. And on the same principle, because he has never suspected her before, therefore he suspects her all the more vehemently now: that his confidence has hitherto stood unshaken, he attributes to extreme artfulness on her part; for even so, to an ill-disposed mind perfect innocence is apt to give an impression of consummate art. A passion thus groundless and self-generated might well be full-grown as soon as born. The more greedy and craving, too, that it has nothing real to eat; it therefore proceeds at once to 'make the meat it feeds on', causing him to magnify whatever he sees, and to imagine many things that are not. That jealousy, however, is not the habit of his mind, appears in that it finds him unprepared, and takes him by surprise; insomuch that he forthwith loses all self-control, and runs right athwart the rules of common decency and decorum, so that he becomes an object at once of pity, of hatred, and scorn.

I think the Poet hardly anywhere shows a keener and juster insight of nature than in the behaviour of this man while the distemper is upon him. He is utterly reason-proof, and indeed acts as one literally insane. For the poison infects not only his manners, but his very modes of thought: in fact, all his rational and imaginative forces, even his speech and language, seem to have caught the disease. And all the loathsome filth which had settled to the bottom of his nature is now shaken up to the surface, so that there appears to be nothing but meanness and malignity and essential coarseness in him. Meanwhile an instinctive shame of his passion and a dread of vulgar ridicule put him upon talking in dark riddles and enigmas: hence the confused, broken, and disjointed style, an odd jumble of dialogue and soliloquy, in which he tries to jerk out his thoughts, as if he would have them known, and yet not have them known. I believe men generally credit themselves with peculiar penetration when they are in the act of being deluded, whether by themselves or by others. Hence, again, the strange and even ludicrous conceit in which Leontes wraps himself. 'Not noted, is't,' says he, referring to the Queen's imaginary crime,—

> not noted, is't,
> But of the finer natures? by some severals
> Of head-piece extraordinary? lower messes,
> Perchance, are to this business purblind?

Thus he mistakes his madness for a higher wisdom, and clothes his delusion with the spirit of revelation; so that Camillo rightly says—

> you may as well
> Forbid the sea for to obey the moon
> As or by oath remove or counsel shake
> The fabric of his folly, whose foundation
> Is pil'd upon his faith.

I must note one more point of the delineation. When Leontes sends his messengers to Delphos, he avows this as his reason for doing so:

> Though I am satisfied and need no more
> Than what I know, yet shall the oracle
> Give rest to th' minds of others.

Which means simply that he is not going to let the truth of the charge stand in issue, and that he holds the Divine authority to be a capital thing, provided he may use it, and need not obey it; that is, if he finds the god agreeing with him in opinion, then the god's judgment is infallible; if not, then, in plain terms, he is no god. And they who have closely observed the workings of jealousy, know right well that in all this Shakespeare does not one whit 'overstep the modesty of Nature'.

The Poet manages with great art to bring Leontes off from the disgraces of his passion, and repeal him home to our sympathies, which had been freely drawn to him at first by his generosity of friendship. To this end, jealousy is represented as his only fault, and this as a sudden freak, which passes on directly into a frenzy, and whips him quite out of himself, temporarily overriding his characteristic qualities, but not combining with them; the more violent for being unwonted, and the shorter-lived for being violent. In his firm, compact energy of thought and speech, after his passion has cleared itself, and in his perennial flow of repentance after his bereavement, are displayed the real tone and texture of his character. We feel that, if his sin has been great, his suffering is also great, and that if he were a greater sinner, his suffering would be less. Quick, impulsive, headstrong, he admits no bounds to anger or to penitence; condemns himself as vehemently as he does others; and will spend his life in atoning for a wrong he has done in a moment of passion; so that we are the more willing to forgive him, inasmuch as he never forgives himself.

H. N. HUDSON, *Shakespeare: his Life, Art, and Characters* (1872)

Hermione

HERMIONE is a queen, a matron, and a mother; she is good and beautiful, and royally descended. A majestic sweetness, a grand and gracious simplicity, an easy, unforced, yet dignified self-possession, are in all her deportment and in every word she utters. She is one of those characters of whom it has been said proverbially that 'still waters run deep'. Her passions are not vehement, but in her settled mind the sources of pain or pleasure, love or resentment, are like the springs that feed the mountain lakes, impenetrable, unfathomable, and inexhaustible. . . .

There are several among Shakespeare's characters which exercise a far stronger power over our feelings, our fancy, our understanding, than that of Hermione; but not one—unless, perhaps, Cordelia—constructed upon so high and pure a principle. It is the union of gentleness with power which constitutes the perfection of mental grace. Thus among the ancients, with whom the *graces* were also the *charities* (to show, perhaps, that while form alone may constitute beauty, sentiment is necessary to grace), one and the same word signified equally *strength* and *virtue*. This feeling, carried into the fine arts, was the secret of the antique grace—the grace of repose. The same eternal nature—the same sense of immutable truth and beauty—which revealed this sublime principle of art to the ancient Greeks, revealed it to the genius of Shakespeare; and the character of Hermione, in which we have the same largeness of conception and delicacy of execution—the same effect of suffering without passion, and grandeur without effort— is an instance, I think, that he felt within himself, and by intuition, what we study all our lives in the remains of ancient art. The calm, regular, classical beauty of Hermione's character is the more impressive from the wild and Gothic accompaniments of her story, and the beautiful relief afforded by the pastoral and romantic grace which is thrown around her daughter Perdita.

ANNA JAMESON, *Characteristics of Women* (1832)

Perdita

THE qualities which impart to Perdita her distinct individuality are the beautiful combination of the pastoral with the elegant, of simplicity with elevation, of spirit with sweetness. The exquisite delicacy of the picture is apparent. To understand and appreciate its effective truth and nature we should place Perdita beside some of the nymphs of Arcadia, or the Clorises and Sylvias of the Italian pastorals, who, however graceful in themselves, when opposed to Perdita, seem to melt away into mere poetical abstractions. . . .

ANNA JAMESON, *Characteristics of Women* (1832)

IN the midst are Florizel and Perdita, like two rose-trees in a garden of herbs. They are high-born, and they become their rank. Shakespeare, in an age when high-birth honoured itself,

makes their birth shine in their words and ways. Florizel is
known by Camillo and Polixenes, who are now present in disguise, for what he is; but Perdita is not known, save as a girl
who has always lived among the shepherds. Shakespeare keeps
her a princess at every point but pride. To Florizel, as he looks at
her, the sheep-shearing is as a meeting of the petty gods, and
she the Queen of it. Polixenes, though angry with her, cannot
resist her charm. . . .

Her talk belongs to her native nobleness. She has, like the
shepherdesses of Sidney's pastoral, drunk from the classic
spring, and this little learning is exalted into poetic beauty
by her gracious character, her imagination of beauty, and by
the uplifting impulse of her love. All the world knows how
exquisite, how creative is her speech as she comes to meet her
guests, half-buried in her flowers [Brooke quotes IV. iv. 116 ff.].

Added to this poetic beauty is the grace of native intellect.
She holds her own with Polixenes when he discusses the mutual
relation of nature and art. Her sight of the knot of a difficulty
is always clear, and so is her solution of it. This is the mother's
intellect in the child. Then, her love for Florizel is confessed as
simply, with as little care for what others think of her, as her
mother confessed her friendship with Polixenes. In his handing down of similarity of character, Shakespeare is perhaps
scientifically and certainly poetically right; and he supports
this idea of his throughout the rest of the play. Perdita, with a
difference, descends from her mother. . . .

Her passionate love, her soft tenderness do not affect her
intellect. Like Hermione, she is quite clear-eyed; keen to
divide the true from the false; quiet, through good sense, in
hours of confused trouble. In the midst of the hurry of flight
and of changing plans, Perdita, like her mother—whose intellect, even in the deepest grief, is always detached to meet with
coolness the point at issue—can stay to correct a view of life
put forward by Camillo [Brooke quotes IV. iv. 570–7].

And finally, when all is ready, Camillo and Florizel both
excited to depart, Perdita is quiet. She has made up her mind
as well as her heart. She sees that there is no other way for her,
and takes it, undelaying.

STOPFORD A. BROOKE, *On Ten Plays of Shakespeare* (1905)

Paulina

PAULINA . . . is a character strongly drawn from real and common life—a clever, generous, strong-minded, warm-hearted
woman, fearless in asserting the truth, firm in her sense of right,
enthusiastic in all her affections; quick in thought, resolute
in word, and energetic in action; but heedless, hot-tempered,
impatient, loud, bold, voluble, and turbulent of tongue; re-
gardless of the feelings of those for whom she would sacrifice
her life, and injuring from excess of zeal those whom she most
wishes to serve. How many such are there in the world! But
Paulina, though a very termagant, is yet a poetical termagant
in her way; and the manner in which all the evil and dangerous
tendencies of such a temper are placed before us, even while
the individual character retains the strongest hold upon our
respect and admiration, forms an impressive lesson, as well as
a natural and delightful portrait.

ANNA JAMESON, *Characteristics of Women* (1832)

Autolycus

AUTOLYCUS is the incarnate rogue. He has come down from
Greekland, but he is English also, and Elizabethan. He lives on
the simplicity of the world, and thinks he is right in that. The
world, he thinks, exists for rogues. And indeed, he is so frank
of his roguery, and enjoys it so heartily, that it is easy not to
be angry with him. We begin to think that he and his fellow-
sinners are of use in the world. . . .

But the best excuse for him, and his excellent use, is his
gaiety. Nothing interferes with that, nothing darkens it. He
has been degraded from the court for dishonesty; he is a piece
of a coward; he is, now and then, for practice of his art, something of a sneak, but he is as gay as a cuckoo who has been
a fraud from the beginning. And the world is so stupid, that it
is thankful for the rogue, provided he makes it mirth; so un-
inventive, that it likes the imaginative liar; so lazy, that the
hustling of the rogues is excellent for its activity. Nothing
can be better done than his fooling and robbing of the Clown,

especially if we read what is said with our eyes on the stage. All he says supplies by-play for the actor. . . .

He has entered on the scene, singing; and the song shows he is not without some enjoyment of nature. Shakespeare knew that if a man be naturally merry, and has good health, and also the want of conscience which, in slight natures, so often accompanies good health, roguery does not prevent him from having pleasure in sweet air and the songs of birds, from feeling the charm of the spring dancing in his blood, from having a vague happiness in the beautiful world. . . . Yet Shakespeare felt that he must say something about conscience, give us some hint how it happens that Autolycus is happy, and yet such a rascal. And one pregnant touch explains it. 'Beating and hanging are terrors for me (*sic*); for the life to come, I sleep out the thought of it.' Coleridge objects to that; I think it hits the very white of the matter. Moreover, Autolycus, if a whiff of conscience troubles him, gets rid of the trouble of it, as many of us do, by confession of his roguery to himself— priest and penitent in one—by absolving himself, after he has blamed himself. The moral burden is lifted off when he describes himself, to the Clown, by name, as a rascal, whipped out of the court for his vices, and settled into roguery.

It is not only bodily health, but intellectual quickness that makes his life happy. There is not one touch of noble thought or delicate feeling from end to end of Autolycus. He is strictly kept within his low, monkey-inspired range; but within that he is clever, imaginative when he is lying, and always ravished with his own tricksy intelligence. His quickness gives as much pleasure to the world as to himself. When the servant comes to report his arrival at the feast, we see how he has ravished the simple rustics [Brooke quotes IV. iv. 204 ff.]. When he is among them, he boldly risks their unbelief with marvels of lying, preferring the fun of his rogue-imagination to even the money he wins by it. He is the life and soul of all the homely foolery of the feast; and though he robs everybody, he makes everybody happy. . . .

Lastly, his self-delight in his roguery raises it almost into the dignity of a profession. He is Hermes, fallen from his high estate, into evil times, and modern ways.

STOPFORD A. BROOKE, *On Ten Plays of Shakespeare* (1905)

The Songs

AUTOLYCUS does not appear until the scene following the Prologue in the Fourth Act. His entrance is one of the most effective in the comedies—the gay, careless, and unscrupulous character of the man is at once conveyed. Even for the reader sitting in his library, all the descriptions, with which modern dramatists fill up their play-books, could not do it more effectually. It is the song used as a soliloquy, whereby the audience can have intimate information as to Autolycus's point of view, and never has any man been limned more tersely and vividly than in the two opening songs, which are separated only by a few spoken words. From them we are led to suspect that, when the Clown enters, he is to be shorn some way or another. Robbed the Clown is and in the meanest manner possible, but the songs deprive the theft of half its villainy, and we are actually inclined to laugh at his discomfiture and to attribute the blame to his own foolish simplicity. The naïve confidence of Autolycus reminds us of 'I am a poor fellow that would live' (a remark from which Pater derived delight) of that other entertaining rascal, Pompey, in *Measure for Measure*. At the end of the scene, Autolycus leaves the stage singing in a strain no less careless than that in which his opening songs were cast and with a conscience not in the slightest degree ruffled. . . .

All the songs are essential, for they are songs of character, and were it not for them the audience would conceive the most violent antipathy to Autolycus as an intolerable scamp without any relish of salvation. The songs put his would-be judges in good humour and there is not one of them that would not be his advocate. Shakespeare did not go out of his way to provide these humorous situations for nothing, he had of course to amuse, but he did not allow the incidents to go to waste. Consequently whatever cuts may be necessary in representing the play, the songs must not be among them.

The songs of Autolycus are in Shakespeare's final form of dramatic song; they are character songs of a type hitherto unused by him. *When daffodils* is the autobiographical song, used as a soliloquy, and it ranks, in this respect, with *Where the bee sucks* in *The Tempest*, which is also practically a soliloquy. The two songs in the assumed character of the pedlar are parallels to the two which Ariel, as the spirit of the air, sings to Ferdinand. In the study of the development of Shakespeare in his use of song, there are many reasons for associating Autolycus with Ariel and *The Winter's Tale* with *The Tempest*.

RICHMOND NOBLE, *Shakespeare's Use of Song* (1923)